Trade Policy Review

Trinidad and Tobago
1998

World Trade Organization
Geneva, January 1999

PREFACE

The Trade Policy Review Mechanism (TPRM) was first established on a trial basis by the GATT CONTRACTING PARTIES in April 1989. The Mechanism became a permanent feature of the World Trade Organization under the Marrakesh Agreement which established the WTO in January 1995.

The objectives of the TPRM are to contribute to improved adherence by all WTO Members to rules, disciplines and commitments made under the Multilateral Trade Agreements and, where applicable, the Plurilateral Trade Agreements, and hence to the smoother functioning of the multilateral trading system, by achieving greater transparency in, and understanding of, the trade policies and practices of Members. Accordingly, the review mechanism enables the regular collective appreciation and evaluation of the full range of individual Members' trade policies and practices and their impact on the functioning of the multilateral trading system. It is not intended to serve as a basis for the enforcement of specific obligations under the Agreements or for dispute settlement procedures, or to impose new policy commitments on Members.

The assessment carried out under the TPRM takes place, to the extent relevant, against the background of the wider economic and developmental needs, policies and objectives of the Member concerned, as well as its external environment. However, the function of the review mechanism is to examine the impact of a Member's trade policies and practices on the multilateral trading system.

Under the TPRM, the trade policies of all Members are subject to periodic review. The four largest trading entities in terms of world market share, counting the European Union as one, are reviewed every two years, the 16 next largest trading entities every four years, and other Members every six years; a longer period may be fixed for least-developed countries.

The reviews are conducted by the Trade Policy Review Body (TPRB) on the basis of two documents: a policy statement by the Member under review and a comprehensive report drawn up by the WTO Secretariat on its own responsibility.

TABLE OF CONTENTS

PART A

CONCLUDING REMARKS BY THE CHAIRPERSON

OF THE TRADE POLICY REVIEW BODY,

H.E. MR. ALI SAID MCHUMO

AT THE TRADE POLICY REVIEW OF

TRINIDAD AND TOBAGO

12-13 NOVEMBER 1998

CONCLUDING REMARKS BY THE CHAIRPERSON

1.   The first Trade Policy Review of Trinidad and Tobago was conducted by the TPR Body on 12-13 November 1998.   These remarks, prepared on my own responsibility, are intended to summarize the main points of the discussion; they are not intended as a full report. Further details of the discussion will be fully reflected in the minutes.

2.   The discussion developed under three main themes: (i) economic environment; (ii) trade policy measures; and (iii) sectoral policies.

(i)   Economic environment

3.   Members congratulated Trinidad and Tobago on its recent liberalization and economic reforms, which had resulted in steady growth rates, low inflation and had attracted substantial foreign investment.   However, challenges remained, including dependency on the energy sector, high unemployment and a still sizeable participation of the State in key sectors. Also, the traditional trade surplus had turned to deficit in 1997, primarily as a consequence of a surge in imports. There was also concern about the effect of lower oil prices on export earnings and government revenue. Members welcomed the steps taken by Trinidad and Tobago to develop a legal framework for competition policy and encouraged its prompt implementation.   There was some worry about the range, cost and coherence of the various incentive schemes, particularly with respect to investment, for which procedures were also sometimes cumbersome. Members encouraged Trinidad and Tobago to continue to seek the diversification of economic activity and to accelerate the process of privatization, particularly in the agriculture and energy sectors.

4.   Members commended Trinidad and Tobago on its commitments to the multilateral trading system particularly as seen by the implementation of WTO agreements in some cases ahead of schedule. They acknowledged the importance of Trinidad and Tobago's role within CARICOM.

5.   The representative of Trinidad and Tobago expressed his country's firm adherence to a rule-based multilateral trading system. His country had willingly assumed the obligations resulting from the Uruguay Round. However, he felt that the WTO needed to address the particular interests and needs of developing country members and to ensure that sustained efforts were made towards balancing the obligations assumed and the benefits derived from the system. He stressed the need for new approaches to deal with the special and differential treatment for developing countries in the WTO, for example through the provision of technical assistance and through technology transfer. As a small island economy, Trinidad and Tobago fully supported initiatives in international fora to identify measures to integrate small states into the global economy.

6.   On the issues raised by Members, the representative of Trinidad and Tobago said his Government had undertaken a trade reform programme to diversify the economy away from the petroleum sector and to improve employment opportunities. Unemployment had already declined significantly. On the trade deficit, capital imports had been an important factor. He identified several sectors with the potential for sustainable export-led growth, including financial services, agro-processing, software development, specialty chemicals, engineering goods and services, and cultural tourism. Future economic strategies would include continued efforts to attract foreign investment and to foster the development of small businesses, tourism and light manufacturing sectors.   The representative noted that the process of amending investment legislation would lead to a simplification of procedures and enhance transparency.

(ii)   *Trade policy measures*

7.   Members welcomed Trinidad and Tobago's trade liberalization, including a lowering of tariffs, virtual elimination of quantitative restrictions and a reduction in the scope of import licensing. In encouraging Trinidad and Tobago to continue with these efforts, Members raised a number of questions particularly with respect to: the gap between applied and bound tariff rates; high import surcharges on agricultural products; import licensing; notification of legislation dealing with anti-dumping and countervailing measures; standards and technical regulations; tax allowances for exports; and intellectual property rights, especially with respect to enforcement of copyrights.

8.   In reply, the representative of Trinidad and Tobago stated that the maximum tariff rate had been reduced from 45% to 20% over five years, and that there were no immediate plans to lower tariffs further. Any alteration of the Common External Tariff would require approval from the CARICOM Heads of Government. With regard to the gap between applied and bound tariffs for agricultural products, the Government intended to re-examine bindings upon completion of a review of agricultural policies. The representative noted that only a few items were currently subject to licencing, mainly for public safety and national security reasons, as well as under CARICOM Treaty obligations. Trinidad and Tobago had amended its anti-dumping legislation to ensure conformity with its WTO obligations; a notification in this respect would shortly be submitted to the WTO. Apart from anti-dumping, Trinidad and Tobago had amended its legislation and procedures in a number of areas, including TRIPS and customs valuation, and was in the process of drafting or revising legislation in other areas. The procedure for setting standards was also explained.

9.   With regard to export allowances, involving a tax credit based on certain export earnings, the representative of Trinidad and Tobago said that, in accordance with the Budget Speech of 1998, they would be eliminated in 2002. Trinidad and Tobago was addressing the problem of enforcement of intellectual property rights, particularly regarding video and audio cassette piracy. The representative of Trinidad and Tobago stressed the need for technical assistance to strengthen the capacity of small trading partners to meet reporting obligations under the WTO and to fully exercise their rights.

(iii)   *Sectoral policies*

10.   Members acknowledged Trinidad and Tobago's efforts to diversify its economy, reducing its dependency on the energy sector by facilitating activity in non-petroleum manufacturing and services. On agriculture, Members posed questions with regard to issues such as: high import surcharges, quantitative restrictions applied to imports of live poultry, and the role of state-owned enterprises in the sector. Regarding the energy sector, Trinidad and Tobago was encouraged to implement a more transparent pricing structure for natural gas. On services, Members welcomed Trinidad and Tobago's commitments in the GATS and encouraged a broadening of their scope, particularly in financial services. A number of questions were raised on specific issues, including "exclusive rights" provisions in telecommunications; banking sector regulations and licensing requirements; transparency in the work permits regime; and licensing and cargo handling in both maritime and airline services.

11.   The representative of Trinidad and Tobago stated that the high surcharges applied to the agricultural sector would be reviewed before 2004 with a view to ensuring compliance with WTO commitments. Regarding maritime transport services, the Government was considering a proposal for the restructuring of port operations. On financial services, national treatment was accorded to foreign providers, and the Government was finalizing an offer on banking to be presented by January 1999. The Government was pursuing the matter of exclusive rights on basic telecommunication services

with the provider, with a view to advancing liberalization in this sector. Amendments were being made to the Telecommunications Act; these were expected to be approved by June 1999, allowing Trinidad and Tobago to meet its GATS obligations. Detailed answers were also provided regarding civil aviation and the issuance of work permits.

Conclusions

12.   In conclusion, Members expressed appreciation for Trinidad and Tobago's liberalization efforts, and prompt compliance with their obligations under the WTO. Members strongly welcomed the many steps that Trinidad and Tobago had already taken in becoming a more open and outward-oriented economy that was integrated into the multilateral system; they acknowledged the challenges faced by Trinidad and Tobago as a small resource-based economy and appreciated the reform programme to diversify the economy. It was felt that a continuation of Trinidad and Tobago's trade-opening efforts would consolidate the basis for economic diversification and for steady, sustainable growth; in this respect, the support of Trinidad and Tobago's trading partners would also be important.

PART B

REPORT BY THE WTO SECRETARIAT

CONTENTS

CHARTS

TABLES

APPENDIX TABLES

I.   THE ECONOMIC ENVIRONMENT

III.   TRADE POLICIES AND PRACTICES BY MEASURE

SUMMARY OBSERVATIONS

1.   Since the mid 1980s, Trinidad and Tobago has engaged in a process of liberalization and deregulation, which has led to the elimination of a number of restrictions to trade and to a reduction in the average level of tariff protection. Few non-price border restrictions to trade remain, and the amendment of domestic legislation to incorporate Trinidad and Tobago's commitments under the different WTO agreements has been virtually completed. No direct export subsidies are granted; however, a complex system of investment incentives remains in place. Regional trade liberalization undertaken in the Caribbean Community and Common Market (CARICOM) has gone hand-in-hand with commitments under the multilateral trading system. Trinidad and Tobago has been in the forefront of compliance with CARICOM's Common External Tariff (CET) reduction commitments for industrial goods. Tariffs on agricultural goods remain above average, however, and some products are subject to high import surcharges.

(1)   ECONOMIC ENVIRONMENT

2.   Trinidad and Tobago's economy relies heavily on production and export of oil and natural gas. Proven oil reserves are estimated at 12 years' supply at the current level of production, while proven natural gas reserves have been estimated as sufficient for 55 years of output. Related industrial activities include oil refining, gas processing and production of ammonia, urea, methanol, iron and steel.

3.   The economy grew rapidly between 1973 and 1982, triggered by high oil prices, leading to a substantial increase in investment and consumption. Falling oil prices thereafter led to contracting output, declining per capita income, high unemployment, rising current account deficits and loss of foreign exchange reserves. In response, Trinidad and Tobago introduced in 1988 a programme of structural reform and liberalization, aimed at restoring external balance, reducing the public sector

deficit, and improving financial intermediation. This reform process was strengthened in the 1990s, when price controls were virtually dismantled, import duties were reduced under CARICOM provisions and the role of the private sector in economic activity enhanced. However, there remains a large participation of the State in the oil/natural gas sector; overall, government consumption and investment represent between one-fourth and one-third of GDP.

4.   Annual economic growth accelerated to over 3% a year between 1994 and 1997, as trade and investment liberalization took hold. Tariffs were cut as a result of the implementation, starting in 1995, of the four-phased reduction programme of CARICOM's CET, which has lowered the maximum tariff on industrial goods from 35 to 20%; capital controls were removed; the fixed exchange rate régime was replaced by a managed float; and a programme of privatization and liquidation of public enterprises was put in place. GDP growth reached 3.2% in 1997, fuelled by an investment and consumer spending boom. Initial forecasts point to an acceleration of growth in 1998, reflecting the effects of massive investment in the oil/natural gas sector. These forecasts may, however, need to be revised downward, to take into account the negative effect of the recent decline in oil prices. Although below its peak, unemployment remains high, at 13.5% at the end of 1997.

5.   As a result of improvements in tax collection, proceeds from privatization, and reductions in government subsidies and transfers, Trinidad and Tobago has posted a budget surplus since 1995; the surplus reached 1.8 % of GDP in 1997. Lower oil prices may, however, have a negative impact on public finances in 1998 and 1999.

6.   External transactions in goods and services represent over 100% of GDP, with exports of fuels, the main earner of foreign exchange, accounting for over 20%. Low export diversification and strong dependence on the oil/natural gas sector make Trinidad

and Tobago vulnerable to external shocks. The strong decline in oil prices occurring in 1998, while imports continue to increase, is likely to have a negative impact on the current account. Moreover, Trinidad and Tobago's heavy reliance on a single market, the United States, for exports may add to this vulnerability, should the U.S. economy slow down.

7.   Until 1997, Trinidad and Tobago generally posted a trade surplus. Recently, however, imports have grown much faster than exports, fuelled by rapid increases in consumer and capital goods, as the economy has expanded and the local currency has appreciated in real terms. Between 1993 and 1997, imports more than doubled, while exports increased by around 50%, and in 1997 a trade deficit of US$610 million was registered. In 1998, a trade deficit, albeit smaller than in 1997, is again forecast. The current account, in surplus for most of the 1990s, recorded a deficit of US$708 million (12.1% of GDP) in 1997. The capital account, fed by direct investment flows mainly to the oil/natural gas sector, has registered a surplus since 1996, peaking at US$619 million in 1997, leading to a substantial accumulation of net foreign exchange reserves, which stood at the equivalent of over four months of imports at end-1997.

(2)   TRADE POLICY REGIME AND OBJECTIVES

8.   One of the Government's main policy concerns is to diversify the economy away from its dependence on the petroleum sector, by developing non-oil manufacturing activities as well as services, such as transhipment and trading. Other concerns include increasing the level of foreign and domestic investment, generating   permanent   employment opportunities, and promoting food security. The Government also aims to improve the regulatory, legal and fiscal framework for growth in the energy sector; to maximize local crude oil production; to increase refining capacity; and to develop downstream natural gas-based industries.

9.   Trinidad and Tobago, a GATT contracting party since October 1962, became a WTO Member on 1 March 1995. MFN treatment is accorded to all its trading partners. As a result of the Uruguay Round, most industrial tariffs are bound at a ceiling rate of 50%; some products are bound at 70%. There is a substantial gap between bound rates and applied tariffs, which peak at 30%. All agricultural lines are bound, mostly at 100%. Other duties and charges are bound at 15%. Trinidad and Tobago has revised and amended several pieces of domestic legislation to comply with its obligations under the WTO. Thus, anti-dumping legislation and regulations have been amended to conform to the WTO Anti-dumping Agreement; new Patent and Copyright Acts have been adopted, and legislation   regarding   trademarks   and industrial designs amended to conform to the TRIPS Agreement. Legislation with respect to trade secrets and unfair competition has also been put in place.

10.   Under the GATS, Trinidad and Tobago made specific commitments on tourism, business (including professional), educational, health-related, research and development, recreational, cultural and sporting, transport and financial services. Trinidad and Tobago's Schedule includes horizontal commitments on commercial presence and the presence of natural persons. Trinidad and Tobago also participated and presented offers in the subsequent WTO negotiations on telecommunications and financial services.

11.   To date, Trinidad and Tobago has not been involved directly, as either plaintiff or defendant, under the GATT or WTO dispute settlement mechanisms.

12.   Trinidad and Tobago, a founding member of CARICOM, adopted CARICOM's CET in 1991, implementing the four-phase schedule of CET rate reductions between 1995 and 1 July 1998. Deeper integration among CARICOM countries is expected to result from reforms aimed at consolidating the CARICOM Single Market and Economy (CSME). Two

protocols amending the CARICOM Treaty signed in 1997, are expected to lead to free movement of goods, services and capital, while further steps are being taken to liberalize movement of persons. Schedule I of the CARICOM Treaty allows a few national exceptions to the duty-free entry of goods from other CARICOM member states; for Trinidad and Tobago these are milk and cream, tyre repair materials, and rubber tyres. However, Trinidad and Tobago has chosen not to use this exception, and is in the process of eliminating Schedule I.

13. CARICOM has preferential trade agreements with Colombia and Venezuela. Under the Agreement with Colombia, Trinidad and Tobago, as a CARICOM medium-development country, has bound duty-free access bilaterally as of 1 June 1998 on a number of products, most of which are already imported duty free. Actual concessions have been granted on a small number of products, including skipjack and bonito, and knives and cutting blades for kitchen appliances and lawn mowers. Phased, bound duty reductions will be extended from 1 January 1999 to another group of products, including precious stones, some kinds of coated electrodes and rods, and a group of non-competing inputs and capital goods. Unilateral preferential market access to Venezuela is granted under the CARICOM/Venezuela Agreement on Trade and Investment.

14. The Foreign Investment Act of 1990 is expected to be replaced by a new Investment Promotion Act, now in draft, which seeks to diversify export-related foreign investment. Currently, more than half of foreign investment is in the energy sector and related downstream activities; the United States is the largest foreign investor, mainly in the petroleum sector. There are no restricted sectors for foreign investment; however, approval is required for acquisition of commercial and residential land exceeding a certain area, or where a licence is needed (e.g. for drilling, mining or establishment of a bank by any investor, domestic or foreign; or for acquisition of more than 30% of a publicly

held local company by a foreign investor). Trinidad and Tobago has bilateral investment agreements with Canada, France, the United Kingdom and the United States; agreements with Argentina, Hungary, Italy, the Netherlands and Venezuela are under negotiation. Investment issues are also covered in CARICOM's agreements with Colombia and Venezuela. In addition to the treaty with other CARICOM members, double taxation treaties have been signed with Canada, Denmark, France, Germany, Italy, Norway, Sweden, Switzerland, United Kingdom, United States and Venezuela.

(3) TRADE POLICY BY INSTRUMENT

(i) Border measures

15. Trinidad and Tobago adopted CARICOM's CET for all goods, except a group of mainly agricultural products (List A) and industrial goods (List C) in 1991. Between 1995 and 1998, maximum import duties for industrial products were lowered from 35% to 20% in four phases. Maximum applied rates for agricultural goods have remained at 40% during the whole implementation period. As a consequence of these reductions, Trinidad and Tobago currently has an unweighted average MFN tariff of 9.1% (slightly higher if ad valorem equivalents of specific duties are included). Nominal protection is higher for agricultural products, with an average rate of 19.1%, while industrial imports face an average tariff of 7%. The tariff structure offers higher protection to final consumption goods and agricultural products than to inputs and capital goods, which are either duty-free or subject to a 2.5 % tariff. Final goods that compete with domestic or CARICOM production face the highest rates. Exceptions to the CET, including some motor vehicles, electrical appliances, and jewellery, are charged rates of up to 30%.

16. Quantitative restrictions have largely been dismantled since 1990. Import surcharges are currently applied on a number of agricultural products. These were originally expected to be eliminated by December 1994,

but this elimination was postponed, although certain surcharges were gradually reduced or phased out. Under a schedule established in 1995, surcharges on bovine meat and milk were to be eliminated by 1998; and those on vegetables and fruit are to be eliminated by 1999. Import surcharges on certain other products will remain after that date; some will be subject to reductions by 2004, but some will remain. For example, import surcharges of 60% on sugar, 75% on icing sugar, and 86% on some poultry cuts are expected to remain in place beyond 2004, considerably exceeding the 15% level bound during the Uruguay Round and included in Trinidad and Tobago's schedule of concessions.

17. According to the authorities, Trinidad and Tobago is de facto applying the WTO Agreement on Customs Valuation, although, under the Agreement, Trinidad and Tobago, as a developing country, has until end-1999 to bring its valuation system into conformity with the Agreement.

18. The Trinidad and Tobago Bureau of Standards (TTBS), under the Ministry of Trade and Industry is the enquiry point under the WTO Agreement on Technical Barriers to Trade. Standards are compulsory where they affect the health and safety of consumers or where they can prevent fraud and deception. The TTBS has also the right to test against standards for quality and grading, and is authorised to accept foreign certificates. Environmental standards, using ISO 14000 guidelines, were adopted in 1997, and are the domain of the Environmental Management Authority.

19. Trinidad and Tobago is not a party to the plurilateral Agreement on Government Procurement. Government procurement is not included in the scope of CARICOM, although an action plan to create a central regional information-coordinating agency has been launched. Procurement for governmental agencies is regulated by a Central Tenders Board. Tenders are either selective or competitive, and are open to foreign suppliers. However, a preferential margin of 10% is accorded to local suppliers of goods and services, and, in some cases, if tenders go to foreigners, a local agent may be required.

20. According to the authorities, anti-dumping legislation has been brought into conformity with the relevant WTO Agreement. The Anti-Dumping and Countervailing Duties Act (No.11 of 1992), notified to the WTO in March 1995, was substantially amended in 1995; however, the amendment has not yet been notified. To date, the only anti-dumping action taken by Trinidad and Tobago has been an investigation on imports of cheddar cheese from New Zealand, initiated in September 1996. In this case, a margin of dumping of 13.93% was calculated; however, no duty was imposed, since the New Zealand Dairy Board undertook to increase its price of cheddar cheese exported to Trinidad and Tobago by the amount of the calculated margin of dumping.

21. Licences are still needed for the importation of some products, namely those included in the Import Negative List, originally used to manage a system of quantitative restrictions to protect infant industries, and now used mainly for licensing purposes. Currently, the List includes livestock, meat, fish, sugar, oils and fats, motor vehicles, cigarette papers, small ships and boats, and pesticides; it does not apply to CARICOM imports, except of oils and fats.

(ii) **Measures affecting exports, production and trade**

22. Trinidad and Tobago applies no export taxes, but a system of export licensing for a number of products, mainly for security and health purposes but also to control the re-export of capital goods imported under preferential conditions, is in effect. There are no export quotas, except those determined under bilateral arrangements, nor specific export performance requirements.

23. Trinidad and Tobago has notified the WTO that it maintains no export subsidies. However, a number of incentives are applied,

including tax concessions and duty-free access for imports of inputs and capital goods. Some are geared to promoting exports, such as export allowances (in the form of tax credits) under the Corporation Tax Act and the Finance Act; others are designed to promote the development of specific industries or sectors, such as the customs duty concessions for imports of capital goods for a wide range of approved manufactured activities. The Government plans to eliminate export allowances by the year 2000, although Trinidad and Tobago, as a developing country, is required to comply fully with the disciplines of the WTO Agreement on Subsidies and Countervailing Measures only in 2003. Duty concessions under these schemes have, in some cases, already been wiped out by the elimination of tariffs on non-competing inputs and capital goods.

24. *The establishment and administration of Free Zones is regulated by the Trinidad and Tobago Free Zones Company, which reviews applications taking into account foreign exchange earning capacity and employment generation potential. No sectoral limitation is applied. Companies granted approved status are allowed to supply domestically a maximum of 20% of goods produced, subject to the payment of import duties. Since 1997, certificates of origin have been required for goods manufactured in the Free Zones. There are currently 24 companies operating under the free-zone régime, with exports totalling US$38 million in 1996.*

25. *Although most price controls have been eliminated, and only the prices of sugar, pharmaceuticals, and school books remain directly regulated, a number of goods and services are subject to administered prices. These include certain agricultural products (i.e. coffee, milk, cocoa, etc.), for which guaranteed prices are paid to producers; the ex-refinery prices of certain fuels; and utility fares.*

26. *Trinidad and Tobago has updated its domestic legislation regarding intellectual property rights to bring it in line with the*

TRIPS Agreement. The registration of patents, trademarks and industrial designs is administered by the Intellectual Property Registrar-General, within the Ministry of Legal Affairs.

(4) MEASURES BY SECTOR

(i) Agriculture

27. *The contribution of agriculture and food processing, beverages and tobacco to GDP, is just above 5%, but the sector employs some 14% of the labour force. Agricultural exports are dominated by sugar. The main exports of processed products are beverages and prepared cereals. Trinidad and Tobago is a net importer of agricultural products; the main imported goods are cereals, dairy products, oil seeds and vegetables.*

28. *In the Uruguay Round, Trinidad and Tobago bound its tariffs on all agricultural products at ceiling rates of 100%, with the exception of seven items bound at higher levels; these include poultry, cabbage, lettuce and coffee. Applied tariffs on agricultural products vary between 0 and 40%; in 1998, Trinidad and Tobago's simple average MFN tariff on agricultural products was 19.1%. The highest tariffs are applied to edible fruit and nuts, fish products, edible vegetables, animal and vegetable fat and oil, and meat and edible meat offal.*

29. *Quantity-based measures, previously applied under the Negative List, were converted to equivalent tariffs in accordance with the Uruguay Round Agreement on Agriculture. Some agricultural products are subject to import surcharges; in 1998, surcharges are applied to various parts of poultry (100%), sugar and icing sugar (60-75%), vegetables (15%) and fruit (5%). Surcharges on fruit and vegetables will be removed by 1999, and those on poultry parts will be reduced in 2004; surcharges on sugar and icing sugar are not subject to reduction. Import duties on alcoholic beverages are set at specific rates, ranging from TT$4.75 per litre for beer to TT$40.00 per litre for cordials and*

liqueurs. Alcoholic beverages that are locally and regionally produced face excise duties.

30. Sugar is the main agricultural crop. Exports depend primarily on the quota arrangements with the European Union and the United States, which offer guaranteed prices above world levels. Trinidad and Tobago has been allocated an export quota of 47,556 tons of raw sugar by the European Union under the Sugar Protocol to the Lomé Convention, and an additional 10,000 tonnes under the Special Preferential Sugar Arrangement. The United States allocated Trinidad and Tobago a quota of 14,201 tonnes of raw sugar for fiscal year 1997, of which 13,576 tonnes were exported. Refined sugar is exported to other CARICOM countries, but is also imported when domestic production is insufficient to meet export quotas and domestic demand. Some 29,000 tonnes of raw sugar and 9,105 tonnes of refined sugar were imported in 1997. As noted, imports of raw sugar are subject to a customs duty of 40%, and an additional charge of 60%. Imports of refined sugar face a 15% import tariff.

31. Agricultural incentives include subsidies for soil conservation, equipment and machinery, agricultural vehicles and wheel tractors, as well as price support for sugarcane, coffee, cocoa, milk, oranges, grapefruit, paddy, copra and sorrel. Payments granted for price support reached TT$35.97 million in 1997, while input subsidies totalled TT$0.4million; together these payments account for some 1.8% of agricultural GDP.

(ii) Manufacturing

32. The manufacturing sector is heavily dependent on oil refining and petrochemicals; petroleum-related manufacturing accounts for two-thirds of total manufacturing GDP. The 1998 average MFN tariff on imports of industrial products (HS Chapters 25-97, covering both manufacturing and mining) was 7.0%, with a peak of 30% and a minimum rate of zero. The highest tariffs are applied on arms and ammunition, clocks and watches, works of art, clothing and apparel articles, carpets, furniture, toys, footwear, soap and leather goods. A number of incentive schemes are available for manufacturers; thus, customs duty concessions are granted to imports of machinery, equipment and materials for a wide range of approved manufacturing activities. Relief from corporation tax and customs duty is granted to approved enterprises for a period of up to 10 years.

33. Petroleum-related manufacturing includes a refinery, 13 petrochemical plants, a natural gas liquid recovery plant and electricity power plants. Refining activities have fallen considerably from their peak in the 1960s, but the decline has been reversed in the mid 1990s. On the other hand, petrochemical output has been rising considerably; currently Trinidad and Tobago is the world's second largest producer of ammonia, and third largest producer of urea. Non-petroleum manufacturing activities are concentrated in cement, iron and steel.

(iii) Mineral extraction

34. The extractive sector contributed 14.4% to GDP in 1996, while employing under 4% of the labour force; the sector also generates most foreign investment inflows. Hydrocarbons account for almost the whole of the sector's output. Oil production has declined from its peak in the 1970s; conversely, natural gas production has been increasing since 1978. However, the sector still accounted for 22% of government revenue and 73% of foreign exchange earnings in 1997.

35. The tax régime in the petroleum industry is based on a three-tier system consisting of two profit-based corporation taxes (the Petroleum Profits Tax, set at 50% of taxable profits, and an Unemployment Levy, set at 5% of taxable profits), three production-based taxes (a Royalty, a Petroleum Production Levy, a Petroleum Impost) and an income-based tax, (the Supplemental Profits Petroleum Tax. Profits accruing from

exploration, production and refining activities are subject to the Petroleum Profits Tax and taxed at 50%, while profits accruing from petroleum marketing and distribution, for which the state-owned National Petroleum Marketing Company of Trinidad and Tobago and the National Gas Company have the monopoly, are taxed, since 1997, at a rate of 35%, since they are subject to the Corporate Profits Tax. A system of incentives and tax allowances are used to encourage investment in the energy sector, including import duty and VAT exemptions, and deduction of capital expenditures incurred on workovers, heavy oil projects and on a development dry hole for the computation of the Petroleum Profits Tax.

(iv) **Services**

36.   The services sector accounts for over 60% of GDP and around 75% of total employment. Financial services are particularly important, accounting for 11.5% of GDP. Activity in services has been largely liberalized, and market access is fairly open in most sub-sectors; national treatment is granted to foreign suppliers in most areas. The regulatory frameworks for financial services, transport, and telecommunications have been strengthened. In telecommunications, partial privatization had led to a temporary de facto monopoly in the provision of basic telephony services by Telecommunication Services of Trinidad and Tobago (TSTT); this monopoly is expected to be dismantled by 2009. Value-added services must use the network of TSTT.

37.   Under the General Agreement on Trade in Services (GATS), Trinidad and Tobago scheduled horizontal commitments regarding commercial presence and the movement of natural persons for all sectors included in its Schedule. With respect to commercial presence, the acquisition of over 30% of the equity of publicly traded companies is subject to approval. Specific commitments were scheduled in business

services (including professional services, computer and related services, research and development services, real estate and other business services); educational services; financial services; health related and social services; tourism and travel-related services; recreation, cultural and sporting services; and transport services. Trinidad and Tobago Trinidad and Tobago presented a Schedule of Specific Commitments in the Negotiations on Telecommunications, binding full competition in value-added services, using TSTT's network, full competition on satellite-based mobile services and fixed satellite services for public use. Trinidad and Tobago also submitted an additional offer in the 1997 Negotiations on Financial Services, making commitments only in reinsurance.

Conclusions

38.   The economy of Trinidad and Tobago has experienced considerable liberalization and deregulation since the mid 1980s, and particularly since 1993. Strong investment in the oil/natural gas sector has fuelled growth since the mid 1990s, at the same time leading to a substantial increase in imports, which added to high investment income outflows, has resulted in a current account deficit. The recent strength of the Trinidad and Tobago dollar, which has resulted from the stringent monetary policy conducted by the Central Bank, may aggravate the current account deficit. Despite the current weakness of oil prices, Trinidad and Tobago's economy has been partly shielded from negative effects by large direct investment inflows. However, the economy remains vulnerable to external shocks due to its excessive dependence on the production and export of fuels, and a prolonged situation of lower oil prices is likely to take its toll on growth. Hence, to ensure long-run economic stability Trinidad and Tobago needs to reinforce its current policy of diversifying away from the oil sector. This effort will be helped by open access to markets for its non-fuel exports.

I. THE ECONOMIC ENVIRONMENT

(1) MAJOR FEATURES OF THE ECONOMY

1.   Trinidad and Tobago is a resource-based economy. The economy derives most of its income from oil and oil-based products and petrochemicals, although its dependence on this single commodity has declined as industrial diversification has been pursued in the last few decades. Proven oil reserves are estimated at 534 million barrels, about 12 years' supply at current production rates. Trinidad and Tobago also has significant deposits of natural gas (proven reserves are enough to last 55 years), on which it has based its petrochemicals industry. In addition to primary energy products, related industrial activities include oil refining, gas processing and the production of ammonia, urea, methanol, iron and steel. Total GDP in 1997 was roughly US$5.8 billion (Table I.1).

Table I.1
Major features of the Trinidad and Tobago economy, 1996 and 1997

	1996	1997[a]
Area: 5,130 square kilometres		
Population (thousands	1,264.0	1,271.0
Population growth rate (%)	0.3	0.6
Labour force (thousands)	530.4	541.0
Unemployment	16.3	15.0
GDP at current prices (US$ million)	5,653.4	5,843.4
GDP per capita (US$)	4,472.6	4,597.5
Share in GDP (%)		
Agriculture	3.0	2.8
Industry	36.3	35.6
Petroleum sector	28.1	26.6
Manufacturing	8.2	9.0
Services	60.0	61.1
Construction	7.8	8.4
Distribution, hotel	16.1	17.0
Government	9.1	8.3
Financial services	11.3	11.5
Other services	15.7	15.9
Other	0.7	0.5
Merchandise exports f.o.b. (US$ million)	2,506.0	2,427.0
Merchandise imports c.i.f. (US$ million)	2,159.0	3,038.0
Merchandise exports to GDP (%)	44.3	41.5
Merchandise imports to GDP (%)	38.2	52.0
Non-factor services (US$ million)	245.0	213.0
Exports of goods and non-factor services GDP (%)	52.6	49.4
Imports of goods and non-factor services GDP (%)	42.2	56.3

a   Estimates.

Note: All figures are based on current market prices, unless otherwise stated.

Source: IMF, International Financial Statistics, (various issues).

2.   Trinidad and Tobago imports some 75% of its domestic food requirements. Agriculture employs 9.6% of the labour force but contributes 2.3% to GDP. The main crops are sugar, coffee, cocoa and, more recently, citrus fruit. Manufacturing, despite attempts at diversification, continues to

depend heavily on petroleum-related industries, and employs around 8% of the labour force. The service sector is the major contributor to GDP and employment, the public sector being the dominant employer. However, as many state enterprises have been privatized, employment in the public sector has fallen from 30% of the labour force in 1987 to 25% in 1997.

3.   After a period of fast economic growth between 1973 and 1982, triggered by the increase in oil prices, the economy of Trinidad and Tobago experienced a decade of contracting output and falling per capita income. In 1988, as a response to economic contraction, high unemployment, and the loss of foreign exchange reserves, Trinidad and Tobago introduced a programme of structural reform and liberalization, aimed particularly at restoring its external balance. The programme provided for the relaxation of price controls, improvement in financial intermediation, and a reduction of the public sector deficit, particularly through expenditure-cutting measures.

4.   Structural reform has been strengthened during the 1990s: import duties have been reduced, and the role of the private sector in economic activity has been enhanced. However, due to the importance of the oil sector, there remains a large participation of the State in the economy: it is estimated that government consumption and investment represent between one fourth and one third of GDP. As a member of CARICOM, Trinidad and Tobago adopted in 1993 the Common External Tariffs (CET) four-phased schedule of rate reductions aimed at lowering the maximum rate for industrial goods from 35% to 20% by 1998.

5.   The economy grew at an average annual rate of 1.7% between 1989 and 1997; population growth averaged 1.2% a year, implying annual average growth in per capita income of 0.5% for the period. Two distinct sub-periods can be identified: the first one of low or negative growth (1989-1993), and a subsequent sub-period (1994-97) with growth rates above 3%. The second sub-period coincides with an increase in the degree of openness of the economy, as evidenced by the implementation of the CET's four-phased tariff reduction programme, the removal of capital controls, the floating of the exchange rate, and the privatization or liquidation of public enterprises. GDP growth was 3.2% in 1997, and is expected to accelerate in 1998, reflecting the effects of massive investment in the oil/gas sector. The recent decline in oil demand and prices may temper, however, initial forecasts. By the end of 1997 unemployment had fallen from its peak levels but remained high at 13.5%.

6.   Apart from oil and natural gas, Trinidad and Tobago has large deposits of asphalt, andesite, argillite, chromium, clay, copper, fluorspar, graphite, gypsum, iron, limestone, sand, and porcellanite. Among these, clay is the most abundant and extensively utilized. It also has one of the largest natural sources of asphalt in the world. There is a large variety of agricultural crops, exports of which are concentrated mainly in sugar, cocoa and, until recently, coffee. The main exports of processed products are beverages and preparations of cereals. Tourism is not as important as in other Caribbean islands (282,000 arrivals in 1995, and 3,874 hotel rooms), but the Government plans to enhance its contribution to economic activity. There are two major airports - the Piarco Airport in Trinidad and the Crown Point Airport in Tobago - which are owned and managed by the government-controlled Airport Authority of Trinidad and Tobago. The major sea ports are Port of Spain and Point Lisas, in Trinidad, and Scarborough in Tobago. The supply of water is adequate and electricity is mostly generated from domestically-produced natural gas. Constraints to growth have arisen in the past from a dependence on the oil sector, labour market rigidities and excessive government intervention in the economy. High unemployment is partly due to the capital-intensive character of some of the main production and export activities, especially oil/gas and mining which are encouraged by investment incentives.

7.   One of Trinidad and Tobago's recent concerns is the effectiveness of monetary policy, since the extensive use of unremunerated high reserve requirements for banks is proving inadequate to prevent credit expansion. Open-market operations have been increasingly used to complement the effectiveness of reserve management. The strong inflow of foreign exchange as a consequence of oil-related investments is partly behind the increase in the money supply. Another factor is the enhancement of financial intermediation which has led to circumvention of legal reserve requirements and thereby to a higher money multiplier. The surge in private consumption spending, estimated at about 20% in 1997, is largely explained by credit expansion.

8.   Imports and exports of goods and services together amount to over 100% of GDP, over 20% of which are exports of fuels. Foreign exchange receipts rely heavily on the oil/natural gas sector, with investment in that sector being the major force behind the strong capital account surplus (US$837 million) posted in 1997. The concentration of exports in the oil/natural gas sector places Trinidad and Tobago in a vulnerable position to external shocks. Reliance on a single market, the United States, for almost half of its merchandise exports adds to this vulnerability. Attempts to diversify have resulted in a substantial increase in trade with other CARICOM countries which now absorb almost a quarter of total exports.

(2)   RECENT ECONOMIC PERFORMANCE

(i)   GDP and employment

9.   Economic performance can be divided into three phases: the oil boom, lasting roughly from 1973 to 1982; a period of severe recession from 1982 to 1993 when per capita income fell to pre-1973 levels; and a period of growth since 1994, during which stabilization policies and an increased openness of the economy have succeeded in attracting foreign investment, particularly in the energy sector.

10.   During the oil boom the economy grew by 5.5% a year, boosted by an improvement in the terms of trade. Nominal per capita income rose from US$4,200 to US$6,200; savings and investment averaged 30% of GDP. Meanwhile, industrial policy based on protection against imports focused on shifting manufacturing output towards products with higher value added. With the collapse in oil prices after 1982, the economy suffered over the next decade an almost uninterrupted decline in output. Per capita income fell by an average 5% per annum, returning to its 1973 level. Gross fixed capital formation fell from an average 22.6% in 1983-86 to 15.2% in 1987-93, having a negative effect on labour productivity and labour demand. Unemployment rose from 10% in 1982 to 22% in 1989. Output decline continued in 1992 and 1993.

11.   Since 1994, the economy has recorded positive growth (Table I.2). In 1994 and 1995, export growth and private investment fuelled the expanding economy whereas in 1996, as direct and indirect taxes were cut, consumption overtook investment as the main impetus to growth. The decline in investment stopped in the early 1990s, and its share in GDP is estimated to have reached 21.8% in 1997. Gross national savings, however, have been declining since 1995, reflecting a sharp increase in consumer spending (estimated at over 19% in 1997) and an increase (until 1996) in net factor payments. The savings/GDP ratio, which stood at over 20% between 1994 and 1996, fell to slightly under 10% in 1997, well below the investment /GDP ratio. The large investment/savings gap posted in 1997 (the counterpart of which was a large current account deficit) was financed by external savings - mainly by foreign direct investment in the fuel sector.

Table I.2
Economic performance, 1992-97
(Per cent)

	1992	1993	1994	1995	1996	1997[a]
	Percentage change (based on 1985 prices)					
Real GDP at market prices	-1.6	-1.5	3.6	3.8	3.5	3.2
Private consumption	-2.2	2.3	-11.6	5.4	13.0	19.4
Government consumption	-2.7	-8.9	5.1	-0.6	-2.9	-8.2
Gross national investment	-24.8	3.0	44.7	-13.9	11.5	0.0
Exports of goods and non-factor services	13.2	-4.4	16.9	15.2	-6.9	3.9
Imports of goods and non-factor services	4.1	3.9	-9.6	16.9	13.4	50.6
Unemployment (annual average rate)	19.6	19.8	18.4	17.2	16.3	15.0
Consumer price index (1990=100)	6.5	10.8	8.8	5.2	3.4	3.7
Government finance	Percentage of GDP					
Government revenue	26.3	27.6	25.8	27.0	28.1	27.1
Government expenditure	29.1	27.3	26.1	26.8	26.4	25.3
Government surplus/deficit(-)	-2.8	0.2	-0.3	0.2	1.7	1.8
Government domestic debt	21.7	21.9	19.0	20.0	18.6	22.3
Public external debt	40.7	45.8	41.6	35.9	33.2	26.1
Memorandum:						
Gross National Investment/GDP	13.8	14.3	20.2	16.0	17.2	21.8
Gross National Savings/GDP	14.4	12.0	24.8	21.0	18.4	9.6

a   Estimates.

Source: IMF, International Financial Statistics (various issues).

12.   While unemployment has been a persistent challenge for the Government, in the last few years, the more labour-intensive segments of the economy have outperformed the petroleum sector. By the fourth quarter of 1997, unemployment had fallen to 13.5%, the lowest level in 13 years.[1] This rate remains high, however, and is not likely to fall significantly in the near future because growth is expected to be concentrated mainly in the capital-intensive oil/natural gas sector.

13.   The non-petroleum sector has performed in a more stable fashion, having achieved a fairly steady average annual growth rate of around 3.8% between 1994-97. The petroleum sector increased at an average annual rate of 2.4% in the same period, but annual growth rates were subject to large fluctuations (Chart I.1). In the non-petroleum sector the fastest growing activities were hotels, distribution, and construction. In the petroleum sector the most dynamic area was the production of petrochemicals.

---

[1] The average unemployment rate for the year was 15 %.

Chart I.1
GDP growth rates, by sector, 1992-97

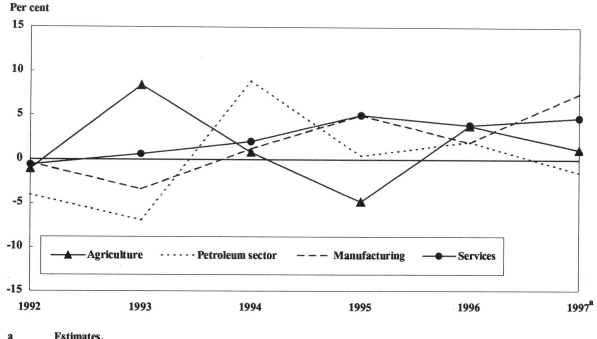

Per cent

a   Estimates.
Source: IMF, International Financial Statistics (various issues).

14.   Tight fiscal and monetary policies, especially tight management of bank reserve requirements and other policies aimed at curtailing credit expansion, have proved ineffective in stopping a sharp increase in consumer spending, which accounted for some 75% of GDP in 1997. Imported goods, particularly motor vehicles and other consumer durable goods, account for a considerable part of this spending. The expansion in private consumption observed in 1997 has lowered the private savings GDP ratio to an estimated 2%. Spending on imported goods and services in the 1995-97 period grew at a faster rate than that on domestically produced goods; in 1997 alone, it is estimated to have increased by over 50% compared to the previous year. The real effective appreciation of the Trinidad and Tobago dollar observed in 1997 may have contributed to an expenditure-switching effect, leading to a greater increase in consumption of imported goods over domestically produced goods. This, together with lower export prices, resulted in a negative contribution of net exports to GDP growth of around 7%, reversing the trend of the previous year.

15.   Although unemployment has increased throughout most of the 1990s, and productivity growth has been weak at best, real wages have risen.[2] Real wage increases are the result of skilled labour shortages, particularly in the oil refining sector[3], strong union bargaining power, and wage indexation.

---

[2] As an example, real wages for all industries increased by 7 % in the first nine months of 1995, and by 5.1 % in the first nine months of 1996. Central Bank of Trinidad and Tobago (1997a), p. 9.
        [3] Real wages in the oil refining sector increased by 43.2% in the first nine months of 1995, and by 12.3% in the first nine months of 1996.

(ii)   Prices

16.   The rate of inflation has been falling since 1993, from an annual average of 13.1% to 3.7% in 1997, mainly as the result of the positive effect of trade liberalization measures, including tariff reductions, exchange rate stability, and the removal of the value-added tax (VAT) for certain food items. These positive effects have partly countered the inflationary pressure stemming from high wage increases.

17.   Monetary and fiscal policies have also helped to keep inflation under control. The restrictive fiscal policy applied by the Government since the beginning of the 1990s has led to several years of central government surpluses.   The current increase in consumption added to the relative ineffectiveness of monetary policy in curtailing credit growth could pose a future inflationary threat. However, tariff reductions under Phase IV of the CET (Chapter III(2)(iii)) could have a welcome effect in tempering inflationary pressures.

18.   Since 1993, most price controls have been eliminated.   Only the prices of sugar, pharmaceuticals and school books continue to be regulated.   Maximum retail prices for drugs distinguish between imported and locally manufactured products (Chapter III (4) (vi)).

(iii)   Monetary policy

19.   The Central Bank of Trinidad and Tobago, established in 1964 by the Central Bank Act (since amended), is in charge of monetary policy and acts as lender of last resort to the Government. The Bank must report to and act under the authority of the Ministry of Finance, although this authority is seldom exercised.[4]   The Government is currently considering enhancing the Central Bank's independence. The main policy instrument for monetary control has been the use of high legal reserve requirements for commercial banks in order to sterilize the inflow of foreign currency associated with foreign direct investment. In addition, until the late 1980s, restrictions on consumer credit and a ban on borrowing by foreign corporations were applied. Local banks were not allowed to open foreign currency accounts for residents. Moreover, the Central Bank encouraged banks to lend to selected sectors at preferential rates; credit ceilings were placed on loans to state-owned enterprises. Beginning in the late 1980s, the Central Bank started to move away from selective intervention in credit markets while strengthening its prudential powers.[5]

20.   After the floating of the Trinidad and Tobago dollar and the removal of capital controls in 1993, monetary policy focused on exchange rate stability and low inflation. By early 1994, all selective credit controls and guidelines had been abolished. Open-market operations were launched in September 1996, an initiative aimed at reducing reliance on reserve requirements. Since the transition away from monetary controls, interest rates have become positive in real terms after many years of negative real rates of return on savings (which may help to explain Trinidad and Tobago's low savings rate) (Chart I.2).[6]

---

[4] The Minister of Finance's authority to give the Central Bank a written directive in respect of monetary and fiscal policy has been exercised only once since 1964.

[5] Clarke and Leon, 1996.

[6] The spread between deposit and lending rates has been traditionally very high in Trinidad and Tobago (Chart I.2), as the market for loans is basically local and the costs of operating high reserve requirements is passed on to the customer. In 1997, the spread between loan rates and time deposits shrank somewhat, due to a reduction in the former and an increase in the latter. The existence of high spreads my be due to inefficiencies in the banking system.

Chart I.2
Deposit and lending rates, 1981-97

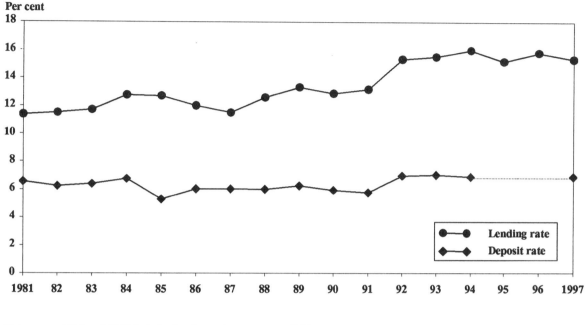

Note: 1995 and 1996 data for lending rates are not available.

Source: IMF, International Financial Statistics (various issues).

21.   In an attempt to keep credit expansion under control, monetary policy was tightened further in 1997. The rate of unremunerated reserve requirements for banks was increased from 21% to 24% in the fourth quarter (it had been reduced by 2 percentage points at the beginning of the year), while the rate for non-banks was raised from 6% to 9%.[7] The increase in reserve requirements was accompanied by open-market operations withdrawing TT$100 million (US$16.1 million) out of the financial system.

22.   Although monetary policy was tightened in 1997, broad money M3 continued to expand at a rate exceeding 15%, well above the rate of inflation; liabilities to the private sector increased by 23%. Domestic credit continued to be the main source of money creation, despite tight reserve requirements, with credit extended to the private sector expanding by over 30%. There was also a steep increase in domestic financing of the Central Government. The accumulation of net external assets was another important source of money creation. To contain the expansion of the money supply, the Central Bank resorted heavily to open-market operations, increasing substantially (by over 70%) Treasury Bill holdings by the private sector and pushing up yields.[8] Due to negative real

---

[7]The Central Bank estimates that the increase in reserve requirements for banks and non-banks amounted to withdrawing TT$484 million (US$77 million) from the system. Central Bank of Trinidad and Tobago (1997b).

[8]The average yield for Treasury Bills issued for open-market operations in the fourth quarter of 1997 was 10.84%, while the yield for those issued for the purpose of refinancing maturing treasury debt was 10.69%; both yields are above those observed in the second and third quarters of 1997. Despite the fourth quarter increase, however, annual Treasury Bill yields in 1997, at 9.8% on a weighted-average basis for both types of issues, were below average yields in 1996 which stood at 10.45%.

returns, banks have tended not to keep excess reserves.[9] Interest rates remained high in real terms, but loan rates fell in the second half of the year while time deposit rates increased slightly.[10]

(iv)   Exchange rate policy

23.   Until 1993, Trinidad and Tobago maintained a fixed exchange rate regime. In 1976, the Trinidad and Tobago dollar was pegged to the U.S. dollar at the rate of TT$2.40 to US$1. A system of exchange controls was in place, including the allocation of foreign exchange by the Central Bank. The exchange rate remained unchanged until the mid-1980s, leading to a real appreciation of the Trinidad and Tobago dollar. In 1985, the Trinidad and Tobago dollar was devalued (to TT$3.60 per US$1) and again in 1988 (to TT$4.25 for US$1). From 1988, the foreign exchange regime was gradually liberalized: net earners of foreign exchange were exempted from the allocation process starting in 1989, and the Government eliminated most restrictions on import payments by the end of 1990. From mid-1992, non-residents were allowed to open foreign currency accounts with local banks.

24.   On 13 April 1993 the Trinidad and Tobago dollar went on to a managed float and was devalued by 26%. Following passage of the Central Bank Amendment Act of 1993, remaining exchange controls were removed and foreign investors were no longer required to obtain approval to repatriate capital, interest, dividends or capital gains. Capital account transactions were liberalized and Trinidad and Tobago accepted the obligations of the IMF's Article VIII, 2, 3 and 4 on 13 December 1993. In an attempt to curtail the "dollarization" of the economy, the Government imposed a 10% tax on interest earned on foreign currency accounts held locally by individuals. Foreign exchange transactions are conducted through authorized dealers, requiring a licence; foreign exchange dealers may be commercial banks or *bureaux de change*.

25.   A goal of the Central Bank is to achieve nominal exchange rate stability. This goal has been largely achieved: between 1994 and 1997, nominal exchange rate fluctuations were generally less than 2% (Chart I.3). Due to the fact that inflation has remained subdued, movements in the real exchange rate have been moderate in that period. One of the Central Bank's key concerns has been to convince the main earners of foreign exchange to keep the market supplied on a regular basis. Insufficient supply of foreign exchange has led in the past to a trend towards depreciation of the Trinidad and Tobago dollar, with the Central Bank intervening to stabilize the exchange rate. In 1997, this situation changed because strong capital inflows led to an increase in the availability of foreign exchange. This resulted in a real effective appreciation of the Trinidad and Tobago dollar of around 2%.

---

[9]The average balances with the Central Bank/deposits ratio for commercial banks was 17.6 %, below the 21% statutory cash reserve requirement applicable in most of 1997. This included special deposits in the Central Bank, which are remunerated at 4%.

[10]Median loan rates were 15% in the second half of 1997, half a percentage point below rates in 1996 and three quarters of a percentage point higher than on the first half of 1997. The median rate for time deposits ended the year at 6.75%, compared to 6.44% in 1996.

Chart I.3
Selected indicators of external performance, 1992-97

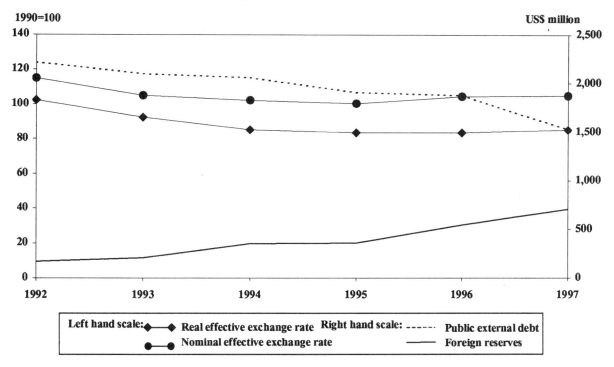

Source: IMF, International Financial Statistics (various issues).

(v)   Public finances

26.   During the oil boom, revenue from oil taxes provided the Government with the capacity to intervene on a large scale. Much of these revenues were used to subsidize public enterprises. After the fall in oil prices in the early 1980s, the Government tried to maintain expenditure levels despite reduced revenues. As a result, the public sector went into deficit, which was financed by the accumulation of external debt. With a further drop in oil prices in 1986 and the exhaustion of foreign exchange reserves by 1987, a strict regime of import licensing (Negative Import List) and foreign exchange controls was put into effect. As a part of the structural adjustment programme launched in 1988, the Government introduced a series of austerity measures intended to control expenditures and reduce the budget deficit: cost-of-living allowances for public servants were suspended, salaries reduced by 10%, government subsidies and transfers were cut, and the direct tax structure was modified. In 1992, the pace of structural adjustment was intensified with the revamping of taxation of the oil and natural gas sector to encourage exploration, and large scale divestment of public enterprises (Box I.1).

27.   As a part of the programme of structural adjustment, a value-added tax was introduced in 1990 and, as a result, the revenue base has broadened. Customs duties were reduced in 1991, when the Common External Tariff was introduced; they were reduced further in 1993, 1995, 1997, and 1998. Since 1993, revenue collection has been much improved and, in the last few years, the maximum corporate and income tax rates have been lowered progressively. In 1996, the corporate tax rate was reduced from 38% to 35%, the same as the top marginal tax rate on individuals. The threshold for commercial suppliers subject to VAT was increased from TT$100,000 to TT$150,000 and the number of zero-rated foods was increased. Between 1993 and 1997 (except in 1994), the

Central Government balance has been in surplus.[11] Central Government revenue during the 1994-97 period remained stable at around 27% of GDP, of which 23 percentage points stem from non-oil revenue; expenditure averaged 26% of GDP in the same period. Income tax and VAT receipts accounted for over 50% of revenue. Customs duties accounted for 5.2% of revenue in 1996, increasing to 6.2% in 1997 following a rise in imports (section(3)(ii)).

Box I.1: Privatization

By the late 1980s, state-owned enterprises accounted for one fifth of GDP in Trinidad and Tobago. In May 1987, the Government appointed a team to review the performance and assess the viability and future prospects of public enterprises and make recommendations for their restructuring and reform. In 1990, 49% of the telephone company, Telco, was sold. As of 1 January 1992, the Government's portfolio of investments included shareholding in 87 enterprises with a value of TT$6.5 billion. Of these 37 were wholly owned, 17 majority-owned, 2 minority-owned and 17 indirectly owned. In addition, the government held investments in the four statutory public utilities supplying water, power, transport and port facilities. State enterprises have been important contributors to the economy, accounting for 23.3% of GDP, 30.3% of capital investment, 9.8% of employment and 56.3% of foreign exchange earnings in 1992. Of the 87 entities in the Government's portfolio in 1992, 61 were slated for divestment or liquidation, 7 for restructuring and 19 were to be retained. As explained below, this goal has not been attained yet.

In 1993 the Government outlined the role of state enterprises, limiting state participation to areas of strategic importance such as oil and natural gas and to enterprises providing social services. The Divestment Secretariat, a unit of the Ministry of Finance but located in the Central Bank, was established in 1993 as the executing body for the government divestment programme. In the period 1992-97, the Divestment Secretariat was engaged in 36 assignments, including the national carrier BWIA International (51%), Fertilizers of Trinidad, Trinidad and Tobago Urea Company, Trinidad and Tobago Methanol Company, Iron and Steel Company, National Flour Mills (49%), Power Generation Company of Trinidad and Tobago (49%), Point Lisas Industrial Port Development Corporation (49%). Other companies partly or wholly privatized between 1993 and 1996 include Trinidad and Tobago Packaging and Printing, Trinidad and Tobago Fruit Processors, Airline Caterers, Trinidad and Tobago Cement, National Poultry, Trinidad and Tobago Mortgage and Finance Company, Maritime Life, National Fishers, National Television and Broadcasting, Reinsurance Company of Trinidad and Tobago, Shipping Corporation of Trinidad and Tobago, and Telecommunication Services of Trinidad and Tobago, among others. Much of the privatization has been effected by sales to foreign interests. As of 1 January 1998, the Government still had direct equity holdings in 36 enterprises, including the Petroleum Company of Trinidad and Tobago (Petrotrin), the National Gas Company of Trinidad and Tobago and Caroni. Petrotrin and Caroni, both of which ran heavy losses in 1997, remained completely in Government hands.

---

28.   Public external debt declined between 1993 and 1997, from 45.8% of GDP to 26.1%. External debt service fell accordingly, from 30.8% of exports of goods and services in 1993 to 15.8% in 1997.

---

[11]The overall public sector balance was in surplus between 1993 and 1996. In 1997, it registered a small deficit due to the losses incurred by Petrotrin and Caroni.

(3)   EXTERNAL PERFORMANCE

(i)   Balance of payments

29.   Until 1997, Trinidad and Tobago normally had a trade surplus, primarily from fuel exports. Imports have, however, been expanding much faster than exports during the 1990s, and in 1997 a trade deficit of US$610 million was posted due to a strong increase in imported consumption and capital goods.[12]   The capital-intensive nature of the oil sector has created an increasingly strong dependence on imported capital goods.   Imports of goods represented 52% of GDP in 1997, heavily outweighing exports (41.5%) (Table I.3).   Imports of merchandise expanded by 41% in 1997, while exports declined by 3%, mainly due to lower oil prices.   Between 1993 and 1997, imports have more than doubled, while exports have increased by around 50%.   Fed by the investment and consumption spending sprees and by the recent real appreciation of the Trinidad and Tobago dollar, import growth is expected to continue outpacing export growth, and a trade deficit, albeit smaller than in 1997, is forecast for 1998.

30.   Traditionally, the balance of non-factor services posts a small surplus, primarily from travel and transportation.   The traditional deficit in investment income reflects remittances of profits and dividends by oil companies and interest payments abroad.   In 1997, the deficit declined, partly reflecting a reduction in interest payments on the external debt, and partly lower profit repatriation by oil companies.

31.   The current account, in surplus for most of the 1990s, recorded a deficit of US$708 million (12.1% of GDP) in 1997.   The deficit is expected to be slightly lower in 1998.   The structure of Trinidad and Tobago's capital account is dominated by direct investment flows.   Private capital inflows which hovered between US$200-US$300 million a year during 1992-96, increased to US$814 million in 1997.   The total stock of foreign direct investment is estimated at nearly US$4 billion or 75% of GDP.[13]   An additional US$1 billion, related to gas exploration, is expected to flow into the country before the end of the decade.   The capital account has registered a surplus since 1996, peaking at US$619 million in 1997, leading to a substantial accumulation of net foreign exchange reserves, which stood at the equivalent to over four months of imports at end-1997.

(ii)   Evolution, composition and direction of trade

32.   Total merchandise exports in 1997 amounted to US$2.4 billion, 3% below 1996 levels.   The share of energy products (in value terms) is still high, but declining (from close to 93% in 1980 to 52.6% by 1996) (Table AI.1).   For the same period, crude oil declined from 40% of total exports to 17.9%.   Meanwhile, processed energy products have increased in importance.   Manufactured goods, representing only 5% of exports in 1980, grew to 38.7% in 1996, led by petrochemicals, which account for two thirds of the total (Trinidad and Tobago is the second largest exporter of ammonia), and iron and steel, which account for a quarter.   Export-to-production ratios of cement and steel, industries privatized some years ago, have improved significantly.   Exports of chemicals more than doubled between 1985 and 1996.

---

[12]Imports of capital goods more than doubled in 1997, from US$652 million to US$1.4 billion, as a direct consequence of the investment boom in the oil sector.

[13]UNCTAD, (1997).

Table I.3
Balance of payments, 1992-97
(US$ million)

	1992	1993	1994	1995	1996	1997[a]
Merchandise trade balance	422.0	163.0	598.0	592.0	347.0	-611.0
Exports f.o.b.	1,622.0	1,662.0	1,972.0	2,477.0	2,506.0	2,427.0
Imports c.i.f.	1,200.0	1,499.0	1,374.0	1,885.0	2,159.0	3,038.0
Services, net	-355.0	-264.0	-370.0	-306.0	-270.0	-103
Non-factor services	89.0	61.0	43.0	159.0	245.0	213
Factor services	-444.0	-325.0	-413.0	-465.0	-515.0	-316.0
Current transfers, net	-16.0	-7.0	-6.0	-16.0	-7.0	5.0
Current account balance	91.0	-108.0	221.0	270.0	69.0	-708.0
Capital account, net	-139.0	89.0	-34.0	-36.0	36.0	619.0
Memorandum items:						
Current account balance/GDP (%)	1.7	-2.4.0	4.5	5.1	1.2	-12.2
Direct investment, net	177.9	379.2	516.2	298.9	356.3	979.7
Net official reserves	-83.0	74.0	262.0	296.0	510.0	688.0
Public external debt	2,214.90	2,096.0	2,058.0	1,905.0	1,876.0	1,527.0
Public external debt/GDP (%)	40.7	45.8	41.6	35.9	33.2	26.1
Debt service ratio (% of exports)	29.8	30.8	26.3	17.6	13.2	16.6
Exchange rate (TT$/US$)	4.3	5.4	5.9	6.0	6.0	6.3
Nominal effective exchange rate (Index; 1990=100)	115.0	105.1	102.2	100.5	104.4	104.9
Real effective exchange rate (Index; 1990=100)	102.4	92.4	85.3	83.6	83.6	85.2
Terms of trade (percentage change)	-6.9	-5.5	9.3	7.0	2.5	7.9
Trade balance/GDP	8.0	3.6	12.1	11.2	6.1	-10.5
Exports/GDP	34.4	36.3	39.9	46.7	44.3	41.8
Non-oil exports/GDP	18.3	19.4	24.6	26.1	22.9	24.0
Imports/GDP	26.4	32.7	27.8	35.5	38.1	52.3

a   Estimates.

Source: IMF, International Financial Statistics, (various issues).

33.   Imports (c.i.f.) were US$3 billion in 1997, some 41% higher in value terms than in 1996. Import growth in 1997 was triggered by an increase in foreign direct investment and, to a lesser extent, by the real appreciation of the Trinidad and Tobago dollar. Imports of consumer and capital goods progressed rapidly in 1997 imports of motor cars were particularly dynamic. Almost two thirds of imports are manufactures, especially machinery and equipment (one third of the total). Trinidad and Tobago is also a large importer of agricultural goods and of fuels (for refining purposes) (Chart I.4 and Table AI.2).

34.   Trinidad and Tobago's most important trading partner is the United States, accounting for 48.3% of exports and 38.1% of imports in 1996 (Chart I.5 and Table AI.3) CARICOM, especially Jamaica, is also an important market, absorbing almost a quarter of Trinidad and Tobago's exports, but supplying less than 4% of its imports. The European Union accounts for 10% of total exports and supplies 17.2% of imports.

Chart I.4
Product composition of merchandise trade, 1992 and 1996

Per cent

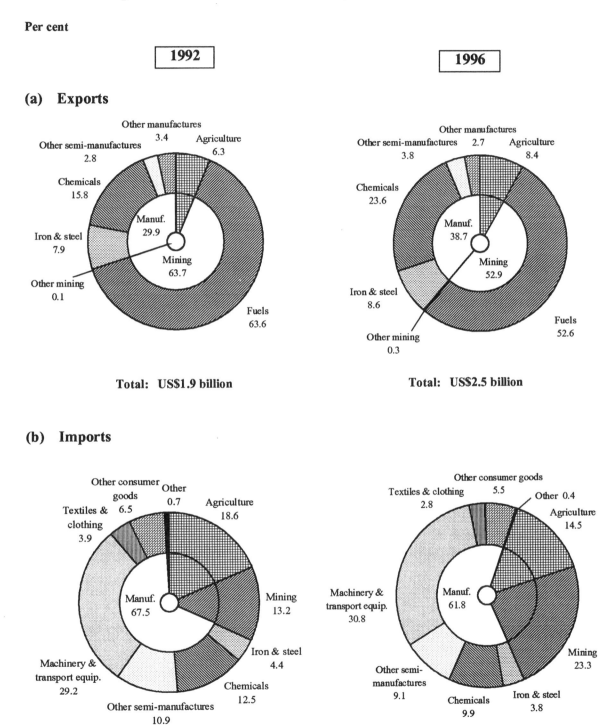

1992

1996

(a) Exports

Total: US$1.9 billion

Total: US$2.5 billion

(b) Imports

Total: US$1.4 billion

Total: US$2.2 billion

Source: UNSD, Comtrade database (SITC Rev.1).

Chart I.5
Merchandise trade by main origin and destination, 1992 and 1996

Per cent

| 1992 | 1996 |

(a) Exports

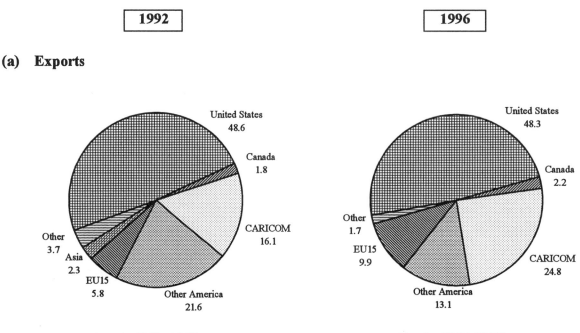

Total: US$1.9 billion

Total: US$2.5 billion

(b) Imports

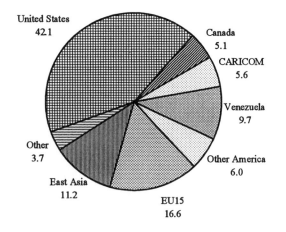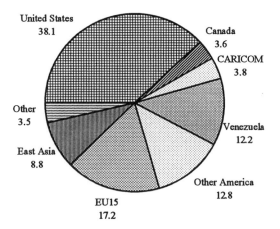

Total: US$1.4 billion

Total: US$2.2 billion

Source: UNSD, Comtrade database (SITC Rev.3).

35.   Trinidad and Tobago has a trade surplus with CARICOM. The surplus was about TT$3 billion in 1996, 16% higher than in 1995; imports were TT$493.7 million, exports totalled TT$3.5 billion. Figures for the first half of 1997 showed a surplus of TT$1.7 billion. The main CARICOM trading partner is Jamaica, which absorbs almost 37% of Trinidad and Tobago's exports to CARICOM partners and supplies around 23% of its imports. Other important trading partners in CARICOM are Barbados and Guyana.

(4)   ECONOMIC OUTLOOK

36.   Lower oil prices should temper GDP growth, limiting it to 3-4% in 1998 and 1999. Lower growth will have an impact on consumption and imports, and will probably contribute to a reduction in the current account deficit in both 1998 and 1999; however, lower oil prices will mean lower export earnings, so the final effect on the trade and current account balances remains uncertain. If the effect on imports is larger, this will translate into lower demand for credit, which should enhance monetary policy effectiveness. The implementation of Phase IV of the CET will contribute to controlling inflation. Lower oil prices will affect oil-sector revenues and hence public finances, which are likely to post a deficit in 1998. Despite important investment inflows, unemployment is expected to remain high.

II. TRADE AND INVESTMENT POLICY REGIME: FRAMEWORK AND OBJECTIVES

(1) INSTITUTIONAL STRUCTURE OF POLICY FORMULATION

(i) Form of Government

1.   Trinidad became Britain's first crown colony in 1802 and Tobago came under British rule in 1877; in 1888, the two were joined administratively. Under self rule since 1956, Trinidad and Tobago won independence in 1962 and became a Republic, within the British Commonwealth, under a new Constitution on 1 August 1976. The Constitution provides for a President and a bicameral Parliament, comprising a Senate and a House of Representatives.

2.   Executive authority is vested in the President, the Head of State who, generally, is to act in accordance with the advice of Cabinet.[1] The head of Government is the Prime Minister, who is the leader of the majority party in the House of Representatives and presides over the Cabinet which is collectively responsible to Parliament. The Prime Minister is appointed by the President, who can revoke his appointment following a vote of non-confidence. Ministers are appointed by the President, on advice from the Prime Minister, from among members of the House and the Senators. The President, acting in accordance with the Prime Minister, may dissolve or prorogue Parliament.

3.   Presidential and parliamentary elections take place every five years. The Constitution requires Parliament to be dissolved every five years. The House consists of 36 members elected by universal adult suffrage. The Senate consists of 31 members appointed by the President: 16 on the advice of the Prime Minister, six on the advice of the leader of the opposition and nine at the President's own discretion from among outstanding persons from economic, social or community organizations. The President is elected by an Electoral College, voting by secret ballot, of members of the Senate and the House of Representatives. Ten Senators, the Speaker of the House and twelve other members of the House, constitute a quorum of the Electoral College.

4.   Tobago has its own House of Assembly to which powers over local affairs have been delegated by Parliament.

5.   In the hierarchy of domestic legislation, the Constitution is the supreme law. International treaties have no legal effect unless they have been incorporated into domestic law. According to the authorities, the Marrakesh Agreement did not become part of domestic law in its entirety, but parts of it are being ratified in laws that Trinidad and Tobago has passed. Private individuals may not invoke WTO provisions directly before national courts, but only provisions in domestic legislation, patterned after WTO provisions. Parliament enacts laws based on bills passed by the House and the Senate and assented to by the President. According to practice, the President acts on advice of the Attorney General regarding the legislation to be assented. A bill, other than a money bill (dealing with tax and financial matters, public grants and loans, etc.) may be introduced in either the House or the Senate. Money bills may not be introduced in the Senate. In order to be passed, laws require a simple majority in both Houses of Parliament, except legislation that seeks to alter the entrenched provisions of the Constitution, which requires a two-thirds majority in each House or in some cases, a three-fourths majority in the House of Representatives and a two-thirds majority in the Senate.

6.   The legislative process begins with the introduction of proposals involving legislation by Ministers. If the Cabinet agrees, it issues drafting instructions to the Chief Parliamentary Counsel. A draft bill is prepared on the basis of those instructions and in consultation with the Ministry

---

[1]The Constitution, Article 80.

concerned. It is then reviewed by the Legislation Review Committee of the Attorney General's Ministry to ascertain whether it is in a suitable form for presentation to Parliament. Once the bill is introduced in Parliament it undergoes two readings. As soon as the bill has gone through all its stages in both Houses, it must be submitted to the President for his assent. A bill does not become law until the President has assented thereto, and does not have effect until it is proclaimed by the President.

7. The judicial system, whose independence is guaranteed by the Constitution, is similar to that of the United Kingdom, with a High Court and Appeal Court. Final appeal is to the Judicial Committee of the Privy Council, a group of judges from Commonwealth countries, which sits in London.

(ii)   **Policy-making and administration**

8. The Ministry of Trade and Industry is in charge of trade policy matters, including negotiating trade agreements and approving import licensing applications (Table II.1). The Ministry also approves activities accorded incentives, including duty concessions, which are subject to legislative approval. However, under the Fiscal Incentives Act, the President may, by order, declare a product an approved product or an enterprise an approved enterprise. The Ministry is currently being reorganized and will create an International/Hemispheric and Regional Trade Unit which will be responsible for trade policy formulation, implementation and review, participation in multilateral fora such as the WTO, negotiations of bilateral and regional agreements, and CARICOM issues.

9. The Tourism and Industrial Development Company of Trinidad and Tobago, Ltd. (TIDCO), established in 1995 in the portfolio of the Minister of Trade and Industry, has a number of trade-related responsibilities. The Division of Trade and Industry is, *inter alia*, involved in trade negotiations, the analysis of trade agreements, and the promotion of export activities of local manufacturers. Its Certification Department is the certifying body for various regional trade agreements facilitating concessions to exporters. The Government Policy and Special Projects Division is responsible for promoting the implementation of relevant government policy through legal, regulatory, informational and institutional reforms.

10. The Government or the private sector may propose changes to the tariff structure but the Cabinet is the final arbiter for introducing such changes. According to the Customs Act, Parliament may impose import and export duties. The Department of Customs and Excise, within the Ministry of Finance, handles such matters as duty collection, the imposition of surcharges, duty concessions and export rebates; it also issues certificates of origin for exports under various preference schemes, including the Generalized System of Preference, and the Caribbean Basin Initiative.

11. The registration of patents, trademarks and industrial design is administered by the Intellectual Property Registry of the Registrar General who reports to the Attorney General within the Ministry of Legal Affairs.

12. The Cabinet Sub-Committee, headed by the Minister of Energy and Energy Industries, comprises also the Ministers of Finance, Planning and Development, Trade, Industry and Consumer Affairs, Foreign Affairs and Public Utilities to take decisions in respect of the energy industry. A Fiscal Incentives Committee has recently been set up, as mandated by the Energy Sub-Committee, to evaluate the costs of the incentives and analyse the extent to which concessions are necessary.

13. In December 1997, the Cabinet agreed to the establishment under the responsibility of the Ministry of Trade and Industry of a Technical Coordinating Committee (TCC) and supporting sub-committees on access, competition policy, intellectual property rights, etc. The function of the TCC is to ensure that Trinidad and Tobago's position in the various negotiations is informed by

government policies. The responsibility of the specialist sub-committees is to provide advice to the TCC on functional subject areas.

Table II.1
Government agencies involved in the formulation or administration of trade or trade-related policies and area of responsibility

Agencies	Responsibility
Ministry of Finance	Double taxation agreements
Controller of Customs	Changes to the Common External Tariff (CET)
	Administration of rules of origin and procedures
	Administration of the Common External Tariff
Ministry of Agriculture	Plant and animal quarantine
	Sanitary and phytosanitary measures
Ministry of Trade and Industry	Formulation of trade policies
	Negotiation of free-trade agreements
	Co-ordination of trade in services
	Administration of anti-dumping and countervailing duties
	Bilateral Investment Treaty
	Administration of competition policy
Tourism & Industrial Development Company Limited (TIDCO)	Implementation of trade and investment policy
	Administration of certificates of origin
Trinidad and Tobago Bureau of Standards (TTBS)	Implementation and development of standards
Ministry of Legal Affairs	Administration of intellectual property (patents, trademarks, etc.)
Intellectual Property Office	Drafting of legislation and agreements
Office of the Attorney General	Environmental impact assessment
Chief Parliamentary Council	Co-ordination of overall economic policy framework
Ministry of Planning	
Ministry of Works	Air services agreements
(Standing Committee on Air Services Agreement)	
Office of the Prime Minister	Telecommunications Agreement
Telecommunications Division	Negotiations related to telecommunication services
Ministry of Health	Food and drug certification
Food and Drug Division	

Source: Information provided by the authorities of Trinidad and Tobago.

(iii)   Advisory and review bodies

14.   The Government has appointed a Standing Advisory Committee on Trade and Related Matters. This Committee comprises representatives of the major private sector bodies, the Trinidad and Tobago Manufacturers' Association, Chambers of Commerce, the University of the West Indies and representatives of the labour movement. This Committee meets at least once a month.

(iv) Trade laws and regulations

15.   The main legislation affecting trade is encompassed in the Customs Act, dating from 1936, but amended frequently (last in 1996). Merchandise trade is also regulated via the Imports and Exports Control Regulations of 1941 and ordinances issued thereunder. There are also numerous provisions in a variety of laws that relate to trade matters. These laws include the Miscellaneous Taxes Act which is the underlying legislation for the imposition of surcharges or the Animal (Diseases and Importation) Act (1954) incorporating regulations governing the import of animal products. Much of the legislation affecting trade in both goods and services is under review including the Foreign Investment Act of 1990 and the Fiscal Incentives Act of 1985. Other pieces of legislation have also been revamped to conform with international obligations, such as the Standards Act 18 of 1997, or the legislation for antidumping and intellectual property.

(2) TRADE POLICY OBJECTIVES

(i) General policy objectives

16.   The emphasis of trade policy, reflected in the shift from import substitution to a more outward orientation in the last ten years, has graduated from extracting maximum value from preferential arrangements to advancing Trinidad and Tobago's own competitiveness under conditions of sustainable growth. A cornerstone of Trinidad and Tobago's current development policy is the encouragement of foreign and domestic investment. Since 1988, when a concerted effort at structural adjustment began, the Government has progressed in the direction of trade liberalization to foster development of the non-oil manufacturing sector driven by export-led growth. The authorities have identified many areas where improvements are still needed: *inter alia*,

-        the streamlining of bureaucratic procedures;

-        the removal of temporary import surcharges on agricultural products;

-        a competition policy to regulate restrictive business practices in the domestic market;

-        the development of international standards on imported goods; and

-        the adoption of international environmental standards.

17.   In the Uruguay Round negotiations, Trinidad and Tobago bound all of its tariffs (Chapter III (iii)(b)), and made specific commitments under the General Agreement on Trade in Services (GATS) in a number of subsectors including business services, insurance, telecommunications, transport and tourism. Since joining the WTO, Trinidad and Tobago has fulfilled a number of its notification obligations (Table II.2).

18.   The Government has a regional and bilateral approach to negotiating free-trade agreements. As a member of CARICOM, Trinidad and Tobago will be seeking trade agreements with the Dominican Republic, the Andean Pact, the Central American Common Market, and MERCOSUR. Bilaterally, Trinidad intends to pursue a free-trade agreement with Mexico[2] In 1994, Trinidad and Tobago formally declared its desire to accede to the North American Free Trade Agreement (NAFTA), signing a bilateral agreement with the United States on the protection of intellectual property rights to further its cause but it considers accession by CARICOM as a group the preferred option.

---

[2]Ministry of Finance, (1997), p. 3.

Table II.2
Notifications by Trinidad and Tobago to the WTO

Legal basis, instrument or provision	Periodicity	WTO documents	Subject
General Agreement on Trade in Goods 1994			
Art. XXVIII:5	Triennial	G/MA/42 10.01.97	Reservation of right to modify schedule for a 3-year period commencing 1.1.97
Agreement on Agriculture			
Art. 10 and 18.2	Annual	G/AG/N/TTO/1 31.01.96	No export subsidies
Art. 18.2	Annual	GT/AG/N/TTO/2 27.07.98	Domestic support measures
Agreement on the Application of Sanitary and Phytosanitary Measures			
Art. 7, Annex B	Ad hoc	G/SPS/N/TTO/1 10.10.95	Regime for mealybug infested fruit and vegetables
Agreement on Textiles and Clothing			
Art. 6.1	Once	G/TMB//N/117 14.08.95	Retention of right to use safeguard measures
Agreement on Technical Barriers to Trade			
Art. 2.10	Ad hoc	G/TBT/NOTIF.97.675 13.10.97; G/TBT/NOTIF.97.676 13.10.97	Notification of technical regulations
Art. 10.6	Ad hoc	G/TBT/Notif.98.161 25.03.98	
Annex 3C	Once	G/TBT/CS//N/37 29.04.96	Acceptance of Code of Good Practice on voluntary standards
Agreement on Trade-related Investment Measures			
Art. 5.1	Once	G/TRIMS/N/1/TTO/1 15.04.96	No laws or regulations inconsistent with the Agreement
Agreement on Implementation of Art. VI of the GATT 1994 (Anti-dumping)			
Art. 16.4	Ad hoc	G/ADP/N/2/ADD.1/Rev.1 28.08.95	Anti-dumping actions (taken within the preceding six months)
Art. 18.5	Once	G/ADP/N/1/TTO/1 06.04.95; G/ADP/N/1/TTO/1/Corr.1 31.10.95	Anti-dumping laws and regulations (and changes thereto, including changes in the administration of such laws)
Agreement on Rules of Origin			
Art. 5.1	Once	G/RO/N/7 12.02.96	Does not maintain any non-preferential rules
Annex II(4)	Once	G/RO/N/7 12.02.96	Preferential rules (Treaty of Chaguaramas)
Agreement on Import Licensing Procedures			
Art. 7.3	Annual, by 30 September	G/LIC/N/3/TTO/1 16.02.96	Replies to questionnaires on import licensing procedures

Table II.2 (cont'd)

Legal basis, instrument or provision	Periodicity	WTO documents	Subject
Agreement on Subsidies and Countervailing Measures			
Art. 32.6	Once	G/SCM/N/1/TTO/1 22.11.95; G/SCM/N/7/Add.1 08.12.95	Notification of laws and regulations
Art. 25.1	Annual	G/SCM/N/3/TTO 09.01.96	Trinidad & Tobago provides no subsidies
Art. 25.11	Ad hoc	G/SCM/N/4/Add.1/Rev.2 22.11.95; G/SCM/N/12/Add.1 18.04.96	Countervailing duty actions (taken within the preceding six months)
Agreement on Safeguards			
Art. 12.6	Once	G/SG/N/1/TTO/1 04.10.95	No safeguard legislation in force

Source: WTO Central Registry of Notifications.

(ii)   Sectoral policy objectives

19.   For the last few decades, the Government has had a policy of diversifying the economy away from its dependence on the petroleum sector. At present, industrial-development policy aims to expand the range of business activity in the non-oil business sector, increase levels of foreign and domestic investment, generate permanent employment opportunities and attain food security objectives.[3] Industrial policy focuses essentially on the development of the non-oil business sector, the non-financial services sector and the small business sector.

20.   In agriculture, goals include the evaluation of commodities with agro-processing potential, improving access to farm credit, continuing trade and price policy reforms and the provision of appropriate incentives to export agriculture.

21.   A Green Paper on energy policy identified the following overall policy objectives:

- the development of an efficient administrative, regulatory, legal and fiscal framework, to promote sustainable growth and development;

- the maximization of local crude oil production;

- the further development of refining capacity;

- the optimal exploitation of natural gas resources;

- the development of downstream natural gas-based industries;

- security of energy supplies, both for consumption and supplies to the refining industry; and

- state participation in the sector as a promoter and facilitator[4].

---

[3]Ministry of Trade and Industry (1996).
[4]Ministry of Energy and Energy Industries, (1997).

22.   Proposed regulatory measures include the establishment of a petrochemical licence and the creation of a more transparent gas pricing structure, critical to petrochemical production and the industries consuming large quantities of fuel.

23.   In the provision of public utilities, reform of the regulatory environment focuses on improving performance and pricing services to reflect their economic and environmental costs. In the services sector, Trinidad and Tobago seeks both to capitalize on its location to act as a regional transhipment and trading centre and to transform it into an international financial services centre. Off-shore banks would participate in the domestic financial system and the local capital market would be developed to provide a broader range of investment instruments.

(3)   TRADE AGREEMENTS AND ARRANGEMENTS

(i)   Multilateral trade agreements

24.   Trinidad and Tobago joined the GATT in October 1962 and ratified the WTO Agreements on 30 January 1995, with the Agreement entering into force on 1 March 1995[5]. Trinidad and Tobago grants at least MFN treatment to all its trading partners.

(ii)   Regional trade agreements

(a)   CARICOM

25.   Trinidad is a founding member of the Caribbean Community and Common Market (CARICOM) established by the Treaty of Chaguaramas (Trinidad) which entered into force on 1 August 1973. CARICOM currently comprises fifteen member states (Box II.1)[6]. CARICOM was notified to GATT under Article XXIV as an interim agreement for the formation of a customs union and reviewed by a working party that produced a report adopted on 2 March 1977[7]. Since then, no further notifications have been made on the part of CARICOM.[8]

26.   Trinidad and Tobago is the second most populous member of CARICOM, after Jamaica. It accounts for the largest share member, of intra-regional exports (over 20% mainly petroleum and its by-products), and is the only member with a consistently positive balance on intra-CARICOM trade. In 1996, CARICOM accounted for nearly one quarter of its exports but less than 4% of its imports.

---

[5]WT/LET/7, 14 February 1995

[6]The founding members were: Barbados, Guyana, Jamaica, and Trinidad and Tobago. Bahamas, Belize, Dominica, Grenada, Montserrat, St. Lucia and St. Vincent acceded in May 1974; Antigua and Barbuda and St. Kitts and Nevis joined in July 1974. The first non-English-speaking country to join CARICOM was Suriname, followed by Haiti in July 1997.

[7]BISD 24S/68.

[8]Article XXIV:5(c) of GATT 1947 states that "any interim agreement...shall include a plan and schedule for the formation of a customs union or free-trade area within a reasonable period of time". Discipline under the WTO has been tightened: paragraph 3 of the Understanding on the Interpretation of Article XXIV of the GATT 1994, states that "...the reasonable length of time referred to in par. 5(c) of Art. XXIV should exceed 10 years only in exceptional cases".

Box II.1: CARICOM

The Caribbean Community and Common Market (CARICOM), preceded by the Caribbean Free Trade Association (CARIFTA), was established in 1973 under the Treaty of Chaguaramas. Its initial objectives included economic integration and a unified foreign policy. Progress towards integration was slow; for the first eighteen years CARICOM was a preferential trading area and subsequently a free-trade area. In 1991, CARICOM started to operate as a customs union when the Common External Tariff (CET) was implemented. The original objectives were redefined in 1989 and endorsed in 1991 as a "Single Market and Economy" characterized by the free movement of goods, services, labour and capital, and to be achieved by the end of the decade. The CARICOM Treaty was amended in 1997 with the signature of the Protocol Amending the Treaty Establishing the Caribbean Community, Protocol I. The Protocol restructures the organs and institutions of CARICOM to deepen the process of integration, and sets the foundations for the CARICOM Single Market and Economy (CSME). Protocol I has been ratified by some CARICOM countries, and is currently applied provisionally. Trinidad and Tobago ratified Protocol I on 12 June 1997. Protocol II, referring to the right of establishment, services and capital, was signed in July 1997 but has not yet been ratified.

At the institutional level, the major decision-making body, guided by the unanimity principle, is the Conference of the Heads of Government; it meets annually and, in recent years, in Inter-Sessional Conference. The Conference is also responsible for the conclusion of treaties and agreements with international organizations and with states. The Community Council of Ministers is responsible for decisions related to the functioning of the economy and the single market. The Community Council was created in October 1992 to replace the Common Market Council as the second highest organ of the Community; it is composed of Ministers designated by each member state. A number of Standing Committees share responsibility for specific subject areas, including Agriculture, Foreign Affairs, Legal Affairs, Industry, Transportation and Tourism.

In order to accelerate the pace of implementation of common market objectives, the 1992 Special Conference, held in Trinidad and Tobago, established the Bureau of CARICOM, comprising three rotating Heads of Government and the Secretary General of the CARICOM Secretariat. The Bureau was given competence to initiate proposals and ensure implementation of decisions and the Secretary General was vested with "appropriate executive power". Under the 1997 Protocol amending the Treaty, the functions of the Secretariat were upgraded by authorizing it to "initiate or develop proposals for consideration and decisions by competent Organs in order to achieve Community objectives."

---

27.   For intra-CARICOM trade in goods, most tariffs and non-tariff barriers to trade have been virtually eliminated. Intra-regional trade in services has not, however, been liberalized, although Article 36 of the Annex to the Treaty provides for preferential treatment of CARICOM service providers over third-country suppliers. Rules of origin are complex and modelled on the Lomé Convention; they typically, but by no means always, require 50% regional value-added content to benefit from preferential treatment. Article 13:1 of the CARICOM Treaty allows members to apply quantitative restrictions or duties to products included in Annex I of the Treaty. These restrictions to trade should be listed in Annex I, where their duration shall be stated. In certain cases members are allowed to waive this obligation, but their action may be challenged by other members who deem their benefits under the Treaty to have been impaired. There is no general policy regarding export subsidies, but they are not allowed in principle, with the exception of certain agricultural products. Exports taxes are also prohibited. No export incentives are allowed, and a member may refuse to grant preferential access to exports from another member who benefits from tax breaks. There are no provisions preventing double taxation, but eleven states, including Trinidad and Tobago have signed the Intra-Regional Double Taxation Agreement.

28.   The Special Conference of Heads of Government in October 1992 set a ceiling for the Common External Tariff (CET) of 35% from January 1993, with the exception of agricultural goods which could command a 40% duty to take account of subsidies by trading partners. The plan was to reduce the maximum tariff in four phases from 35% in 1995 to 20% by 1998. It is estimated that the

CET covers 95% of extra-CARICOM imports. National exceptions to the CET are allowed. Furthermore, the Community Council is entitled (Art. 56 of the Treaty) to temporarily suspend the application of the CET or of any measure of internal liberalization if it considers this to be necessary to develop a certain industry in a member state[9]

29.   Trade among CARICOM countries has been limited by an inadequate infrastructure. Efforts to enhance trade, encourage integration and pool capital have been made in the past few years. These include the implementation, in April 1991, of a system of securities cross-trading among Jamaica, Trinidad and Tobago, and Barbados, and the establishment of a Regime for CARICOM Enterprises (CER). The CER is aimed at drawing resources from any participating state to an enterprise of another state in order to integrate production and capital at a regional level and develop stronger multinational enterprises. The regime is currently restricted to a few services, including: banking and finance, construction and engineering, air and sea transportation, and consultancy and international marketing.

30.   Through the move to create the CARICOM Single Market and Economy (CSME), members are expected to coordinate their commercial relations with third countries. Although individual members are in principle entitled to conduct an independent trade policy, the CSME is geared towards achieving harmonization. Members are expected to coordinate and harmonize their exchange rate and monetary policies, as well as their tax and incentives regimes. The ultimate goal is to achieve economic convergence, which may lead to the adoption of a common currency. The CSME is expected to be fully implemented by December 1999.

31.   Under Protocol II for the consolidation of the CSME there were modifications to the CARICOM Treaty for the removal of restrictions on the right of establishment,[10] the provision of services, and the movement of capital. Regarding services, Protocol II includes standstill, national treatment and rollback provisions. Members are given a year from the date of entry into force of the Protocol to present a programme for the removal of existing restrictions on the provision of services. Although banking and insurance are included in the commitments, Protocol II allows for the exclusion of certain financial services from national treatment.

32.   Prior to Protocol II, CARICOM had no specific engagement regarding services, except that any measure taken by a member had to be notified to the Council for Trade and Economic Development, and could not be more restrictive than existing legislation. Under Protocol II, capital movements are to be subject to national treatment and MFN, and to standstill and rollback commitments; the coordination of foreign exchange policies is encouraged. The goal is to achieve total freedom of capital flows, as well as currency convertibility in all member states.

33.   Protocol II also introduces changes to the Treaty of Chaguaramas to allow members to adopt safeguard measures for balance-of-payments purposes[11] Safeguards for balance-of-payments purposes must be non-discriminatory, last not more than 18 months, and may include quantitative restrictions on imports, restrictions on services, restrictions on capital movement and on payments and transfers needed for the provision of services. They must be notified to the Council for Finance and Planning and to the Council for Trade and Economic Development. The balance-of-payments situation of the member concerned will be assessed through periodic consultations. All findings

---

[9]There are safeguards for agricultural products. Additionally, Guyana maintains, a special sectoral safeguard on the importation of oil products from the Caribbean Common Market.

[10]Under the Treaty of Chaguaramas, there was no engagement regarding the free movement of natural persons.

[11]Article 28 of the Caribbean Common Market Annex is replaced by Article 37c(bis), which draws on the WTO Understanding on Balance-of-Payments Provisions of the GATT 1994.

related to foreign exchange, monetary reserves and balance of payments provided by the CARICOM Committee of Central Bank Governors must be accepted. The Protocol also introduces the possibility of adopting safeguards when difficulties arise for the exercise of rights under the Treaty. Safeguards may be applied to resolve the difficulties in a specific sector or in a region. In line with the WTO, the Protocol introduces security exceptions and special provisions for less-developed countries, for whom some of the obligations under the CARICOM Treaty may be waived.

(b)   Bilateral agreements between CARICOM and other countries

34.   CARICOM has signed bilateral trade agreements with Colombia and Venezuela. Additionally, CARICOM intends to negotiate bilateral trade agreements with MERCOSUR, the Andean Pact, the Dominican Republic and with some countries in Central America.

35.   The CARICOM-Colombia Agreement on Trade, Economic and Technical Cooperation was signed on 24 July 1994 and renegotiated in 1997. Colombia granted unilateral preferential access for four years to its market to a group of products originating in CARICOM after which the preferential trade scheme is to become reciprocal, taking into account development differences. Colombia identified a list of 227 products (Annex I of the Agreement) for which imports from the CARICOM would be duty-free as of 1 January 1995, the date of the official coming into force of the Agreement[12] Additionally, there would a phased, three-year tariff reduction for a list of 207 other products (Annex II), starting from 1 January 1995. Finally, a third group of products, included in Annex III, would qualify for preferential treatment from the beginning of 1999. Other Colombian imports from CARICOM receive MFN treatment. Non-tariff barriers are to be phased out. It was initially agreed that duties on a group of Colombian exports to Jamaica and three other CARICOM states (Barbados, Guyana, and Trinidad and Tobago) would be subject to phased reductions as of 1 January 1998. In December 1997, CARICOM and Colombia agreed to postpone this part of the Agreement for a year, during which the list of Colombian products to be granted preferential access to the four CARICOM countries would be decided. The phase-out of duties is now expected to start being implemented on 1 January 1999.

36.   The scope of the Agreement with Colombia goes beyond merchandise trade and includes provisions regarding the harmonization of standards, as well as cooperation in services, particularly tourism, trade financing and transport, and in environmental policies, agricultural development and research. There are no specific commitments, however, in these areas. The Agreement includes a safeguard clause in case of prejudice or threat of prejudice to domestic production or for balance-of-payments reasons. In cases of unfair trade practices, the Parties to the Agreement may apply anti-dumping or countervailing measures. There is no provision, however, dealing with subsidies and anti-dumping disputes, which are to be taken to the WTO. A CARICOM-Colombia Joint Council on Trade, Economic and Business Cooperation is responsible for the administration of the Agreement.

37.   Trinidad and Tobago entered into a Bilateral (Partial Scope) Agreement with Venezuela on 4 August 1989, with the objective of stimulating trade through the granting of tariff preferences and the elimination or reduction of non-tariff barriers. The Partial Scope Agreement accords preferential import duty status on certain products from both countries. Tariff preferences granted consist of percentage reductions. The Agreement also contains a standstill clause on non-tariff barriers to the importation of the negotiated products, except for measures aimed at: protection of public morals; application of safety rules and regulations; regulation of the importation or export of arms, ammunition and other war materials and, in exceptional circumstances, all other military material;

---

[12]The share of preferential imports in Colombia's total imports from CARICOM was 73% (US$ million) in 1995 (WTO 1996, Trade Policy Review of Colombia).

protection of human, animal and plant life and health; imports and exports of gold and silver in bullion form; protection of the national patrimony of artistic, historic or archaeological value; and export, use and consumption of nuclear materials, radio-active products or any other material used in the development or exploitation of nuclear energy. At the signing of the Agreement, 11 products from Trinidad and Tobago and 12 products from Venezuela were identified to enjoy preferential tariff rates. In November 1989 the parties expanded the list by a further 24 products for each signatory. Subsequent reductions of the CET have, however, wiped out the preferential access for Venezuelan products, with the exception of three products: leather footwear, excluding men's footwear; wrought aluminium bars, profiles and angles; and disposable syringes.

38.   The CARICOM-Venezuela Agreement on Trade and Investment was signed in October 1992 and entered into force on 1 January 1993. It is a one-way preferential agreement which aims at promoting CARICOM exports into Venezuela, by giving some products duty-free access or phased reductions in tariffs. The phased reductions were concluded on 1 January 1996, and currently CARICOM products included in Annex I and Annex II of the Agreement receive duty-free treatment.[13]   Other CARICOM exports enter Venezuela under MFN conditions. Any change in CARICOM's tariff structure is subject to consultations with Venezuela. The Agreement also aims at promoting investment in the region and facilitating the creation of joint ventures[14] The Agreement contains a safeguard clause which may be applied by Venezuela in case of prejudice to domestic production or in case of balance-of-payments difficulties. Safeguard measures may be applied for no longer than a year and must be approved by the CARICOM/Venezuela Joint Council on Trade and Investment. The signatories are allowed to apply measures to counter unfair trade practices, such as export and domestic subsidies and dumping. Compared with the Partial Scope Agreement, the CARICOM/Venezuela Agreement provides increased market access for products from Trinidad and Tobago since it embodies a larger range of products and offers lower tariff rates. However, a number of products of export interest to Trinidad and Tobago, such as urea, ammonia, and a variety of iron and steel products are excluded from preferential access. According to the authorities, the Partial Scope Agreement has not been superseded by the CARICOM-Venezuela Agreement.

(c)   Association of Caribbean States

39.   Trinidad and Tobago has assumed full membership in the Association of Caribbean States (ACS), an organization for economics and trade, launched by the Heads of State of CARICOM on 29 July 1994 and comprising 25 countries of the Caribbean Basin. The ACS will have a total market of 200 million people, estimated GDP of US$500 billion and annual trade worth some US$180 billion. Its mandate includes developing strategies for convergence of trade policies among its member countries, new initiatives aimed at boosting trade and strengthening private sector participation in regional development and trade.

40.   Its Plan of Action adopted at the Inaugural Summit in August 1995 seeks to advance the process towards strengthening integration, concrete action and consultation among Member States, particularly in areas of trade, tourism and transportation.[15]   The Trade and External Economic Relations Committee was mandated to follow up the Trade Action Plan. Specific to trade, the Plan of Action instructed the Secretariat, headquartered in Trinidad and Tobago, to *inter alia*, disseminate amongst members information regarding the WTO Agreements and its implementation in each State

---

[13]Goods in these Annexes include fresh produce, confectionery, cosmetics, jams and jellies, medicines, wooden furniture, horticultural products, spices, processed foods and toilet preparations.
[14]This is to be implemented through bilateral treaties between Venezuela and each CARICOM member.
[15]Ministry of Trade and Industry, (1997).

and to coordinate efforts between the different secretariats regarding efforts toward harmonization of trade rules and regulations.

(d)   Free Trade Area of the Americas

41.   The 1994 Summit of the Americas called for the completion of negotiations for an FTAA by 2005. The Government of Trinidad and Tobago participates in the Working Groups and collaborates with CARICOM member states in coordinating a common regional position. In keeping with the decision of the CARICOM Conference, Trinidad and Tobago participates in developing a common negotiating position with Central American States in the FTAA process.

(e)   Preferential trade agreements

Caribbean Basin Initiative

42.   Under the Caribbean Basin Economic Recovery Act (CBERA), the Caribbean Basin Initiative (CBI) came into effect on 1 January 1984. All Caribbean and Central American countries are beneficiaries except Cuba and the French overseas departments of Guadeloupe, Martinique and French Guiana. The CBI provides for duty-free access to the U.S. market for a wide range of exports. However, there are exclusions, notably textiles and clothing, footwear, leather goods, canned tuna and petroleum and petroleum products. Sugar remains subject to quotas. To qualify for duty-free access, goods have to be exported directly to the United States and a minimum of 35% of the value has to be locally added (of which 15% may be of U.S. origin).

43.   A revised CBI (CBI II), through the CBERA, came into effect in August 1990, improved trade and tax benefits and made them permanent. Trade improvements included a 20 per cent tariff reduction on certain leather products and expanded duty-free treatment to include twenty-eight additional tariff categories.[16] Continued eligibility for benefits depends on countries' efforts to cooperate on transparency in government procurement in various international fora, including the WTO. According to U.S. trade statistics, Trinidad and Tobago ranks fifth as CBERA supplier, accounting for US$184 million, 6.6% of CBERA imports by the United States in 1996.[17]

44.   A number of products are excluded from duty-free treatment under CBI II. These are: textile and apparel items subject to textile agreements; footwear, handbags, luggage, leather wearing apparel, work gloves, flat goods; tuna prepared or preserved in airtight containers; petroleum or petroleum products; sugar syrup and molasses; watches and watch parts.

45.   A proposal to temporarily grant CBI countries similar access on certain products to the United States as the treatment given to Mexico under NAFTA was abandoned before being submitted to Congress. The proposal would have granted imports of textiles and apparel meeting NAFTA rules of origin, or manufactured in a CBI country with material cut or manufactured in the United States, duty-free and quota-free access to the U.S. market.

CARIBCAN

46.   Under CARIBCAN, which entered into force on 15 June 1986, Canada extends duty-free treatment to imports of eligible products (excluding textiles, clothing, footwear, luggage and other leather goods) into Canada from beneficiary Commonwealth Caribbean countries. In 1998, methanol and lubricating oil were extended preferential treatment. To qualify for duty-free access to Canada,

---

[16]WTO, G/L/25, 15 September 1995.
[17]WTO, WT/L/233, 10 October 1997.

products from the Commonwealth Caribbean countries and territories must meet the requirement that 60% of their ex-factory price (including factory overhead and a margin for profits) originates in any beneficiary country or in Canada. CARICOM currently runs a trade surplus with Canada.

Lomé Convention

47.   Trinidad and Tobago is a beneficiary of the Lomé IV and Lomé IV-B Convention, which was signed on 15 December 1989 for a period of ten years.[18] Products originating in Trinidad and Tobago generally enjoy preferential access to the EU, either duty-free (manufactures) or at conditions more advantageous than MFN treatment. Rules of origin for preferential entry to the EU under Lomé IV stipulate that agricultural goods be wholly produced in an African, Caribbean or Pacific (ACP) country and that at least 50% of the value added of manufactured goods originate in an ACP country or jointly in an ACP and EU country.[19] Exports of sugar and rum have been the main traditional export products from Trinidad and Tobago to the EU. Recently, share in the EU has been won for petroleum and fertilizers.

48.   Trinidad and Tobago and other Caribbean countries may benefit from some changes in rules of origin requirements agreed at the mid-term review of Lomé IV in 1995. These now allow for cumulation with Colombia, Costa Rica, El Salvador, Guatemala, Honduras, Nicaragua, Panama and Venezuela. The possibility of cumulation with Colombia and Venezuela is particularly interesting for CARICOM countries as they have free-trade agreements with those two countries and as such it may encourage joint ventures and combined production schemes.

49.   Other features of the Lomé Convention that concern Trinidad and Tobago include the Rum Protocol and the Sugar Protocol. The Rum Protocol gives duty-free access to the EU to a certain quantity of rum every year. Through the Sugar Protocol annual export quotas are agreed for ACP producers. Trinidad and Tobago benefits from the special undertakings in sugar, for which the EU pays guaranteed prices.

50.   The Fourth Lomé Convention between the European Union and the 71 African, Caribbean and Pacific (ACP) States expires in 2000. Formal negotiations on a successor agreement started in September 1998.

Global System of Trade Preferences

51.   Trinidad and Tobago is a member of the Global System of Trade Preferences (GSTP). Tariff concessions are received from Brazil (sponge iron, granted a 100% reduction in the tariff base rate) and Venezuela (sponge iron, granted a 50% reduction in the tariff base rate and methanol, granted a tariff binding of 20%, compared to a 50% MFN binding).

Generalized System of Preferences (GSP)

52.   Trinidad and Tobago's products are eligible for the GSP schemes of Australia, Canada, Czech Republic, European Union, Japan, New Zealand, Poland, Russia, Slovak Republic, Switzerland and the United States.

---

[18]The European Union was granted a waiver (under Article XXV:5) to its obligations under Article I:1 of GATT 1947 by the CONTRACTING PARTIES on 9 December 1994, and up to 29 February 2000. However, following the Uruguay Round Understanding in respect of Waivers of Obligations under GATT 1994, the waiver should have terminated by end 1996. On 9 September 1996, the EU asked the Council for Trade in Goods for an extension of the waiver until 29 February 2000 (WTO document G/L/107). The case was submitted to the General Council and approval was granted on 14 October 1996 (WT/FC/M/15).

[19]Rules of origin requirements vary from product to product. A complete list of the requirements by tariff heading may be found in: The Courier, No. 155, Jan-Feb 1996, pp. 117-144.

(4) INVESTMENT REGIME[20]

53. The Government is scrutinizing and reviewing its policy towards foreign investment, intending to harmonize incentives across sectors and in general to improve the business environment in order to facilitate foreign, along with local, investment. A number of fiscal incentives are offered to investors under various pieces of legislation, such as the Fiscal Incentives Act, Income Tax Act.

54. The Tourism and Industrial Development Company of Trinidad and Tobago Ltd. (TIDCO), established in 1995, includes an Investment Facilitation and an Investment Promotion Department. The former is responsible for the evaluation of applications from investors for industrial and tourism investment incentives final approval lies with the Ministries and assists in processing licenses. The latter is responsible for promoting Trinidad and Tobago as a suitable location and participates in trade fairs and other promotional projects.

55. While the bulk of foreign investment has been in the energy sector and downstream industries, the Government is anxious to develop the non-oil manufacturing sector. Policy makers aim to upgrade investment incentives, provide a neutral package of investment incentives across business sectors, remove disincentives to investment and attract investment for export-oriented production targeted towards markets with which it has negotiated free-trade agreements. The Government recognizes that there is an absence of transparent criteria for approving investments and is in the process of a radical reform to ensure that the process is transparent, simple and efficient. Applications for investment incentives (Chapter III(3)(4)(ii)) are currently evaluated on the basis of a number of criteria, including local value added, net foreign exchange, potential export sales, and environmental impact.

56. The Foreign Investment Act of 1990 is due to be replaced by the Investment Promotion Act now in draft.[21] Under current legislation, a foreign investor is defined as an individual who is neither a citizen of a CARICOM country nor a resident of Trinidad and Tobago, while a foreign company with both domestic and foreign capital is considered a foreign company if foreign ownership or control is in the majority.[22] There are no regulations governing the entry of foreign investment capital nor restrictions on the repatriation of profits, dividends or income.

57. While no sectors are closed to foreign investment, approval is required for the acquisition of commercial and residential land over a certain minimum (foreigners are automatically allowed to own five acres and one acre for business and residential purposes, respectively); approval is also required where a licence is needed. For certain activities licenses are required by both nationals and non-nationals. Approvals are granted by the Ministry of Energy for drilling or mining activities, by the Ministry of Trade and Industry for certain commercial activities, and by the Central Bank for the establishment of a bank or other commercial institutions. In the case of portfolio investment, where a foreign investor would be acquiring more than 30% of a publicly held local company, approval is required. In some cases, incentives are only made available if the company is locally owned, e.g. in the construction sector.

58. Trinidad and Tobago is a signatory to the International Convention on the Settlement of Investment Disputes (ICSID) and the Multilateral Investment Guarantee Agency (MIGA). Bilateral investment promotion and protection agreements are in place with the United States (1994), the

---

[20]The Constitution provides for "the right of the individual to enjoyment of property" and the right not to be deprived thereof except by due process of law.

[21]The current Act which significantly liberalized the previous investment régime does not apply to financial institutions covered by the Financial Institutions Act.

[22]InterAmerican Development Bank , (1996).

United Kingdom (1993), France (1993), and Canada (1995). Similar agreements are currently being negotiated with Argentina, Hungary, Italy, the Netherlands, and Venezuela.

59.   In 1978, Trinidad and Tobago established a permanent team to develop guidelines and negotiate double taxation treaties, including prevention of tax evasion. The negotiations are based on its position as a developing country.[23] In addition to the treaty with other CARICOM members, double taxation avoidance treaties have been signed with Canada, Denmark, France, Germany, Italy, Norway, Sweden, Switzerland, United Kingdom, United States and Venezuela; these are being renewed and additional treaties are to be negotiated with Latin American and Asian countries.

60.   The United States is the largest foreign investor in Trinidad and Tobago, mainly in the petroleum sector.

(5)   TRADE CONSULTATIONS AND DISPUTES

61.   Trinidad and Tobago has never invoked the dispute settlement provision of the GATT or WTO, nor have any complaints been brought against it in these fora.

62.   Amongst CARICOM member States, dispute settlement procedures are defined in Art. 11 and 12 of the Treaty. Members are encouraged to find bilateral solutions to their disputes. If this is not the case, the dispute is brought to the CARICOM Council, which then calls for the setting of a Tribunal comprised of three referees. The plaintiff and the defendant are allowed to appoint one referee each from a roster maintained by the CARICOM's Secretary General. Both referees choose a third one who will act as President. The Tribunal will then study the dispute and inform the Council of its conclusions. There is no time limit for this. The Council, through majority vote, may then make recommendations to the member affected by the Tribunal's conclusions. If the member does not comply with the recommendations, the Council may authorize, again through majority vote, that any member suspend its obligations with regard to the non-complying member. According to Art. 12.9, CARICOM members may only make use of this dispute settlement procedure and may not, for trade disputes among themselves, use any other dispute settlement mechanism.

63.   Under the CARICOM-Venezuela Agreement on Trade and Investment, disputes may be resolved through the Joint Council on Trade and Investment, although this recommendation is not binding. Disputes between Trinidad and Tobago and Venezuela on fishing rights have given rise to diplomatic tensions.[24] Under the CARICOM-Colombia Agreement, dispute settlement is also under the responsibility of a Joint Council.

---

[23]According to the authorities, this implies that the investment flow tends to be from the developed to the developing country and the income flow from the developing country to the developed one.

[24]According to the authorities, these incidents have now been resolved. A joint Trinidad and Tobago/Venezuela Commission for the Presentation, Investigation and Resolution of Fishing Incidents was established on 31 July 1996. The Commission is in charge of holding periodic meetings for the exchange of information, as wells as coordinating and supervising procedures for the prompt resolution of any incident.

III. TRADE POLICIES AND PRACTICES BY MEASURE

(1) OVERVIEW

1. Trinidad and Tobago adopted the CARICOM Common External Tariff (CET) on 1 January 1991. Trade between CARICOM Members is duty free. Since the implementation of the CET, the maximum external tariff for industrial goods (with the exception of products for which minimum rates have been agreed within the CARICOM) has been lowered from 35% to 20%. The average 1998 applied MFN tariff has been calculated as 9.1%. The vast majority of customs duties are *ad valorem* rates: there are no seasonal tariffs or alternate duties; only a few specific duties apply.

2. During the Uruguay Round, with the exception of seven items bound at higher levels, Trinidad and Tobago bound all of its tariffs on agricultural goods at 100% ceiling bindings; under the CET, maximum agricultural tariffs are 40%. Most industrial products have been bound at 50%, with certain exceptions where items are bound at 70%. Trinidad and Tobago's Schedule of Concessions includes a binding of 15% with respect to "other duties and charges".

3. Import surcharges, which replaced quantitative restrictions in 1990, still apply to a handful of products: e.g. poultry, sugar and assorted fruits and vegetables. For some products they will be eliminated in 1999, for others they will continue to apply. Excise duties on beer and wine are levied at apparently higher rates on third-country imports.

4. A Negative List containing all products which were subject to quantitative restrictions still exists but it has been constantly reduced. In 1997, it included only livestock, meat, fish, sugar, oils and fats, motor vehicles, cigarette papers and small ships and boats. Sugar was removed from the Negative List in June 1992 but, along with school books and pharmaceuticals, is still subject to price control. Although there are some *de facto* monopolies in both goods and services trade, the State has liquidated or sold off much of its stake in productive activities.

5. Trinidad and Tobago applies no export taxes, no direct subsidies and no export performance requirements. An export allowance in the form of a tax credit is granted to companies exporting processed or manufactured products (excluding petrochemicals and certain other products) to non-CARICOM markets. The tax credit covers the profits on the proportion of export sales to total sales so that profits on exports are effectively tax exempt[1] Other forms of export promotion to extra-regional markets include assistance on a 50/50 cost-sharing basis to eligible exporters to assist them with the cost of entering and competing in export markets. Local tax law also allows for a deduction of 150% of expenses incurred in promoting the expansion into non-CARICOM markets.

6. There are many different kinds of incentives directed at both foreign and local investment ranging from duty concessions, tax exemptions, loss write-offs, training subsidies and export allowances to free-zone incentives for companies exporting a majority (80%) of their production. Under the Fiscal Incentives Act (1979), a tax holiday for a period of up to ten years may be granted at the discretion of the Minister or the President for the manufacture of approved products by approved enterprises. Approved enterprises are classified according to the degree of local value added to be contributed to output; length of tax holidays are granted proportionately, e.g. a company manufacturing a product incorporating 50% or more local value added would be eligible for the maximum tax holiday period.

---

[1] According to the authorities, proposals have been made to remove the existing export allowance by the year 2000.

7.   Trinidad and Tobago has reviewed and updated several of its trade-related laws and policies to comply with its obligations under the WTO. Anti-dumping legislation has recently been amended and anti-dumping duties were levied in 1998 on imports of cheese. Domestic laws regarding intellectual property rights have been updated in order to bring existing legislation in line with the TRIPS Agreement. Legislation governing investment incentives is under scrutiny, a competition law is before Parliament, and environmental standards are under preparation.

(2)   MEASURES AFFECTING IMPORTS

(i)   Customs regulations

8.   Importers must operate through licensed customs brokers. These prepare the relevant documents for submission to the customs authorities: import declaration (C82), invoice, valuation form, certificate of origin where preference is being claimed and permits if required for health or security reasons. Customs introduced ASYCUDA, an electronic customs document processing system, in the last few years. Under this system, the importer is given a registration number to be used on documentation; the documents are then scanned by the ASYCUDA system and duties are determined accordingly.

9.   The authorities state that it generally takes no more than three days to process an import entry; one day to process an export declaration. Roughly half of all merchandise is inspected at the port of entry. For perishables and emergency goods, importers may post a bond in advance and pay duties after delivery. Importers may appeal a customs decision at the station, further appeal to the Comptroller of Customs and Excise and, failing an agreement, may have recourse to the Tax Appeal Board.

(ii)   Rules of origin

10.   New rules of origin for CARICOM were introduced in 1998. Duty-free treatment is accorded only if goods are shipped directly between member states. Pre-certification of origin is required with a verification process taking place at the importing end. Qualifying conditions may be "wholly produced" and "substantial transformation"; substantial transformation includes a change in tariff heading by the working or processing of extra-regional materials, manufacture in which certain prescribed materials of Common Market origin are used, or the achievement of a prescribed level of regional value added. Origin is based mainly on the use of prescribed regional raw materials, having shifted away from the value-added criterion in 1983, e.g. fruit juices, jams and jellies require the use of regionally produced fruit and sugar (Table III.1). Under a so-called "safeguard" mechanism, a manufacturer may use extra-regional materials when they cannot be found in CARICOM States; the Council may authorize a temporary derogation from the qualifying criterion.

Table III. 1
CARICOM rules of origin

Product	Rules of origin

A range of:
  Meat products
  Fish
  Vegetables (frozen, preserved or dried)
  Fruit (frozen, preserved or dried) and nuts
  Products of milling industry
  Oil seeds
  Vegetables materials (for plaiting, stuffing, etc.)
  Cocoa beans
  Sugar
  Molasses
	Wholly produced

A range of:
  Oils
  Animal products
  Sugar confectionery
  Vegetable, fruit and nuts preparations
  Mineral waters
  Liqueurs and other spirituous beverages
  Vinegar
  Wood, wood products and carpentry work
  Wicker work
  Ceramic products
  Articles of cement
  Articles of plaster
  Articles of glass
  Jewellery, gold and silver in semi-manufactured forms
  Steel products
	Produced from regional materials

A range of: Chemical products included in HS Chapters 28-39	Produced by chemical transformation
A range of: Plastics products	Non-regional material content must not exceed 10% of export price of finished product
Articles of apparel, clothing, accessories and other articles of furskin (HS 43.03)	Produced from materials not included in HS 43.03 and not being fur skins assembled in plates, crosses or similar forms
Dyed or printed fabrics	Production in which the value of extra-regional materials used does not exceed 30% of the export price of the finished product

A group of products including:
  Paper products
 	
  A range of products included in HS Chapters 73-96:
  Copper, nickel and aluminium and articles thereof
  Lead, tin and zinc and articles thereof
  Other base metals; miscellaneous articles of base metal
  Tools
  Machinery and mechanical appliances, boilers
  Electrical machinery and parts
  Railway or tramway locomotives and parts thereof
  Vehicles other than railway and tramway locomotives and parts thereof
  Aircraft and parts thereof
	Production in which the value of extra-regional materials does not exceed 50% of the export price of the finished product

Table III.1 (cont'd)

Product	Rules of origin
Ships and boats and floating structures	
Optical, photographic, cinematographic, measuring, checking, medical or surgical instruments and apparatus and parts and accessories thereof	
Clocks and watches	
Musical instruments	
Furniture	
Arms and ammunitions	
Toys	
Miscellaneous articles	

a   These origin rules apply to the medium-development countries of CARICOM; the less developed are accorded slightly more generous shares of regional value added.

Source: CARICOM Secretariat. List of Conditions to be complied with as provided under Article 14 of the Annex to the Treaty and the rules regarding Common Market origin, Schedule II, 1 January 1998.

(iii)   Tariffs

11.   Trinidad and Tobago adopted the CET on 1 January 1991.[2] The tariff schedule is based on the Harmonized Commodity Description and Coding System of 1996 (HS 96) and is in principle the CARICOM CET Schedule applied at Phase IV of the CET's calendar of reductions, including the national exceptions to the CET listed in Lists A and C (Table AIII.2). Since the adoption of the CET, the maximum external tariff for industrial goods has been lowered from 35% to 20% with the last phase implemented on 1 July 1998. The ceiling rate does not apply to goods included in List C of the CET, for which the CET has been suspended and which are subject to *ad valorem* rates as high as 30% and, in the case of some products (see below), to specific duties.

(a)   Tariff Structure

12.   Trinidad and Tobago introduced tariff structure HS 96 on 1 July 1998; at the same time it put in place the tariff reductions called for in Phase IV of the CET implementation process.[3] The Trinidad and Tobago Customs Tariff as applied as of 1 July 1998 comprises 6,325 tariff lines at the six-digit level.[4] It has nine tiers, with rates of 0, 2.5, 5, 10, 15, 20, 25, 25 and 30% for industrial goods and an additional rate of 40%, which applies only to agricultural products. The vast majority are *ad valorem* rates. (Charts III.1, III.2 and III.3) There are no seasonal tariffs or mixed or alternate duties. Specific duties apply to 27 tariff lines covering alcoholic beverages and film.[5]

---

[2]Trinidad and Tobago, together with Jamaica and Guyana adopted in principle the CET in 1976. However, divergences in its implementation and non-compliance by some members prevented the effective achievement of a CARICOM common external tariff. It was only in 1991 that the CET really went into effect, with the endorsement of the Caribbean Single Market and Economy (CSME). The Government has exercised the option to delay the implementation of the final phase of the reduction of the CET until the latter half of 1998.

[3]As part of the process of converting to HS 96, Trinidad and Tobago has reserved its right to modify its Schedule LXVII, under the provisions of Article XVIII:5 of GATT 1994, during the three-year period commencing 1 January 1997. WTO document, G/MA/42 10 January 1997.

[4]The rates of duty contained in this schedule are in accordance with Phase IV of the CET calendar of reductions for all products except those included in Lists A and C. In the first half of 1998, before HS 96 was implemented, the tariff schedule had 4,078 tariff lines at the seven-digit level.

[5]At a seven-digit level.

Chart III.1
Distribution of MFN tariff rates, 1998

Number of tariff lines

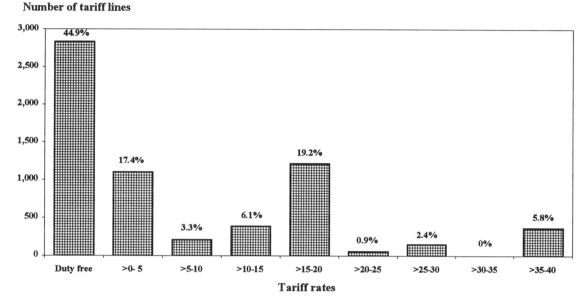

Source: WTO Secretariat calculations based on data provided by the authorities of Trinidad and Tobago.

13.   Tariff rates are established and may be changed by the Cabinet, taking into account Trinidad and Tobago's international agreements, particularly CARICOM. Proposals for changes in the tariff structure may come from the private sector or from Ministries. In practice, proposals for tariff changes – including the list of exceptions to the CET occur at CARICOM level. Tariffs are applied to goods imported from outside the CARICOM or that do not satisfy CARICOM Rules of Origin.

14.   As a result of trade liberalization, the growing importance of the VAT, income taxes on the non-oil sector, as well as corporate taxes and royalties in the oil sector, tariffs have lost importance as sources of government revenue during the 1990s. In 1996, revenue accruing from customs duties reached TT $497.8 million (US$84 million), or 5.2% of total government revenue, four percentage points lower than in 1992 or 1993[6] and around 3.9% of the value of imports.[7]

---

[6]Central Bank of Trinidad and Tobago (1997a).
    [7]A tariff revenue/imports ratio of 3.9% would imply a 35% tariff revenue/average tariff ratio, since the average tariff was 11.2% in 1996 and 1997 (Section (c)).

Chart III.2
Tariffs on agricultural products, 1998

Average tariff rates by HS Chapter (per cent)

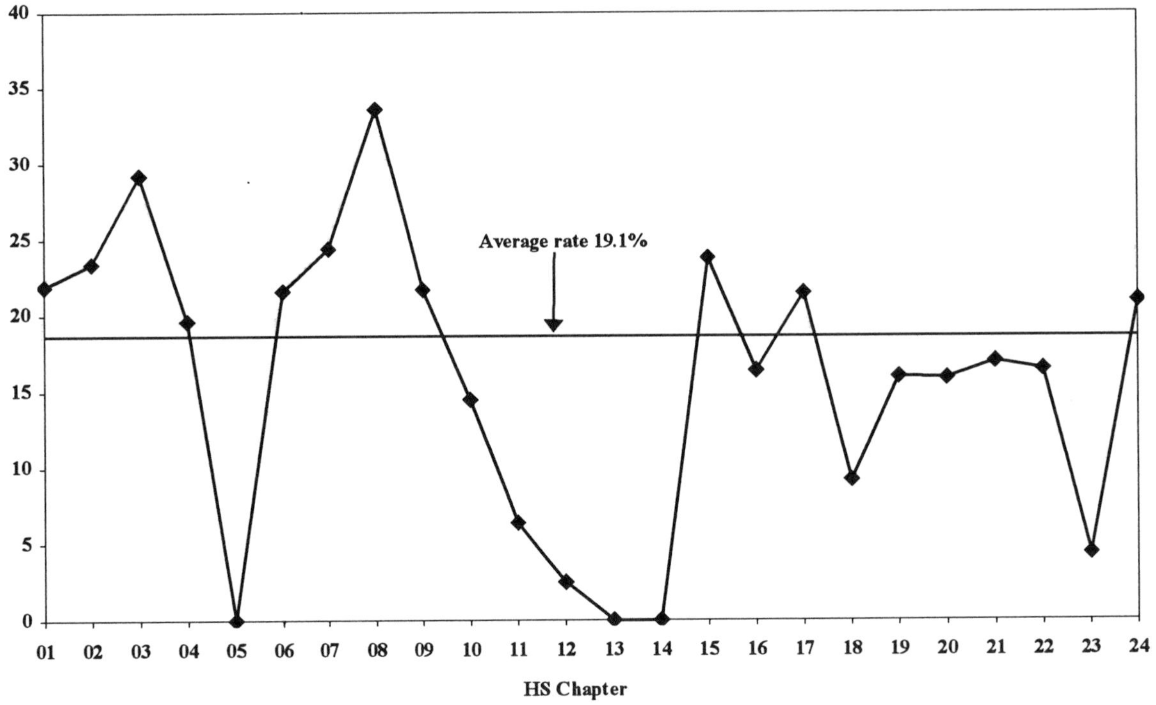

Chapter	Description
01	Live animals
02	Meat and edible meat offals
03	Fish and crustaceans, molluscs and other aquatic invertebrates
04	Dairy produce, birds eggs, natural honey, edible products of animal origin
05	Products of animal origin, n.e.s.
06	Live trees and other plants; bulbs, roots and the like; cut flowers
07	Edible vegetables and certain roots and tubers
08	Edible fruit and nuts; peel of citrus fruits or melons
09	Coffee, tea, mate and spices
10	Cereals
11	Products of the milling industry; malt; starches; wheat gluten
12	Oil seeds and oleaginous fruits; miscellanous grains, seeds and fruit
13	Lacs; gums, resins and other vegetable saps and extracts
14	Vegetable plaiting materials; vegetable products n.e.s.
15	Animal or vegetable fats and oils and other cleavage products; prepared edible fats; etc.
16	Preparations of meat, or fish or of crustaceans, molluscs or other aquatic invertebrates
17	Sugars and sugar confectionery
18	Cocoa and cocoa preparations
19	Preparations of cereals, flour, starch or milk; pastrycooks' products
20	Preparations of vegetables, fruit, nuts or other parts of plants
21	Miscellaneous edible preparations
22	Beverages, spirits and vinegar
23	Residues and waste from the food industries; prepared animal fodder
24	Tobacco and manufactured tobacco substitutes

<u>Source</u>: WTO Secretariat calculations based on data provided by the authorities of Trinidad and Tobago.

Chart III.3
Tariffs on manufactured products, 1998

Average tariff rates by HS Chapter (per cent)

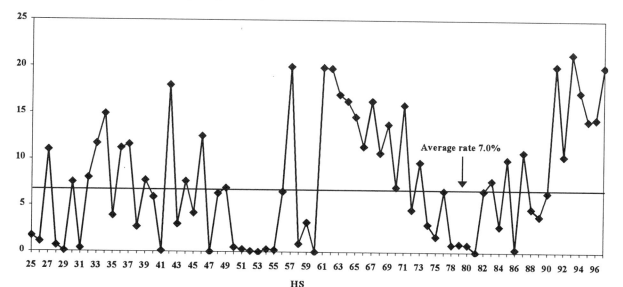

Chapter	Description		Chapter	Description		Chapter	Description
25	Salt; sulphur; earths and stone, etc.		48	Paper and paper board, etc.		72	Iron and steel
26	Ores, slag and ash		49	Printed books, newspapers, etc.		73	Articles of iron and steel
27	Mineral fuels, mineral oils, etc.		50	Silk		74	Articles of iron and steel
28	Inorganic chemicals; organic or inorganic compounds of precious metals, etc.		51	Wool; fine or coarse animal hair, etc.		75	Nickel and articles thereof
			52	Cotton		76	Aluminium etc.
29	Organic chemcials		53	Other vegetable textile fibres		78	Lead and articles thereof
30	Pharmaceutical products		54	Man-made filaments		79	Zinc and articles thereof
31	Fertilizers		55	Man-made staple fibres		80	Tin and articles thereof
32	Tanning or dyeing extracts etc.		56	Wadding, felt and non-wovens; special yarns; twine, cordage, etc.		81	Other base metals, etc.
33	Essential oils and resinoids; perfumery, cosmetic or toilet preparations		57	Carpets; other textile floor coverings		82	Tools, implements, cutlery, spoons and forks, etc.
34	Soap, organic surface-active agents washing prep., etc.		58	Special woven fabrics; lace, etc.		83	Misc. articles of base metals
			59	Impregnated, coated, covered or laminated textile fabrics, etc.		84	Nuclear reactors, boilers, machinery, etc.
35	Albuminoidal substances; modified starches; glues, etc.		60	Knitted or crocheted fabrics		85	Electrical machinery and equipment, etc.
36	Explosives; pyrotechnic products; matches, etc		61	Articles of apparel and clothing accessories, knitted or crocheted		86	Railway or tramway locomotives, etc.
37	Photographic or cinematographic goods		62	Articles of apparel and clothing accessories, not knitted, etc.		87	Vehicles other than railway or tramway rolling-stock; etc.
38	Miscellaneous chemical products		63	Other made-up textile articles; sets, worn clothing, etc.		88	Aircraft, spacecraft, etc.
39	Plastics and articles thereof					89	Ships, boats, etc.
40	Rubber and articles thereof		64	Footwear, gaiters, etc.		90	Optical, photographic, etc. apparatus
41	Raw hides and skins and leather		65	Headgear and parts thereof			
42	Articles of leather, etc.		66	Umbrellas, walking-sticks, etc.		91	Clocks and watches, etc.
43	Furskins and artifical fur; manufactures thereof		67	Prepared feathers and down, etc.		92	Musical instruments, etc.
			68	Articles of stone, plaster, etc.		93	Arms and ammunition, etc.
44	Wood and articles of wood, etc.		69	Ceramic products		94	Furniture, bedding, etc.
45	Cork and articles of cork		70	Glass and glassware		95	Toys, games, etc.
46	Manuf. of straw, of esparto, etc.		71	Natural or cultured pearls, precious or semi-precious stones, precious metals, etc.		96	Misc. manuf. articles
47	Pulp of wood or of other fibrous cellulosic material					97	Works of art, antiques, etc.

Source: WTO Secretariat calculations based on data provided by the authorities of Trinidad and Tobago.

(b)   Tariff bindings

15.   During the Uruguay Round, with the exception of seven items bound at higher levels (Table III.2), Trinidad and Tobago bound all of its tariffs on agricultural goods (those listed in Annex I of the Agreement on Agriculture) at 100% ceiling bindings. Industrial products have been bound at 50%, with certain exceptions bound at 70%: e.g. table salt, Portland cement, some cosmetics, paper products, garments (all of HS Chapters 61 and 62), footwear, some household durables, cars and car parts. The Schedule of Concessions includes a binding of 15% with respect to other duties and charges.

Table III.2
Agricultural products bound above the 100% ceiling binding

		Base rate of duty	Bound rate of duty
		Ad valorem (%)	Ad valorem (%)
020710	Poultry not cut in pieces, fresh or chilled	135	110
020731	Fatty livers of geese or ducks, fresh/chilled	135	110
020739	Other poultry cuts and offal than fatty livers, fresh or chilled	135	110
020741	Cuts of fowl of the species "Gallus Domesticus" frozen	135	110
0704001	Cabbage, fresh	150	126
070510	Lettuce, fresh	180	156
090120	Coffee, roasted coffee beans	130	106

Source: Schedule of Concessions LXVII.

(c)   Average tariff and range

16.   Trinidad and Tobago applies the CARICOM CET according to Phase IV of its implementation, with a number of exceptions, included in Lists A and C.[8] CET rates for industrial products range between 0 and 20%. In the case of agricultural goods, rates range between 0 and 40%. Manufactured goods included in List C are subject to a maximum rate of 30%. Products included in List A are subject to a maximum customs duty of 40%. Tariff rates for industrial goods (barring the exceptions to the CET) were lowered to a maximum of 20% on 1 July 1998, when Trinidad and Tobago moved to Phase IV of the implementation of the CET.

17.   The average applied MFN tariff, excluding specific duties and after implementation of Phase IV of the CET calendar of reductions, has been calculated as 9.1% in the second half of 1998, down from 11.2% in 1997. For agriculture, the average is 19.1% (down from 19.6%), with a maximum of 40%; for industry, 7% (down from 9%). A total of 44.9% of tariff lines are zero-rated and roughly 9% carry duties of over 20%; 5.8% of lines carry a 40% duty (Chart III.1).[9]

18.   A total of 93 seven-digit HS tariff lines are included in List A. Products included in this list (mostly agricultural products, petroleum products, lavatory sets, and household washing machines and dryers) are granted indefinite suspension of the CET (Table AIII.1). A total of 209 seven-digit HS tariff lines are included in List C (automobiles, some electrical appliances, precious metals, beer, wine and spirits) and are subject to tariff rates that may exceed maximum CET rates. 140 tariff lines are subject to customs duty rates of 30%, including products such as cigarettes, motor oil, gas oils and

---

[8]List A includes products on which suspension of the CET has been granted to members under Article 32 of the Common Market Annex for an indefinite period subject to review by the CARICOM Council. List C includes products for which minimum rates have been agreed between members. They are both exceptions to the CET.

[9]WTO Secretariat calculations, based on the customs tariff supplied by the authorities.

other fuels, bituminous mixtures, tyres, precious stones, jewelry, some vehicles and parts, and watches. (Table AIII.2). The average rate for goods included in List C is 26.1%, well above the average tariff, and higher than the maximum CET rate applied under Phase IV of the calendar of reductions. Applied tariff rates for List C products are determined by the different CARICOM member countries: common rates are determined by all members, but only for reference purposes. Applied rates may be modified for budgetary purposes with prior authorization of the CARICOM Council.

19.   Specific duties are applied on a list of products included in List C, including alcoholic beverages and photographic film. Specific duties on alcoholic beverages can result in an *ad valorem* equivalent above the maximum tariff rate of 30%. Some alcoholic beverages pay specific duties equivalent to TT $40 (US$6.40) a litre (vodka) or TT $35 (US$5.50) a litre (whisky or rum). These duties penalize imports of beverages which have lower prices and may compete with domestic production, for example, rum which, depending on the quality, may be facing an *ad valorem* equivalent tariff of 50% or more.[10]

20.   The List of Conditional Duty Exemptions to the CET includes those goods which, when imported for the purposes stated in the List, may be admitted into the importing member state free of import duty or at a rate lower than that set in the Schedule of Rates. In the case of Trinidad and Tobago, this applies mostly to non-competing inputs and capital goods which, according to the CET, should be subject to a tariff of 5%, but are actually imported duty free or subject to a 2.5% rate. Some goods included in the CET's List of Items Ineligible for Duty Exemption may not be exempted (in whole or in part) from duty where they are imported for use in industry, agriculture, fisheries, forestry and mining. The List of Items Ineligible for Duty Exemption includes those items produced in CARICOM countries in quantities which are considered adequate to justify the application of tariff protection (safeguard clause). These items may only be eligible for the exemption from duty if they are imported "for other approved purposes" according to Section XI of the List of Conditional Duty Exemptions, and provided they have been made available as gifts or on a concessionary basis.

(d)   Tariff escalation

21.   Trinidad and Tobago's current tariff structure is likely to provide higher effective than nominal protection to final consumption goods, with imports of non-competing inputs or capital goods granted duty-free access; or facing duties of 2.5%. Imports of semi-processed products are subject to an average tariff rate of 2.2%, while imports of fully processed products pay an average 11.1% tariff. Although raw materials are subject to an even higher average tariff (15%), this is due to the high (40%) rate applied on some agricultural products destined for final consumption and competing with local production (Table III.3).

22.   Most final goods other than capital goods (competing final goods) are subject to tariff rates of 20%, with some products remaining at 30%. Imports of clothing and carpets (HS 57, 61 and 62), and works of art (HS 97) face the highest average rates. Other products facing tariffs above the average include clocks and watches, soaps, essential oils, furniture, footwear, leather products, motor vehicles, electrical appliances, and jewellery, among others.

---

[10]The inclusion of the *ad valorem* equivalent tariff applied on these products in the calculation of the average tariff rate would result in an estimated 0.2 percentage-point increase. The simple average tariff rate would thus be 9.3%.

Table III.3
Main features of Trinidad and Tobago's tariff schedule, 1997

	Simple average %	Range %	Standard deviation[a]	Coefficient of variation[a]
All tariff lines	9.1	0-40	11.6	128.1
By sector[b]				
Agriculture and fisheries	20.0	0-40	19.5	97.5
Mining	3.1	0-30	8.4	268.0
Industry	8.4	0-40	10.4	123.9
By degree of processing				
Primary products	15.0	0-40	18.4	122.8
Semi-processed products	2.2	0-40	5.4	247.2
Finished goods	11.1	0-40	10.2	91.7

a   The standard deviation measures the absolute dispersion of a distribution; the coefficient of variation is a measure of relative dispersion, defined as the standard deviation divided by the average.

b   Based on ISIC classification.

Source: WTO calculations based on data received by the authorities of Trinidad and Tobago.

(e)   Tariff concessions

23.   Customs duty concessions on inputs, capitals goods, machinery and equipment are available under a wide range of incentive schemes and for a wide array of sectors. Duty concessions are mainly used in export-oriented industries or as investment incentives under Section 56 of the Customs Act, the Free Zones Act of 1988 and the Fiscal Incentives Act of 1979. In addition to these concessions, the Minister of Finance is empowered to grant partial or total waiver or relief from import duties on specific goods upon request made by individuals or organizations.

24.   Section 56 of the Customs Act provides for duty concessions on the imports of machinery and equipment, and materials to approved enterprises for approved projects. Enterprises in manufacturing, agriculture, forestry and fisheries, mining/petroleum, and tourism are eligible. Goods exempt from duty are included in the Third and Fourth Schedules of the Customs Act. Goods included in the Third Schedule are totally exempt from customs duties, while goods included in the Fourth Schedule are partially exempt.[11] Applications for approval are made to the Ministry of Trade and Industry via TIDCO. The main criteria for granting a concession are the effects on employment (enterprises must contribute to increased employment to benefit) and the use of local materials to enhance value added.

25.   The different incentive schemes designed to promote investment, production and exports often contain provisions on duty relief. The Free Zones Act grants enterprises located in free zones full exemptions from customs duties on capital goods, parts and raw materials for use in the construction and the equipping of premises in the zones and in connection with the approved activities. The Fiscal Incentives Act grants duty relief on raw material inputs and intermediate goods for the manufacture of approved products by approved enterprises. The Hotel Development Act grants customs duty exemption on building materials and articles of hotel equipment to be used exclusively in connection with construction and equipping of a hotel project.

---

[11]The Fourth Schedule relates to concessions for assembly industries. The tariff reduction schedule eliminated the need for the Fourth Schedule, which is no longer enforced.

26.   The scope of the import-duty relief schemes mentioned above has been eroded by tariff reductions. For example, imports of non-competing inputs are in many cases no longer subject to tariffs or subject to a 2.5% rate.

(f)   Tariff preferences

27.   Within CARICOM, tariff preferences in the form of duty-free access are accorded to other member states. CARICOM started as a free-trade area, as a continuation of the Caribbean Free-Trade Area Agreement (CARIFTA). In 1991, CARICOM moved towards the consolidation of a customs union, with the adoption of the Caribbean Single Market and Economy (CSME).

28.   Under the CARICOM/Colombia Agreement, Trinidad and Tobago (together with Barbados, Guyana and Jamaica) grants preferential treatment to certain imports from Colombia.A first group of goods was granted duty-free access on 1 June 1998, including a range of non-competing inputs and capital goods which are already granted duty-free access on an MFN basis. Actual concessions will be granted on imports of only a few products comprising: skipjack and bonito (HS1604.142), subject to an MFN tariff of 20%; and knives and cutting blades for kitchen appliances (HS8208.301) and for lawn mowers (HS8208.401), subject to an MFN tariff of 2.5%. The list of products to be accorded duty reduction from 1 January 1999 includes another group of goods listed as non-competing inputs or capital goods (hence already enjoying access to Trinidad and Tobago at tariff rates of 2.5% or 5%), plus a few items which currently pay higher customs duties (Table III.4) such as pimento (subject to a 40% MFN tariff rate); mixed bird seeds (20%); rubies, sapphires and emeralds (30%); gauze (15%); spoons plated with precious metals (20%); some types of coated electrodes and rods (15%), etc. In order for goods to benefit from preferential treatment, they must obtain a certificate of origin. Origin is conferred in accordance with the principle of substantial transformation (change of HS tariff heading), or if the c.i.f. value of non-regional inputs does not exceed 50% of the f.o.b. transaction value of the goods produced.[12] All other bilateral agreements signed by CARICOM offer unilateral preferential treatment for CARICOM exports.

29.   The CARICOM Treaty allows a few national exceptions to the duty-free entry of goods from other CARICOM member states. These are included in Schedule I of the Treaty, which allows Trinidad and Tobago to impose import duties or quantitative restrictions on fresh milk and cream, evaporated and condensed milk, tyre repair materials, and rubber tyres. However, Trinidad and Tobago does not impose any restrictions on the entry of these goods, and it is in the process of eliminating Schedule I completely.

---

[12]The determination of the transaction value follows the WTO Agreement on Customs Valuation. The transaction value of the goods produced is determined on a f.o.b. basis, while that of non-originating imports is determined on a c.i.f. basis. The percentage of regional content is calculated as follows: RC = {(TV-MNV)/TV}x100, where RC stands for regional content, TV for transaction value of the goods produced, and MNV for the transaction value of non-originating inputs.

Table III.4
Products to be accorded duty reductions in the markets of CARICOM medium-development countries (MDCs) participating in the agreement on imports originating in Colombia from 1 January 1999

Tariff Heading No.	Description	Applied MFN tariff %
09.04.202	Pimento	40
23.09.901	Mixed bird seed	25
30.04.907	Soft candles	10
38.08.909	Other rodenticides, other than for retail sale only	5
Ex 40.11.91	New pneumatic tyres of rubber having a "herring bone" for tractors	0
41.08.00	Chamois leather	5
49.08.10	Transfers (decalcomanias) vitrifiable	5
49.08.90	Other transfers	5
52.04.20	Cotton sewing thread put up for retail sale	5
59.09.00	Textile hose piping and similar textile tubing with or without lining armour or accessories of other materials	5
71.03.911	Rubies, sapphires and emeralds otherwise worked temporarily strung for convenience of transport	30
71.03.919	Rubies, sapphires and emeralds otherwise worked other than those temporarily strung for convenience of transport	30
72.07.201	Semi-finished products of iron or non-alloy steel weight < 0.25% carbon, blooms and billets only	10
72.10.11	Semi-finished products of iron or non-alloy steel weight = > 0.25% carbon, blooms and billets only	5
72.10.12	Flat-rolled products of iron or non-alloy steel with a width of 600mm or more, clad, plated or coated of a thickness => 0.5mm	5
72.12.302	Flat-rolled products of iron or non-alloy steel with a width of 600mm or more, clad, plated or coated of a thickness < 0.5mm	5
72.12.309	Flat-rolled products of iron or non-alloy steel with a width of less than 600mm, clad, plated or coated, otherwise plated or coated with zinc of a thickness =>3mm	5
72.13.399	Bars and rods, hot-rolled in irregularly wound coils, of non-alloy steel	10
73.01.20	Angles, shapes and sections (of iron or steel)	2.5
73.02.10	Rails	2.5
73.02.20	Sleepers	2.5
73.02.30	Switch blades, crossing frogs, point rods and other crossing pieces	2.5
73.02.40	Fish plates and sole plates	2.5
73.02.90	Other railway and tramway items	2.5
73.07.22	Threaded elbows, bends and sleeves	2.5
73.14.191	Gauze	15
73.23.938	Table and kitchen articles, of iron or steel, parts only	25
73.26.901	Handcuffs	25
74.13	Stranded wire, cables, plaited bands and the like, of copper, not electrically insulated	5
76.14.10	Stranded wire, cables, plaited bands and the like, of aluminium, not electrically insulated with steel core	5
76.14.90	Stranded wire, cables, plaited bands and the like, of aluminium, not electrically insulated, other than those of steel core	5
76.15.202	Parts of sanitary ware of aluminium	5
82.05.30	Planes, chisels, gorges and similar cutting tools for working wood	2.5
82.13.001	Tailors and dress-maker shears	2.5
82.13.009	Scissors, blades and other shears excluding tailors and dress-maker shears	2.5
182.15.91	Spoons, forks, labels, skimmers, cake servers, fish knives, butter knives and similar kitchen or table ware, plated with precious metal	25
83.11.101	Coated electrodes of base metal for electric arc-welding of non-alloy steel	15
83.11.109	Coated electrodes of base metal for electric arc-welding of other base metals	5
83.11.20	Cored wire of base metal for electric arc-welding	15
83.11.30	Coated rods and core wire of base metal for soldering, brazing or welding by flame	15
83.11.90	Other coated electrodes of base metal including parts	5
84.14.60	Hoods having a maximum of horizontal side =<120cm	2.5
84.19.20	Medical, surgical or laboratory sterilizers	2.5
84.80.301	Moulding patterns not of wood	0
85.04.21	Liquid dielectric transformers having a power-handling capacity not exceeding 650 kV	2.5
85.04.22	Liquid dielectric transformers having a power-handling capacity exceeding 650 kV but not exceeding 10,000 kV	2.5
85.04.23	Liquid dielectric transformers having a power-handling capacity exceeding 10,000 kV	2.5
85.15.11	Soldering irons and guns	2.5
85.46.20	Electrical insulators (of ceramics)	5
87.11.101	Motor-cycles (including mopeds) and cycles filled with an auxiliary motor, with or without side cars, with reciprocating internal, combustion engine with a capacity <50cc for transport of goods only	2.5
87.11.201	Motor-cycles (including mopeds) and cycles filled with an auxiliary motor, with or without side cars, with reciprocating internal, combustion engine with a capacity >50cc =<250 cc for transport of goods only	2.5
87.15	Baby carriages and parts thereof	2.5
90.28.20	Liquid meters	2.5
96.06.30	Button moulds and other parts of buttons, button blanks	5

Source: Information provided by the authorities of Trinidad and Tobago and the authorities of Jamaica

(g)   Tariff quotas

30.   Trinidad and Tobago does not use tariff quotas

(iv)   Other duties and taxes

31.   A system of import surcharges was introduced in 1990 to provide protection, on a temporary basis, for locally manufactured goods in the period of transition to a trading regime based on tariffs only. Surcharges, imposed under the Miscellaneous Taxes Act, were initially set at six levels: 10, 15, 25, 35, 50 and 60%. They were expected to offer, when added to customs duties and stamp duties, overall protection not exceeding 100% of the c.i.f. prices of imported goods. Surcharges were expected to be gradually phased out and eliminated by December 1994. However, their elimination was postponed, although rates for certain products have been gradually phased out. Goods subject to import surcharges were listed in the Customs Act Seventh Schedule. For a group of goods included in the Seventh Schedule (fruit juices, some vegetables, soaps, tyres, shoes), rates were reduced in 1993 to a maximum of 25% (from a previous maximum of 55%), at the same time as they were deleted from the Seventh Schedule and included in an Eighth Schedule. For some products, surcharges were eliminated. A Ninth and a Tenth Schedule were subsequently added to the Miscellaneous Taxes Act. Products included in the Tenth Schedule (vegetable oils and rice) were subject in 1994 to a four-year timetable of rate reductions, with surcharges to be eliminated in 1998. In 1995, a schedule for phasing out duties on a group of products included in the Seventh Schedule (bovine meat, milk, some vegetables and fruit) was set out. For meat and milk, surcharges were to be eliminated by 1998; for vegetables and fruit, surcharges, levied at either 5 or 15%, are to be eliminated by 1999.[13] (Table III.5). Import surcharges on certain products will remain after that date; some will be subject to reductions, but some will remain as they are. For example, a 100% surcharge on various parts of poultry (ex HS 0207) will be reduced to 86% by 2004, but an import surcharge of 60% on sugar (75% for icing sugar) will not be subject to reduction. Trinidad and Tobago's schedule of concessions resulting from the Uruguay Round includes a binding of 15% with respect to other duties and charges.

32.   Stamp duties were applied on all imports under the Stamp Duties Act. Rates were at 20% of the c.i.f. price of imports. Imports of capital goods benefiting from tariff concessions under an incentive scheme were taxed at 10%. Stamp duties were eliminated at the end of 1994.

33.   Excise duties are levied on the local production of alcoholic beverages, tobacco and petroleum products. Equivalent rates are set on imports from CARICOM member states. Import duties on alcoholic beverages under the CET are determined as specific rates. For beer and wine, these are set at higher rates than on local and CARICOM goods: for example, sparkling wine imported from outside CARICOM is dutiable at TT$40 per litre; local and CARICOM sparkling wines are excisable at TT$19.28 per litre. In contrast, for spirits the specific rate on extra-CARICOM imports is generally lower. The tobacco tax is applied on cigarettes, cigars and smoking tobacco; rates are identical to those payable on locally manufactured tobacco products. Imports of most tobacco products are subject to a 30% tariff (Table III.6).

---

[13]The Miscellaneous Taxes (Seventh Schedule) (Amendment) Order, 1997, Legal Notice No. 63, 4 April 1997.

Table III.5
Import surcharges

Tariff No.	Description of goods	Rates of surcharge %							
		1997	1998	1999	2000	2001	2002	2003	2004
0201	Meat of bovine animals, fresh or chilled	5	0	-	-	-	-	-	-
0202	Meat of bovine animals, frozen	5	0	-	-	-	-	-	-
0203	Meat of swine, fresh, chilled or frozen	5	0	-	-	-	-	-	-
0204	Meat of sheep or goats, fresh, chilled or frozen	5	0	-	-	-	-	-	-
ex.0206	Edible offal of bovine animals, sheep, goats (fresh, chilled or frozen)	5	0	-	-	-	-	-	-
ex.0207	Chicken, not cut in pieces (fresh, chilled or frozen)	10	5	0	-	-	-	-	-
020730	Poultry cuts and offal (inc. livers), fresh or chilled:								
020731	Fatty livers of geese or ducks	103	100	98	96	93	91	88	86
020739	Other	103	100	98	96	93	91	88	86
020740	Poultry cuts and offal other than livers, frozen								
020741	Of fowls of the species Gallus domesticus:								
0207411	Backs and necks	103	100	98	96	93	91	88	86
0207412	Wings	103	100	98	96	93	91	88	86
0207419	Other	103	100	98	96	93	91	88	86
020742	Of turkeys:								
0207421	Backs, necks and wings	103	100	98	96	93	91	88	86
0207429	Other	103	100	98	96	93	91	88	86
020743	Of ducks, geese, or guinea fowls	103	100	98	96	93	91	88	86
ex0401	Liquid milk (plain or flavoured with the exception of evaporated milk and condensed milk)								
ex0402	Liquid milk (plain or flavoured with the exception of evaporated milk and condensed milk)								
070200	Tomatoes (fresh or chilled)	30	15	0	-	-	-	-	-
0704001	Cabbage (fresh or chilled)	30	15	0	-	-	-	-	-
0704002	Cauliflower (fresh or chilled)	30	15	0	-	-	-	-	-
070510	Lettuce (fresh or chilled)	30	15	0	-	-	-	-	-
0803001	Bananas (fresh)	10	5	0	-	-	-	-	-
0803002	Plantains (fresh)	10	5	0	-	-	-	-	-
ex0804	Dates, figs, pineapples, avocados, guavas, mangoes and mangosteens (fresh)	10	5	0	-	-	-	-	-
ex0805	Citrus fruit (fresh)	10	5	0	-	-	-	-	-
080610	Grapes (fresh)	10	5	0	-	-	-	-	-
0807	Melon (inc. watermelons) and paw-paws (papayas) (fresh)	10	5	0	-	-	-	-	-
0808	Apples, pears and quinces (fresh)	10	5	0	-	-	-	-	-
080900	Apricots, cherries, peaches, (inc. nectarines), plums and sloes (fresh)								
0810	Other fruit	10	5	0	-	-	-	-	-
ex1208	Meals of soya bean	10	-	-	-	-	-	-	-
1701	Cane or beet sugar and chemically pure sucrose, in solid form	60	60	60	60	60	60	60	60
ex1701	Icing sugar	75	75	75	75	75	75	75	75

Source: Miscellaneous Taxes, (Seventh Schedule) (Amendment) Order, 1997.

Table III.6
Excise duties levied on imported and locally produced goods

HS No.	Description of goods	Excise duty levied on local products[a]	Caribbean common market duty[b]	Common external tariff
2202902	Malt beverage	$0.20/l.[c]	$0.20/l[c]	25%
2203001	Beer	$2.81/l.[c]	$2.81/l[c]	$4.75/l.
2203002	Stout	$2.81/l.[c]	$2.81/l[c]	$5.00/l.
2203009	Other	$2.81/l[c]	$2.81/l[c]	$5.00/l.
220410	Sparkling wine	$19.28/l.	$19.28/l.	$40.00/l.
2204202	Other wine	$9.00/l.	$9.00/l.	$25.00/l.
220500	Vermouth and other wine of fresh grapes flavoured with plants or aromatic substances	n.a.	n.a.	$30.00/l.
220600	Other fermented beverages (e.g. cider, perry)	n.a.	n.a.	$20.00/l.
2207	Other potable spirits	$92.10/l. alc./vol.[d]	$92.10/l. alc./vol.[d]	
220710	Undenatured ethyl alcohol of an alcoholic strength by volume of 80% vol. or higher	$92.10/l. alc./vol.[d]	$92.10/l. alc./vol.[d]	$14.30/l.
220720	Ethyl alcohol and other spirits, denatured, of any strength	$92.10/l. alc./vol.[d]	$92.10/l. alc./vol.[d]	$1.32/l.
220810	Compound alcoholic preparations of a kind used for the manufacture of beverages	n.a.	n.a.	$35.00/l.
22082	Brandy and blended brandy	$92.10/l. alc./vol.[d]	$92.10/l. alc./vol.[d]	
2208201	In bottles of a strength not exceeding 46% vol.	$92.10/l. alc./vol.[d]	$92.10/l. alc./vol.[d]	$35.00/l.
2208209	Other	$92.10/l. alc./vol.[d]	$92.10/l. alc./vol.[d]	$35/l. alc./vol.
220830	Whiskies	$92.10/l. alc./vol.[d]	$92.10/l. alc./vol.[d]	
2208301	In bottles of a strength not exceeding 46% vol.	$92.10/l. alc./vol.[d]	$92.10/l. alc./vol.[d]	$35.00/l.
2208309	Other	$92.10/l. alc./vol.[d]	$92.10/l. alc./vol.[d]	$35/l. alc./vol.
22084	Rum and tafia and rum punch	$43.43/l. alc./vol.[d]	$43.43/l. alc./vol.[d]	
2208401	In bottles of a strength not exceeding 46% vol.	$43.43/l. alc./vol.[d]	$43.43/l. alc./vol.[d]	$35.00/l.
2208409	Other	$43.43/l. alc./vol.[d]	$43.43/l. alc./vol.[d]	$35/l. alc./vol.
22085	Gin and Geneva	$92.10/l. alc./vol.[d]	$92.10/l. alc./vol.[d]	-
2208501	In bottles of a strength not exceeding 46% vol.	$92.10/l. alc./vol.[d]	$92.10/l. alc./vol.[d]	$35.00/l.
2208509	Other	$92.10/l. alc./vol.[d]	$92.10/l. alc./vol.[d]	$35/l. alc./vol.
2208901	Vodka	$92.10/l. alc./vol.[d]	$92.10/l. alc./vol.[d]	$40.00/l.
2208902	Cordials and liqueurs	$92.10/l. alc./vol.[d]	$92.10/l. alc./vol.[d]	$40.00/l.
2208903	Aromatic bitters used as a flavouring agent for food and beverages	n.a.	n.a.	$1.10/l.
2208904	Other aromatic bitters	n.a.	n.a.	$14.30/l.
2208909	Other	n.a.	n.a.	$14.30/l.
240220	Cigarettes	$2.50 per pack of 20	$2.50/pack of 20 and in prop. when not so packed	30%
240310	Smoking tobacco	$32.73/kg.	$32.73/kg.	30%
240210	Cigars	$17.24/kg.	$17.24/kg.	30%
ex271013	Premium gasolene	99.696 cents/l.	91 cents/l.	30%
ex271013	Regular gasolene	99.696 cents/l.	91 cents/l.	30%
271031	Diesel oil - auto	19.609 cents/l.	17 cents/l.	30%
	Diesel oil - marine	19.609 cents/l.	10 cents/l.	30%
271092	Lube oil	n.a.	5.5 cents/l.	30%
	Compressed natural gas	24.82 cents/l.		

n.a.   Not applicable.

a   Local excise duties levied via orders issued under the Excise Act; petroleum products are based on 1997 orders; others date from 1992.

b   Act according to orders issued by the President (1992) under Sections 7 and 10 of the Customs Act.

c   At a specific gravity of 1,050 degrees and so in proportion of any difference in quantity or gravity.

d   And so in proportion for any part of a litre or for any greater or lesser strength.

Source: The Common External Tariff (Reduction of Duty) Order, 1995; the Excise Duty (Petroleum Products) Order 1997; The Excise Duty (Composed Natural Gas) Order, 1997.

34.   The value-added tax (VAT) is 15% on non-zero-rated items. On imports, the VAT is levied on the c.i.f. value of imports plus duty and taxes. Zero-rated goods include a number of consumer staples (e.g. rice, flour, milk and milk products, margarine, bread, toilet paper, pasta), any

unprocessed food for human or animal consumption; natural gas, crude oil, agricultural chemicals and equipment; medicines; aeroplanes and ships supplied to the State; books; and steel-band instruments. A number of services are also not subject to VAT, including educational, medical, private transport, real estate; hotel accommodation for more than thirty days; most financial services; air and sea charter services (VAT Act, No 37 of 1989). Financial services are, however, subject to a transaction tax of 15%.

(v)   Customs valuation

35.   In practice, according to the customs authorities, Trinidad and Tobago applies the WTO system of customs valuation and current legislation, Act 34 of 1996,conforms to the requirements of the WTO Agreement. In general, the transaction value is used for the valuation of goods; neither minimum import prices nor reference prices are in use. The Valuations Branch in the Department of Customs and Excise scrutinizes the values of certain sensitive imports; roughly half of all cargo is examined as a large number of discrepancies have been found, particularly where second-hand goods are concerned. The Comptroller, according to Act 6 of 1993, may, within one year of entry, adjust the value if it has been found to be incorrect.

(vi)   Preshipment inspection

36.   Trinidad and Tobago does not carry out preshipment inspections. Due to the absence of foreign exchange controls, this procedure is not deemed to be necessary by the authorities.

(vii)   Import prohibitions and licensing

37.   Section 45 of the Customs Act lists goods that are prohibited from import, inter alia, all goods liable to forfeiture under the Trade Descriptions Act 1983: trademarked goods unless accompanied by a definite indication of the country in which goods were made or produced; counterfeit coins and stamps; arms and ammunition, toy guns resembling firearms; indecent or obscene articles or matter; coin-operated mechanical games; rat poison containing arsenic; saccharin, except to licensed pharmacists and members of the Medical Board; certain alcohols unless of a certain alcoholic volume or a certain packaging; unrefined sugar; and left-hand drive vehicles, except those destined for some specific uses.[14] Quantitative restrictions apply to certain kinds of livestock (live poultry); quantities are determined by the Ministry of Agriculture, Land and Marine Resources. The size of the quota is determined yearly; information regarding the quota is not published but provided directly to the importer.

38.   Licensing is maintained under the Imports and Exports Control Regulations (1941) and the Trade Ordinance of 1958. Applications must be submitted and licences issued for goods which appear on the Import Negative List, for which importation is subject to the granting of a licence. For imports subject to quantitative restrictions, licences are normally not granted to domestic producers of like goods. In the case of goods not subject to quantitative restrictions, in principle an import licence must first be obtained before any order is placed with the supplier. However, goods arriving without a licence may apply for one. An applicant may apply for a licence at any time during the year; depending on the items, allocations are based, if demand exceeds supply, on past performance with a small amount reserved for new applicants. However, eligibility to apply depends on the imported items under consideration. Licences are normally issued immediately unless other agencies are

---

[14] And allowed under Section 45(2) of the Customs Act Chapter 78:01.

involved, then it may take a few weeks. The licensing system is intended to monitor the quantity of imports of those goods which are manufactured locally.[15]

39.   The Import Negative List, established in the 1940s, started as a system of quantitative restrictions to protect infant industries. The list was modified in the 1970s and in the 1980s when, due to balance-of-payments problems, a large number of goods were added to control foreign exchange outflows. In the 1990s the list has been considerably pruned. At the start of the decade it included a wide range of products, from livestock, fish, meat, most agricultural and food products, to chemicals, fuels, cement soaps, plastic products, all motor vehicle imports, footwear, textiles and garments, electrical machinery, furniture, construction materials, etc. In 1992 a group of manufactured items were deleted from the Negative List and were made subject to import surcharges, which were gradually phased-out. The Negative List was modified in 1997 (Table III.7) and again in June 1998.[16] The List, which does not apply to CARICOM imports (with the exception of oils and fats), currently includes livestock, meat, fish, sugar, oils and fats, motor vehicles, cigarette papers and small ships and boats and pesticides.

40.   A second licensing system, the Minister's Licence or Duty Relief System, is applied for the duty-free importation of raw material inputs and intermediate goods to be used by approved manufacturing industries which benefit from concessions under the Fiscal Incentive Act Chapter 85:01, or under Section 56 of the Customs Act. Licences are obtained from the Ministry of Trade and Industry upon recommendation from TIDCO subject to prior approval of the list of materials to be imported duty free. Licences are granted for one year, per shipment or for a certain amount of imports, and must be produced and presented to customs at the moment of importation for the goods to be granted duty-free entry.

(viii)   State trading

41.   Since the beginning of the decade, Trinidad and Tobago has been involved in a major programme of divestment and rationalization of state enterprises (Chapter I). According to the authorities, the government is not aware of the existence of state-trading enterprises in the sense of the GATT 1994. To date, Trinidad has made no notification to the WTO with regard to state-trading. A number of state-owned enterprises participate, however, in the distribution and exportation of certain products.

42.   Caroni, the largest state-owned agricultural enterprise, is the only sugar processor and has a de facto but not a *de jure* monopoly over the purchase, distribution, export and import of sugar. With the approval of the Ministry of Trade and Industry, manufacturers were allowed for a period of time to import sugar, subject to the CET and a surcharge. Being the sole purchaser of sugar cane at guaranteed prices, Caroni holds the quotas under the Lomé Sugar Protocol and for the United States. The National Flour Mills, another government owned agro-business enterprise, was until recently a monopoly producer, importer and distributor of a number of agricultural products including rice, flour and certain edible oils. As part of the divestment programme, the importation of these products was demonopolized in the following years; oil was removed from the Negative List in 1993, flour and rice in 1994. Although cocoa growers are free to sell to other buyers, the Cocoa and Coffee Industry Board purchases the bulk of locally grown cocoa and grinds beans for export. The Board purchases for resale cocoa and coffee beans from farmers through a system of licensed buying agents. (Chapter IV (2)(v)(b)). It also grants export permits to individuals or groups who can accumulate a minimum of 20,000 lbs of product.

---

[15]WTO, G/LIC/3/TTO/1, 16 February 1996.
[16]Notice to Importers No.1 of 1998 – Legal Notice No.180.

Table III.7
Imports requiring licences

Category	Ministry Code No.	Description of goods
		Livestock
00	00000	Live poultry, rearing or breeding
	00001	Live poultry, other than rearing or breeding
		Fish, crustaceans, molluscs
02	02000	Fish, fresh (live or dead), chilled or frozen
	02001	(a) Shrimp (prawn), fresh (live or dead), chilled or frozen;
		(b) Lobster, fresh (live or dead), chilled or frozen;
		(c) Crabmeat, fresh, chilled or frozen
		Oils and fats
12	12000	Coconut in all forms including coconut seedlings, copra, dessicated coconut, coconut milk and coconut cream, but excluding coconut oil
	12001	Oilseed cake, meal and other vegetable oil residues
	12002	Copra
	12003	Oilseeds, beans, nuts etc.
	12004	Animal oils, fats and greases, unrefined
	12006	Fatty acids and solid residues from the treatment of oils and fats
	12007	Vegetable fats
		Motor vehicles
22	22000	Road Motor Vehicles of the following descriptions:
		(a) left-hand drive vehicles imported under section 45(2) (4) of the Customs Act, Chap.78:01 as amended
		(b) Used right-hand drive vehicles
		Paper and paper production
26	26006	Paper for wrapping tobacco or cigarettes
		Miscellaneous manufactured products
35	35015	Ships and boats (under 250 tonnes)
		Pesticides
36	36000	Parathion, ethyl.
	36001	2,4,5 - Trichlorphenyl (s,4,5-T)
	36002	Dichlorodiphenyl – Trichloroethane (DDT)
	36003	Chlordimform
	36004	Dibromocholoropropane (DBCP)
	36005	Ethylene Dibromide (EDB)
	36006	Pentachlorophenol (PCP)
	36007	Lead Arsenate
	36008	Thallium and its salts
	36009	Aldrin, Dieldrin and Endrin

Source: Trade Ordinance (1958): Notice to Importers No. 1 of 1997.

43.   The distribution of energy products has been dominated by fully government-owned companies. Although the National Petroleum Marketing Company still has a monopoly on the distribution of petroleum products in the local market, its marketing operations are now subject to a phased demonopolization plan. The distribution of gasoline is in the process of being demonopolized, with entry allowed to domestic investors in 1998 and to foreign investors in 1999. The Natural Gas Company (NGC) has a monopoly on the purchase, transmission and sale of natural gas in the country. NGC negotiates gas purchasing contracts with suppliers and gas supply contracts with consumers.

(ix)   Government procurement

44.   Trinidad and Tobago is not party to the plurilateral Agreement on Government Procurement. Although government procurement is not included in the scope of the CARICOM Treaty, the Council has launched an action plan to create a central regional information coordinating agency. In February 1994 a "Promotional Program for Increasing Procurement of Regional Goods and Services by Member States from within the Community" was approved.

45.   Procurement for Trinidad and Tobago government agencies is regulated by a Central Tenders Board (CTB) which was established following the enactment of the CTB Ordinance in 1961. Regulations have been issued subsequently to refine the procedures used, including the CTB Ordinance Amendment Acts of 1979, 1987, 1991 and 1993. In principle, similar procedures are followed by all government bodies whether regional or public enterprises. The CTB Ordinance and its amendments allow for the setting up of Tenders Committees within individual agencies and Ministries, where the value of goods, works or services does not exceed TT$500,000. For contracts of TT$500,000 or above, the CTB and the National Insurance Property Development Co. Ltd. act as sole procurers.[17]

46.   All contracts are subject to tendering, which may be either selective or competitive.[18] Selective tenders are solicited from a register of export suppliers or consultants based in Trinidad and Tobago. The CTB decides whether to go selective, in accordance with Article 20(3)(b) of the CTB Ordinance, subject to the approval of the Minister of Finance. If, it is decided that the tender will be selective, names are taken from the register and tenders invited. If the tender is competitive, a notice is posted in the Trinidad and Tobago Gazette and in local or overseas newspapers (required for International Bank for Reconstruction and Development, and Inter-American Development Bank projects only).

47.   Competitive tenders are open and anyone can participate without reference to nationality. They are won by the lowest-evaluated supplier. However, a preferential margin of 10% is accorded to local suppliers of goods and services. In some cases, if tenders go to foreigners, a local agent may be required.

(x)   Anti-dumping and countervailing duties

48.   In March 1995, Trinidad and Tobago notified the WTO, under Article 18.5 of the Agreement, of its legislation, the Anti-Dumping and Countervailing Duties Article (No. 11 of 1992). It was reviewed by Committee members in December 1995 and a number of questions were asked. To date, no responses have been provided. The Act was substantially amended by Act No. 23 of 1995; however, the amendment has not yet been notified to the WTO Committee on Anti-Dumping Measures. Also Anti-Dumping and Countervailing Duties Regulations were issued in 1996 under Section 34 of the Anti-Dumping Act, as amended. Amendments to the 1992 legislation include: new definitions of industry margin of dumping, and subsidy; new detailed provisions on the calculation of normal value, export price, and dumping margins; new detailed provisions on investigation procedures, provisions defining de minimis dumping margins and negligible imports; and new detailed provisions on undertakings and reviews of duties, including a five-year limit on the duration of measures. The new law has added a clause which enables the Minister of Trade and Industry not to impose an anti-dumping duty if he considers that it would not be in the public interest to do so. There is no express provision in the Anti-Dumping and Countervailing Duties legislation for judicial review. The Supreme Court of Trinidad and Tobago, which comprises the Court of Appeal and the High

---

[17]Until 1993, the CTB was the sole procurer; this was amended by Act No.3 of 1993.

[18]According to the authorities, some 50% of contracts are selectively let.

Court, has general inherent jurisdiction to provide relief in the form of judicial review of administrative action. Aspects of the WTO Anti-Dumping Agreement (or any other WTO agreement) not reflected in domestic legislation, do not apply.

49.   An Anti-Dumping Unit was established in January 1996 in the Ministry of Trade and Industry. The Authority may initiate an investigation to determine the existence and effect of any alleged dumping of any goods at the direction of the Minister, on his own initiative or on receipt of a complaint in writing by or on behalf of producers of like goods in Trinidad and Tobago. Before initiating an investigation, the Authority must obtain evidence of dumping and its magnitude; material injury or material retardation; and, where applicable, a causal link between such imports and the alleged material injury or material retardation. Trinidad and Tobago's Act no. 11 of 1992 defines material injury as material injury to the production in Trinidad and Tobago of like goods including, in respect of the subsidization of an agricultural product, an increase in the Government's financial burden. Material retardation is defined as material retardation of the establishment of the production in Trinidad and Tobago of like goods. The issue of conformity of Act No. 11 with the WTO Anti-Dumping Agreement was addressed by the 1995 amendment and the adoption of a set of regulations in 1996.

50.   The 1996 Regulations draw from Article 3 of the WTO Agreement on Anti-Dumping to include, when examining the impact of dumped imports on the domestic industry, relevant factors such as: the volume of dumped or subsidized imports (assessed in absolute terms or relative to production or consumption in Trinidad and Tobago); the effect of dumped or subsidized imports on prices (assessed by reference to whether there has been a significant price undercutting by the dumped or subsidized imports as compared with the price of like goods produced in Trinidad and Tobago), or whether the effect of such imports is to depress to a significant degree, or prevent price increases, that would otherwise have occurred; and the consequent impact of dumped or subsidized imports on the industry that produces like goods (assessed by reference to all relevant economic factors and indices having a bearing on the state of the industry, notably sales, profits, production, market share, productivity, return on investments, rate of use of production capacity, inventories, cash flow, employment, wages, growth, ability to raise capital and investments).

51.   An investigation is terminated at the request in writing on behalf of an industry at whose instance the investigation was initiated either when the margin of dumping on the goods or the actual or potential volume of dumped goods is negligible, or pursuant to an undertaking. A preliminary determination must be made within three months after an investigation has been initiated. This may lead to the application of provisional duties. A final determination must be made within six months after the preliminary determination and final duties may then be imposed. If an anti-dumping duty is imposed, the person affected may appeal to the Tax Appeal Board.

52.   On 19 September 1996 the Anti-Dumping Authority in the Ministry of Trade and Industry initiated an anti-dumping investigation on imports of cheddar cheese from New Zealand. The complaint was lodged by Agrifin, the sole producer of cheddar cheese, claiming dumping and material injury. In January 1998, the Minister of Trade and Industry ordered the imposition of a provisional duty for a period of two months. Imports from the New Zealand Dairy Board had risen from 12.6% to 42.4% of the domestic market between 1991 and 1995. Information cited in the notice of the imposition of the provisional duties noted that cheddar cheese from the New Zealand Dairy Board was imported at prices below Agrifin's cost of production, that Agrifin's market share had fallen from 5% to 3% between 1994 and 1996, and that the company was unable to realize a profit. Since then the company has gone out of business. The authority calculated a margin of dumping of 13.93%. However, no duty has been imposed. The New Zealand Dairy Board undertook to increase its price of cheddar cheese exported to Trinidad and Tobago by the amount of the margin of dumping.

(xi)   Safeguards

53.   Trinidad and Tobago has not used safeguard measures in the sense of GATT Article XIX. It has, however, notified the Textiles Monitoring Body that it reserves the right, during the transitional period of the Agreement on Textiles and Clothing, to apply the transitional safeguard mechanism in accordance with Article 6.1 of the Agreement.[19] At present there is no existing safeguards legislation in accordance with Article XIX.   However, the Caribbean Community Treaty of Chaguaramas contains safeguards legislation (Article 14, Paragraph 6).

(xii)   Standards and technical regulations

54.   The Trinidad and Tobago Bureau of Standards (TTBS), set up in 1974, is the national standards body. Its statutory function is to promote and encourage the maintenance of standards that satisfy criteria for good performance. The organization is under the purview of the Ministry of Trade and Industry and is managed by a Board of Directors.

55.   The TTBS is a member of the International Standards Organization (ISO) and of ISONET, a network of national standards information centres designed to promote the flow of information on standards, technical regulations and related documents. Since March 1996, the Bureau has been designated as the enquiry point under the WTO Agreement on Technical Barriers to Trade.   The Bureau is also a member of the Caribbean Common Market Standards Council and the Pan American Standards Commission. In 1996, the WTO was informed that the TTBS had accepted the Code of Good Practice contained in Annex 3 of the WTO Agreement on Technical Barriers to Trade.[20]

56.   Local standards are created as well as adopted or adapted from existing standards. ISO and IEC standards are the first source for local standards, followed by those of major trading partners. The TTBS is responsible for ensuring that the quality of all goods and services produced in the country conform to international requirements; the same standards are applied to both imports and exports.

57.   The work of the TTBS includes certification, laboratory testing, inspection and monitoring and standardization. Standards, developed by a specifications committee, are published for comment prior to adoption. The Bureau sets standards for all electrical and electronic equipment except for telecommunications equipment (these are set by the operator); there are 60 compulsory national standards, primarily on electrical equipment, labelling requirements and specifications, e.g. for automotive parts. Standards are made compulsory where they affect the health and safety of consumers or where they can prevent fraud and deception. Since becoming the Enquiry Point, TTBS has notified the WTO on three new standards, in accordance with Art. 10.6 of the WTO Agreement on Technical Barriers to Trade.[21] Labelling requirements issued as standards by the TTBS are compulsory; for other products, namely, food, drugs and cosmetics, health and safety regulations, and labelling requirements are issued by the Ministry of Health under the Food and Drugs Act. Within the context of an industrial restructuring loan from the World Bank, the Bureau has expanded its metrology and calibration services. It is also the national laboratory accreditation body. The testing of products is performed in the accredited laboratories; type approval is an accepted practice in determining conformity to a standard. The Bureau of Standards is also the registrar and certifying body for ISO 9000 Quality Management Systems.

---

[19]WTO document G/TMB/N/117, 14 August 1995.
[20]WTO document G/TBT/CS/N/37, 29 April 1996.
[21]These standards concern safety of toys (WTO documents G/TBT/Notif.97.675 and 676, 13 October 1997) and labelling of footwear (WTO document G/TBT/Notif.98.161, 25 March 1998).

58.   The CARICOM Common Market Standards Council was established in 1973 as an Association of all national standards bodies in the region, charged with developing regional standards and advising the Common Market Council on related technical matters. There are currently 72 products to which regional standards apply. For some time, CARICOM has focused attention on harmonizing and regional standards. Recently, the Standards Council recommended that these be made compulsory but the Ministers have postponed this decision; in the interim, all regional standards are voluntary.

59.   The Standards Act 18 of 1997 gave the Bureau the right to test against standards for quality and grading, to require manufacturers/importers to withdraw sub-standard products and introduced the provision to test goods not accepted by other countries. Further, under the Act, the Bureau may recognize a foreign standard for certification and label verification and may accept certificates from laboratories outside the country. Environmental standards, using the ISO 14000 guidelines, were adopted in 1997, but effluent and emission standards are the domain of the Environmental Management Authority.

(3)   MEASURES AFFECTING EXPORTS

(i)   Export procedures

60.   Customs examines all export shipments at the port of exit. Export verification is designed to prevent smuggling, ensure that restricted goods are accompanied by the appropriate certificate, and that goods on which no VAT has been paid are being exported. Thanks to a system of priority, exports normally clear customs within 24 hours.

(ii)   Export taxes

61.   Trinidad and Tobago levies no export taxes on goods.[22]

(iii)   Export licensing

62.   Table III.8 lists the goods which are subject to licensing prior to export. In general, these are controlled for security, health or conservation purposes; however, certain items are subject to licence as a result of domestic subsidies, or import duty concessions (re-exports).

63.   Health certificates for the export of live animals are issued by the veterinary office of the Ministry of Agriculture. Certificates for the export of fresh and processed foods and drugs, if required by the recipient country, are issued by the Food and Drugs Inspectorate of the Ministry of Health.

---

[22]Taxes on exports are prohibited under the CARICOM Treaty.

Table III.8
Exports requiring a licence

		Description of goods
I.	(1)	Coral and other aquatic life found in the country's marine environment or riverine environment:
		(a) coral, turtle, turtle-eggs, fauna;
		(b) aquarium fish;
		(c) shrimp, fish, lobster, crustaceans, molluscs, or other aquatic invertebrates (frozen).
	(2)	Live animals [i.e. mammals, birds, reptiles, amphibians, insects, other species listed in the Convention on International Trade in Endangered Species of Wild Fauna and Flora (CITES) and endangered species of Trinidad and Tobago].
	(3)	Works of art, artefacts and archaeological findings.
	(4)	Clays, crushed limestone, boulders, sand, gravel, plastering sand, porcellanite, argillite, oil, sand.
	(5)	Planting material, including tissue culture and other plant propagation material of (CITES) listed species.
	(6)	Embryos and artificial insemination material.
II.	(1)	Agricultural machinery.
	(2)	Re-export of duty-free capital goods, e.g., mining, construction and other industrial machinery.
	(3)	Re-export of electro-medical or medical electronic equipment.
	(4)	Items which are subsidized either directly or indirectly: rice, baker's flour, gasoline, kerosene, liquid petroleum gas.
III.	(1)	Explosives, firearms, ammunition and ordinance.
	(2)	All goods consigned to a country in which trade restrictions have been imposed as a matter of national policy.
IV.		Human organs.
V.		Non-ferrous metal scrap and ores.

Source: Notice to Exporters No. 1 of 1994, 17 June 1994.

(iv)   Export subsidies and tax and duty concessions

(a)   Direct export subsidies

64.   The Government has notified the WTO that it maintains no subsidies within the meaning of Articles 1 and 2 of the Agreement.[23]

(b)   Tax and duty concessions

65.   Under the Corporation Tax Act, an export allowance, in the form of a tax credit, is granted to locally incorporated companies for exports to non-CARICOM countries of locally manufactured or produced goods, services, and agricultural products.[24]   Branches of foreign corporations are not eligible for this allowance. The tax credit covers the profits on the proportion of exports sales to total sales so that profits on exports are effectively tax exempt.[25]   In 1996, export-allowance claims amounted to TT$18 million (US$3 million), implying a forgone revenue of TT$6.3 million (US$1.1 million) at the 35% corporate tax rate. In 1997, under the Finance Act, this allowancewas

---

[23]WTO document, G/SCM/N/3/TTO, 9 January 1996

[24]The export allowance is calculated as follows: Export allowance = (Export sales/Total sales) x Total sales profit.

[25]Article 1 ((a)(1)(ii)) of the Agreement on Subsidies defines a subsidy as, "government revenue that is otherwise due and that is forgone or not collected (i.e. fiscal incentives such as tax credits)". Annex I provides an illustrative list of prohibited subsidies; relevant here is (e) the full or partial exemption, remission or deferral, specifically related to exports, of direct taxes or social welfare charges paid or payable by industrial or commercial enterprises. Article 27 waives the application of Article 1 for a period of eight years from the date of entry into force of the WTO Agreement, but Article 27.4 states that a developing country Member shall not increase the level of its export subsidies.

expanded to include services connected with the building industry (architectural, engineering, etc.). The Minister of Finance has declared that this export allowance will be eliminated by 1 January 2000.

66.   Imported inputs for companies exporting 100% of their production are exempt from value-added tax.

(c)   Duty drawback

67.   Section 40 (Part IV) of the Customs Act allows goods imported for temporary use (they must be exported within three months) duty-free entry; a deposit or security must however, be paid. Duty drawback is granted under Section 50 of the Customs Act. Part XI of the Customs Act specifies the regulations and products on which drawback of duty on inputs into goods manufactured locally is payable; for example, tobacco used for manufacture, steel used for steel drums, cloth for shorts, materials for shoes, hats, brooms.[26] According to the customs authorities, drawbacks are rarely used. To benefit from a drawback, the value of any export entry must exceed two dollars. In addition, goods must be exported within twelve months of the date of importation. If duties applied on the imported good are reduced during the period between importation and exportation, the drawback will be calculated at the (lower) prevailing rate at the moment or exportation.

68.   Since 1993, exporters have also been eligible for a rebate, amounting to 1.5% of the value of export sales which is valid for the reduction of duty payable on future imports.

(v)   **Export financing and credit insurance**

69.   The recently created Export Import Bank (EXIMBANK) absorbed the existing Export Credit Insurance Company (EXCICO) which was established in 1973 to provide insurance facilities for local exporters against the risks involved in exporting on credit terms. With respect to insurance coverage, the EXIMBANK covers political and commercial risks (including bankruptcy of buyer, *force majeure* causing refusal to accept delayed shipment, payments restrictions arising from controls). A variety of export financing schemes also exist: the EXIMBANK provides pre-shipment financing, allowing the exporter to obtain direct financing at competitive, but not subsidized, rates for purchases of raw materials and other working capital needs against confirmed export orders. Alternatively, it may provide guarantees to commercial banks for advances (for a maximum of 180 days) made to exporters. EXIMBANK also provides post-shipment financing, either directly or in partnership with commercial banks, allowing exporters to convert trade receivables into cash to enhance working capital; previously, exports were funded largely through bank overdrafts. While most of its revenue (TT$165 million of credit insurance business in 1995) comes from insurance activities, financing is expected to grow rapidly. Government shares in EXIMBANK are slated for divestment and the company plans to expand its services, to add export marketing loans, and to increase product coverage. In addition to the current manufactured products, credits will cover agricultural, horticultural, and fresh seafood products as well as services.[27]

(vi)   **Export promotion**

70.   Launched in July 1996, the Export Technical Assistance Facility, a matching grant programme administered by the Trade and Industry Division of TIDCO, provides assistance (on a 50/50 cost-sharing basis) to eligible exporters to assist them with the cost of entering and competing

---

[26]For tobacco, a flat drawback rate of TT$6.28 per kg. of cigarettes exported is used; for cloth for making shorts, the Comptroller establishes an average value which is reviewed annually. (Customs Act, Sections 158 and 160.)

[27]Ministry of Trade and Industry.

in export markets. The Finance Act of 1994 makes provision for a deduction of 150% of promotional expenses incurred in promoting the expansion into non-CARICOM markets for the export of goods shipped in commercial quantities. In 1994 this provision was expanded to include sole traders and persons engaged in agriculture.

71.   The Trinidad and Tobago Export Trading Company purchases products in bulk for sale on the international market from a large number of small producers who individually would find it difficult to access export markets because of their limited resources and know-how. The company works closely with the Small Business Development Company and uses a specific brand name to establish brand loyalty for its exports.

(vii)   Free-trade zones

72.   The administration and operation of free zones is governed by the Trinidad and Tobago Free Zones Act of 1988, subsequently amended in 1995 and 1997. The establishment of free zones was intended to attract export-oriented investments in manufacturing, international trading and service export operations.

73.   Activities which may be carried out in a free zone are prescribed in the First Schedule of the Free Zones Act. These include: warehousing and storage; manufacturing; transhipment; loading and unloading; exporting and importing; service operations including banking, insurance and professional services; packaging and shipping; assembling; processing, refining, purifying and mixing; and merchandising. The 1995 Free Zones Amendment Act widened the range of activities to include petroleum and natural gas, as well as petrochemicals. Activities involving investment of more than US$50 million are not eligible for free-zone status, although these activities may be carried out in a free zone.

74.   The Trinidad and Tobago Free Zones Company, which was established under the Free Zones Act, regulates activities which may be carried out in a free zone. Applications to operate in a Free Zone are made and approved by the Company, which then makes recommendations to the Minister of Trade and Industry for approval. Applications for new areas of activity are sent to the Minister of Trade and Industry on recommendation of the Free Zones Company. The basic approval criteria are whether the activity earns foreign exchange, and whether it creates net employment. Enterprises operating in a free-zone activity are not allowed to carry out other activities in Trinidad and Tobago.

75.   Once approved, a free-zone enterprise is exempted from: customs duties on the importation of goods into free zones; import and export licensing requirements; land and building taxes; fees for work permits; property ownership restrictions; income tax, corporation tax, business levy, value-added tax, withholding tax on profits, dividends and other distributions, and capital gain taxes.

76.   Approved free-zone companies may supply a maximum 20% of goods produced to the customs territory of Trinidad and Tobago after obtaining an approval from the Free Zones Company. These sales are subject to all normal import requirements as well as payment of relevant duties and taxes. Enterprises operating in free zones must maintain accounts including the particulars of materials imported, used in manufacturing, or exported within the free zone. Since 1997, certificates of origin have been issued by TIDCO for goods manufactured in the free zones.

77.   The first free-zone activities commenced in 1993. There are currently 24 companies operating under the free-zone regime; they are located in 11 areas and in one multi-user industrial estate, and account for an estimated 5,000 direct and indirect jobs. A new zone, the Trinicity Free Zone, is being constructed on ten hectares of land. The estimated date of completion is December 1998. Total exports from free-zone enterprises have risen from US$6 million in 1993 to US$38 million in 1996.

Over the same period, purchases of goods and services by free-zone enterprises from the Customs Territory of Trinidad and Tobago have risen six-fold, from roughly US$2 million to over US$12 million (Table III.9).[28]

Table III.9
Direct economic impact of free-zone activities, 1993-96
('000 US$)

	1993	1994	1995	1996
Goods and services purchased from the customs territory	2,356	9,584	9,658	12,697
Total exports by free-trade enterprises	6,569	18,307	23,979	38,053
Payroll taxes paid	106	487	635	738
Licence fees paid	8	63	42	77

Source: Free Trade Zones Company.

(4)   MEASURES AFFECTING PRODUCTION AND TRADE

(i)   Adjustment and regional assistance

78.   With the aim of stimulating job creation and investment in distressed areas of the country, the Ministry of Trade and Industry has proposed an Enterprise Zones Programme. The Programme has not yet been legislated. To qualify as an Enterprise Zone an area must have an unemployment rate at least 50% above the national average or a poverty rate exceeding the national average. This Programme would seem to fall in the category of regional subsidies, defined as non-actionable under the WTO Agreement on Subsidies and Countervailing Measures.[29] Activities qualifying for the zones are assembly, manufacturing, agricultural and agro-processing, research and development, information processing, telecommunication and financial services. Enterprise Zones are operated and managed by TIDCO and SBDC in collaboration with the various regional agencies. Investors in the Enterprises Zones who invest at least TT$50,000 and employ at least two persons are entitled to tax incentives. Such incentives include a tax credit of TT$3,000 for each new employee and TT$3,000 for each TT$50,000 of investment, altogether not exceeding TT$50,000, provided at least 50% of the new employees are zone residents.[30]

(ii)   Investment incentives

79.   Trinidad and Tobago offers a number of tax-related production and investment incentive schemes under different pieces of legislation. These incentive schemes are generally directed at both local and foreign investors; they include duty concessions, tax exemptions, loss write-offs, and training subsidies. In some cases, local incorporation of a company is a prerequisite to be granted an incentive. Applications to benefit from these incentives are co-ordinated through the Investment Facilitation Department of the Division of TIDCO which processes applications and then makes recommendations to the relevant Ministries for final approval. Ministries have total discretion in the granting of concessions. Under the CARICOM Agreement on Harmonization of Fiscal Incentives to Industry, the government is currently reviewing its investment policy with a view towards harmonizing incentives across sectors. Although not legally precluded from applying for tax

---

[28]Trinidad and Tobago Exporter, November 1997.

[29]Article 8(b)(iii) of the Agreement identifies as non-actionable assistance to the disadvantaged regions within the territory of a Member, understood as those with a GDP per capita not above 85% of the average for the whole territory concerned, and/or those with an unemployment rate at least 110% of the average for the territory concerned.

[30]Ministry of Trade and Industry, 1996.

concessions under another incentive scheme, the beneficiary of any investment incentive scheme will not in practice be granted additional incentives under a different scheme.

80.   The Fiscal Incentives Act (1979), grants a tax (corporation and income tax, as well as customs duties) holiday for periods of up to ten years for the manufacture of approved products by approved locally incorporated enterprises. A number of products listed in the First Schedule of the Fiscal Incentives Act (consumer goods such as beer, cigarettes, rum, shirts and hats) are excluded from the definition of approved products. Applications for approved status are presented to the Ministry of Trade and Industry via TIDCO; enterprises are classified in five categories: (i) Group I enterprise, in which the local value added to the product is at least 50%; (ii) Group II enterprise, in which the local value added is between 25 and 50%; (iii) Group III enterprise, in which the local value added is between 10 and 25%; (iv) enclave enterprise, producing exclusively for export to countries outside the CARICOM market; and (v) highly capital-intensive enterprise, in which capital investment is not less than TT$50 million. The length of tax holidays is for a maximum of ten years; enterprises classified as Group I are granted nine years; Group II, seven years; Group III, five years; enclave and highly capital intensive enterprises, ten years. Once it has been granted approved status, an enterprise may enjoy total (or partial) relief from corporate taxes, with the possibility of carrying forward losses for a five–year period following the tax holiday. The Act also grants relief from customs duties as well as from income tax on dividends out of profits derived from the manufacture of approved products. Profits exempt from corporate taxes under the Fiscal Incentives Act amounted to TT$247 million (US$39 million) in 1996 (Table III.10), with forgone tax revenue of TT$86 million (US$13 million).[31] (Total income tax revenue from corporations amounted to roughly TT$900 million (US$145 million) in 1996.)

Table III.10
Tax concessions under the Fiscal Incentives Act
(TT$ million)

	1992	1993	1994	1995	1996
Chargeable Profits	98	116	1,007	523	247
Tax Rate (%)	45	45	45	38	35
Tax Exemption	44	52	483	199	86

Source: Data provided by the authorities of Trinidad and Tobago.

81.   Under the Corporation Tax Act approved in 1988, tax credits are granted to certain categories of locally-owned companies. These include approved small enterprises; approved companies trading in regional development areas; approved activity companies; and approved property development companies.[32] To obtain "approved company" status, an application must be made to TIDCO, except for small companies which must submit their applications to the Small Business Development Company, and for property development companies which must address the Board of Inland Revenue. Once approved, companies, except for property development companies are granted a tax credit of 15% of their chargeable income for seven years. This reduces their effective tax rate to 20% from the statutory 35%. For approved property development companies, a tax credit of 15% is granted on the

---

[31]The top corporate tax rate was reduced from 45% to 35% effective from 1996.

[32]An approved company trading in a regional development area must carry out its operations in the area; undertake at least 75% of its production of manufactured goods or industrial services and hold at least 75% of its fixed assets in the area; and employ twenty or more workers of whom at least 75% must work in the regional area. An "approved activity company" must be capable of earning or effecting savings of foreign exchange, of creating a significant number of permanent jobs or offering prospects for future expansion, and of stimulating technological development or developing new and modern industries making an efficient use of local new materials. An "approved development company" must undertake property development projects in both rural and urban areas.

capital expenditure for the construction of a commercial or industrial property. A 15% tax credit is granted for investment in depressed areas; however, no company has yet applied.

82.   The Income Tax Act grants wear-and-tear allowances on the construction of new buildings or on capital improvement. The allowances are made on the declining balance at the rate of 10% per annum. In addition, income tax deductions are granted to investors in specific areas (25% of the investment made in the equity capital of an approved hotel or tourism development project is tax deductible).[33] Financial institutions may deduct 10% of the net increase of loans to approved small companies as well as 50% of the interest earned in respect of a loan made to an approved small company or for the purchase of agricultural equipment. The Income Tax Act also makes provisions for the write-off of losses. An individual or a company may carry forward losses sustained in the course of its operations to be offset, without limitation, against chargeable profits in succeeding years. The Finance Act of 1997, amending the Income Tax Act, grants a limited form of group relief which allows losses of a company to be set off against the chargeable profits of other companies in the group.[34] Such relief is limited to 25% of the corporate tax that would have been payable in the absence of group relief.

83.   The Income Tax (In Aid of Industry) Act of 1950 grants enterprises engaged in certain specific activities an initial allowance of 10% on the construction of a new industrial building and 50% on the purchase of capital equipment. Companies engaged in the production of sugar, petroleum, or petrochemicals or enjoying concessions under the Fiscal Incentives Act, are granted a 20% annual allowance on the purchase of capital equipment. Companies engaged in petroleum products operations enjoy a first-year allowance of 20% of the expenditure on plant and machinery, with the remaining cost being written off over five years on a straight-line basis.

84.   Sector-specific investment incentives are available under different legislation. The Hotel Development Act provides investment incentives to hotel owners and hotel operators which include a tax holiday for a period of five to ten years as well as customs and excise duty exemption on building materials and articles of hotel equipment to be used exclusively in connection with the construction and equipping of a hotel project. The Ministry of Tourism has discretion on the granting of concessions based on the size and cost of the hotel project.

85.   The Housing Act No. 3 of 1962 grants tax exemptions on profits from the construction of dwelling houses (with a cost of less than TT$300,000) by approved housing companies.[35] Any houses constructed under the scheme may then be exempted from income tax on rentals for a period of ten years from the construction date.

86.   Investment incentives in the petroleum sector are granted in the form of allowances by which various expenses incurred in operations may be deducted in computing petroleum profits taxes and supplemental profits taxes. They include, apart from allowances under the Income Tax (In Aid of Industry) Act: a 100% allowance on the expenditure incurred on workovers, maintenance or repair work on completed wells; and a 100% allowance on capital expenditures on heavy oil projects.

---

[33]Companies enjoying benefits under the Income Tax (In Aid of Industry) Act, or under the Fiscal Incentives Act, the Hotel Development Act, or the Free Zones Act may not take advantage of this incentive scheme.

[34]Group relief is available when the subsidiary company and the claimant company are resident in the country and one company is a 100% subsidiary of the other company or both companies are 100% subsidiaries of a third company throughout an accounting period.

[35]The Housing Regulations Amendment 1998 increased the sum from TT$120,000 to TT$300,000. The Finance Act No.2 of 1989 gives the Minister responsible for housing the authority to designate eligible companies as Approved Mortgage Companies.

87.   The agricultural sector benefits from incentives such as price support schemes (e.g. guaranteed prices); subsidies for soil conservation, expenditure on equipment and machinery, and agricultural vehicles; as well as import duty concessions and VAT exemptions (Chapter IV(2)(iii)).

(iii)   Trade-related investment measures

88.   Trinidad and Tobago has notified to the WTO that it does not have any laws or regulations not in conformity with the Agreement on Trade-Related Investment Measures (TRIMs).

(iv)   Assistance to small enterprises

89.   The Government has identified the development of the small enterprise sector as the primary focus in its trade and industrial policies.[36]   The Corporation Tax Act was amended in 1988 to introduce a category of "approved small companies", and the Finance Act of 1988, amended in 1994, provides for tax incentives to these companies. Small or micro-business companies are defined as those with assets of less than TT$1.5 million (US$250,000), excluding land and building assets. [37] The Task Force on Small and Medium Enterprise Development was established in 1994 by the Cabinet in order to address the specific problems faced by these businesses, such as access to financing, the availability of technical and managerial expertise, and access to technical and marketing information, and to formulate a strategy for the development of the sector.

90.   The Small Business Development Company (SBDC),[38] administered through the Ministries of Finance and Trade and Industry, offers a loan-guarantee scheme to small and micro-businesses. In 1996 alone, the SBDC issued 510 loan guarantees valued at TT$13 million.[39] Loans are distributed mainly through commercial banks, but also through credit unions, finance houses, the Agricultural Development Bank and non-governmental organizations.   Main users of the facility are wholesale/retail trade, manufacture, agriculture as well as general services. The ceiling for loan guarantees is TT$250,000 (recently increased from TT$150,000). The lending rate is set at a market level, currently 15%. In addition to loan guarantees, the SBDC provides business information, training and consultancy services.

91.   The Finance Act of 1988, amended in 1994 grants income and corporate tax relief to small and micro-business enterprises. To be eligible for tax relief, a company must first be approved as a "small company" as defined in the Corporation Tax Act by the SBDC and by TIDCO for activities in (i) regional development, (ii) an approved activity. Under the Income Tax Act, individuals investing between TT$2,500 and TT$200,000 in approved small companies are entitled to a tax rebate.[40] Under the Corporation Tax Act, approved small companies are entitled to a tax credit of 15% of their chargeable income for seven years. This reduces the effective tax rate to 20% from the statutory rate of 35%.[41] Furthermore, financial institutions receive a tax deduction of 10% of the incremental value

---

[36]Ministry of Trade and Industry, (1997) and (1996).

[37]The asset-value threshold for qualification as a small business was increased from TT$500,000 to TT$1.5 million in the 1998 budget.

[38]The government owns 60% of SBDC, while the remainder is held by the private sector. The SBDC's Operations are financed by interest payments, government funding, as well as by grants from the European Union. In 1996, the government provided TT$3 million and the European Union TT$1.5 million.

[39]Small Business Development Company, (1997).

[40]The rebate is calculated by applying to 50% of the investment made the marginal rate of tax for the investor.

[41]TIDCO, (1998).

of loans made to approved small companies; and tax exemptions are offered to financial institutions of up to 50% of the interest earned on loans to approved small companies.

92.   The Venture Capital Investment Programme, which is governed by the Venture Capital Act of 1994 and the Venture Capital Regulation of 1996, was launched in 1996 to mobilize equity financing for small and medium-sized enterprises involved in agriculture, tourism, manufacturing and non-financial services. Under the programme, investors (individuals or corporations) in registered venture capital companies[42] are eligible for a tax credit of 35% of the amount invested. By early 1997, three venture capital companies were registered under the programme.[43]

(v)   Interest rate subsidies and guarantee facilities

93.   Concessionary financing is available from development banks to some sectors. Credits at preferential rates may be obtained from the Agricultural Development Bank (ADB) for the agricultural sector and from Development Finance Limited (DFL) for the manufacturing, tourism, agro-processing and industrial services sectors.[44] The ADB lends to individuals, companies and co-operatives for a wide range of agricultural activities, including crop and livestock production, floriculture, agro-processing and commercial fishing. In 1996, loans totalling TT$37.0 million (some US$6 million) were disbursed, while loan repayments recorded TT$54.6 million (US$9 million). The DFL provides financing for manufacturing, tourism, agro-processing and services enterprises for the purchase of fixed assets, working capital, and in some instances, for debt refinancing.[45] The DFL normally expects a firm's equity to be at least 35% of total assets, but this ratio may be higher for certain industries. Usually the DFL does not lend more than 50% of the total debt requirements of a company. The limit of DFL's financial commitment to any single enterprise is governed by prudential criteria and limited to 15% of its paid-up share of capital and revenues.[46] The DFL's portfolio of TT$172 million (US$29 million) in December 1996 accounted for 9.3% of total loans outstanding to private enterprises involved in manufacturing, tourism and industrial services. The DFL reported that 71% of the companies financed were exporters or earned foreign exchange income from services; approximately 40 % of those exporters were net exporters.[47]

(vi)   Price controls

94.   Until the end of the 1980s, a large number of consumer goods were subject to price controls under the Trade Ordinance of 1958, amended by the Trade Act of 1968. The Price Commission established under the latter, was in charge of the supervision and implementation of price controls

---

[42]Individuals and companies interested in establishing a venture capital company must become incorporated under the Companies Act and have at least TT$50,000 in paid up capital and an authorized capital of between TT$5 million and TT$20 million. The venture capital company must raise at least TT$500,000 in paid up capital and begin making equity investment within 12 months of its registration.

[43]Forde and Joseph *et al.* (1997).

[44]These two development banks were established as wholly government-owned institutions in the late 1960s and early 1970s, respectively, to encourage the development of capital markets and of targeted economic sectors. Private capital was injected in both banks in the late 1980s, after which their lending has become less concessional, with interest rates more in line with market rates.

[45]The distribution of DFL's loan portfolio as at June 1997 was: industrial and commercial services, 17.2%; plastic, metal-working and metal products, 19.0%; tourism-related activities, 19.1%; food processing and beverages, 22.4%; general manufacturing, 6.3%; chemical products, 2.7%; wood and related products, 6.0%; printing, publishing and paper contractors, 5.2%; textiles, garments and footwear, 0.9%; and clay and other building materials, 1.2%.

[46]In the case of a group of companies, the maximum total loans amount is 25% of DFL's share capital and reserves.

[47]Development Finance Limited, http://www.dflpos.com.

until its demise in December 1991. Since then, price controls have been largely removed, and the only goods which continue to be subject to price regulation by the Price Control Inspectorate in the Ministry of Consumer Affairs are sugar, pharmaceuticals and school books. The maximum retail price for certain school books is calculated as the publisher's price plus a mark-up of 15%.

95.   A distinction is made between retail prices for imported and locally manufactured drugs. For imported drugs, the maximum wholesale price is set at landed cost plus 20%. Maximum retail prices are determined as follows: for life-saving drugs, the maximum retail price is the wholesale price plus 25%; for prescription drugs, it is the wholesale price plus 30%; for over-the-counter drugs, it is the wholesale price plus 35%.[48] For locally manufactured drugs, the wholesale price is set at the ex-factory cost plus 30%, and the maximum retail price at the wholesale price plus 35%. Although the mark-up applied for the calculation of the wholesale price is higher for locally produced goods than for imports, and the mark-up on the wholesale price of locally produced goods for the calculation of the retail price is equal to the highest mark-up for imported goods, in many cases the end result is that locally produced goods are effectively protected against imports (Table III.11). The reason for this is that the base value for calculating the wholesale price is lower in the case of locally produced goods. For imported products, the wholesale price is calculated with reference to the landed cost, which is the c.i.f. value plus the customs duty payable.[49] Given the average difference between the c.i.f. and the f.o.b. value of imports, this adds an extra 11% to the f.o.b. value or a comparable ex-factory price, apart from the customs duty which, when applicable, is usually 15%.

Table III.11
Effects of price regulation on pharmaceuticals
(TT$)

	Imported products			Locally manufactured products
	Life-saving drugs	Prescription drugs	Over-the-counter drugs	
Ex-factory price	1	1	1	1
C.i.f. prices[a]	1.11	1.11	1.11	-
Tariff	-	0.15	0.15	-
Landed cost	1.11	1.28	1.28	-
Wholesale markup	0.20	0.20	0.20	0.30
Maximum wholesale price	1.32	1.53	1.53	1.3
Retail markup	0.25	0.30	0.35	0.35
Maximum retail price	1.65	1.99	2.07	1.76

a   Assuming, for simplicity, an equivalence between ex-factory and f.o.b. prices, and freight and insurance costs equivalent to 11% of the f.o.b price.

Source: Calculations by the WTO Secretariat based on information provided by the authorities of Trinidad and Tobago.

96.   Sugar is also subject to maximum wholesale and retail prices, most recently revised in 1993.[50] For example, the wholesale price for 12 two-kilogram packages of granulated sugar is fixed at TT$99.96; the maximum retail price for a package of two kilograms is TT$8.95.

97.   A number of goods and services are subject to administered prices. For instance, certain agricultural products are purchased from growers at guaranteed prices set by the Ministry of Agriculture, Land and Marine Resources. These include sugar cane, cocoa, coffee, milk, oranges,

---

[48]Pharmaceutical products are imported either duty-free or paying a 10% or 15% import duty. Products competing with local production (penicillins, vitamins, analgesics, sulpha drugs, cold preparations, antacids, gauze) are subject to the 15% tariff. This accounts for most prescription and over-the-counter drugs.

[49]The Price of Goods Regulations, 1972.

[50]The Price of Goods (Amendment) (No.1) Regulations, 1993.

grapefruit, paddy, copra and sorrel (Chapter IV(2)(v)). Under the Price of Petroleum Products Order, the Ministry of Energy and Energy Industries is authorized to fix the prices at which the crude oil refinery, Petrotrin, sells to the National Petroleum Marketing Company (NPMC). These ex-refinery prices apply to premium gasoline, regular gasoline, domestic kerosene, auto diesel and marine diesel. Apart from a wholesale margin, the final sale prices of these products include excise duties and filling and handling charges which are fixed by the Ministry of Finance and the Ministry of Energy and Energy Industries, respectively. The NPMC fixes the prices for lubes, greases and small quantities of bitumen and bituminous products which it produces locally. Jet fuel (dual-purpose kerosene) is also sold by the NPMC to a small number of customers on the local market. The price of this product is based on the contracted volumes sold to the respective customers. Natural gas prices at the upstream end are negotiated between the National Gas Company and the respective upstream producers operating in the country. The price at which the gas is sold to end users (base gas price) is related to final product prices (produce reference prices).

98.   The Public Utilities Commission, which fixes rates for water, electricity and domestic telephones, is to be replaced by the Regulated Industries Commission in 1998. The Commission will be operating primarily a price-cap system, under which a maximum rate will be fixed for designated periods, during which the service provider will be allowed to vary rates depending on market conditions. The previous system of differentiated domestic, industrial and commercial rates based on the unit cost of supply, according to the authorities, led some public utility companies, especially the Water and Sewerage Company and the Trinidad and Tobago Electricity Commission to financial difficulties.

(vii)   Competition policy

99.   The introduction of a competition policy framework has been an important component of the country's recent trade policy.[51] Competition policy, in addition to anti-dumping and customs reform, is considered as one of the safeguard measures which the Government has introduced in order to promote free and fair competition in a more liberal economic environment. A proposal for a Fair Trading Act, together with an institutional enforcement mechanism, was presented to Parliament in 1997.

100.   The proposed Fair Trading Act aims to "promote and maintain effective competition throughout the economy, and to ensure that competition is not distorted, restricted or prevented either by private business conduct or by public policy". The proposed legislation prevents the abuse of monopoly power, anti-competitive mergers, and anti-competitive horizontal agreements, i.e. cartels. Vertical agreements are not *per se* prohibited unless they incorporate anti-competitive features, for example, exclusive supply or distribution.

101.   The proposal also envisages the creation of institutional machinery to enforce competition policy. A Fair Trading Commission, reporting to the Ministry of Trade and Industry, will be a quasi-judicial body which will have the power to initiate and conduct investigations under the Fair Trading Act and order and enforce remedies against those who violate the Act. The decisions of the Fair Trading Commission will be open to appeal, to be heard by a Fair Trading Court, which is to be created as a division of the High Court. The Fair Trading Commission will maintain a close working relationship with the Regulated Industries Commission as well as the Consumer Guidance Council.

---

[51]Ministry of Finance, (1997).

(viii)   Trade-related intellectual property rights

102.   Trinidad and Tobago is a member of the World Intellectual Property Organization (WIPO) and a signatory to the major international agreements on intellectual property rights (Table III.12).   It has recently signed the 1978 UPOV Convention for the Protection of New Varieties of Plants and the Trademark Law Treaty.   The former was proclaimed into law on 30 January 1998, and the latter came into force on 18 April 1998.   The Government has expressed its intention to sign the WIPO Copyright Treaty.   Trinidad and Tobago is also a member of the International Union for the Protection of Industrial Property.

Table III.12
Trinidad and Tobago's membership in international agreements on intellectual property rights

The Convention Establishing the World Intellectual Property Organization (1970)
The Paris Convention for the Protection of Industrial Property, Stockholm Text (1883)
The Patent Cooperation Treaty (1970)
The Strasbourg Agreement Concerning the International Patent Classification (1971)
The Budapest Treaty of the International Recognition of the Deposit of Micro-organisms for the Purposes of Patent Procedure (1977)
The Nice Agreement Concerning the International Classification of Goods and Services for the Purposes of the Recognition of Marks (1957)
The Lorcano Agreement Establishing an International Classification for Industrial Designs
The Bern Convention for the Protection of Literacy and Artistic Works, Paris Text (1886)
The Geneva Convention for the Protection of Producers of Phonograms Against authorized Duplication of Their Phonograms (1971)
The Vienna Agreement Establishing an International Classification of the Figurative Elements of Marks (1973)
The Brussels Convention Relating to the Distribution of Programmes-Carrying Signals Transmitted by Satellite and the Universal Copyright Convention, Paris Text (1974)

Source: The Government of Trinidad and Tobago.

103.   Domestic laws regarding intellectual property rights have been updated in order to bring existing legislation in line with the TRIPS Agreement (Table III.13).   Under a Memorandum of Understanding between the Government of Trinidad and Tobago and the Government of the United States of America Concerning Protection of Intellectual Property (the Bilateral Agreement), signed in September 1994, Trinidad and Tobago agreed to provide U.S.-equivalent IPR protection within two years.   As a member of the Caribbean Basin Initiative, the Government is committed to prohibiting unauthorized broadcasts of U.S. programmes.

Table III.13
Intellectual property rights legislation in Trinidad and Tobago

Trade Marks (Amendment) Act, 1997
Copyright Act, 1997
Patents Act, 1996
Industrial Designs Act, 1996
Protection Against Unfair Competition Act, 1996
Layout-Designs (Topographies) of Integrated Circuits Act, 1996
Protection of New Plants Varieties Act, 1997
Geographical Indication Act, 1996

Source: Information provided by the authorities of Trinidad and Tobago.

104.   Changes have been made to trademark law by the Trade Marks (Amendment) Acts of 1996 and 1997.   Copyright legislation has been amended by the Copyright Act of 1997.   In the view of the · authorities, Trinidad and Tobago is fully in conformity with the spirit of the TRIPS Agreement.

105.   The administration of intellectual property laws in Trinidad and Tobago falls under the authority of the newly created Intellectual Property Office, in the office of the Registrar of Companies. The registration of patents, trademarks and industrial designs is administered by the Intellectual Property Registrar General, reporting to the Attorney General within the Ministry of Legal Affairs.

(a)   Trademarks

106.   The Trade Marks (Amendment) Act of 1997, which provides for the registration of trade marks, service marks, collective marks and certification marks, represents the latest change made to modernize the original Trade Marks Act of 1955. The 1994 amendment introduced the international classification of goods and services (34 classes of goods and eight classes of services) of the Nice Agreement, replacing the former national classification based on the U.K. system. The 1996 amendment extended the scope of protection granted to registered marks. The definition of a trade mark was widened to cover the packaging of goods or their shape provided the trade mark did not consist of the shape which resulted from the nature of goods themselves. The term of protection was reduced from 14 years to ten years, renewable within six months of expiry for further periods of ten years. While use is not a prerequisite to renewal, a mark may be removed from the Registry upon application by an interested party if non-use for the preceding five years is proven. Criminal prosecution can now, with this amendment, be brought in cases of unauthorized use of registered marks, including use of well-known marks. The 1997 amendment introduced procedures regarding border measures. Customs authorities are authorized to seize goods coming into Trinidad and Tobago in order to prevent goods infringing marks from entering the territory. In 1996, out of 1,395 applications to register marks, 925 were granted (Table III.14).[52]

(b)   Patents

107.   The Patents Act of 1996 repealed the Patent and Designs Act based on the U.K. system and has significantly changed the patent system regarding procedure as well as substantive law. Under the previous Act the proprietor of any invention could register a patent simply by submitting the required written declaration and specification of the invention describing its nature and its manner of performance; no examination was required. Patents that had already been granted in the U.K. could be registered by the confirmation of U.K. patents. Until 1995, all patent applications were granted (Table III.14).

108.   The 1996 Patent Act introduced the internationally accepted criteria for registration of universal novelty, inventive step and industrial applicability, along with a full search and examination procedure. The Act excludes the patentability for inventions of: (i) a discovery; (ii) any aesthetic creations; (iii) a scheme rule or method for performing a mental act, a game or doing business; (iv) diagnostic, therapeutic and surgical methods for treatment of humans or animals; and (v) the presentation of information. The Act extended the period of protection from 14 years with a possible renewal for seven years under the previous act to 20 years with no possibility of extension. Patent law includes provisions for granting a compulsory licence but such licences have not been granted.

109.   The 1996 Patent Act included a provision for a utility certificate that affords protection to an owner of a useful innovation who may otherwise be unable to fulfil the criteria to obtain a patent certificate. The criteria for the grant of a utility certificate is novelty and industrial application. An applicant for a utility certificate may apply to convert the application to a certificate of patent in prescribed circumstances. The period of protection for a utility certificate is seven years from the date of filing.

---

[52]U.S. Department of State (1997).

Table III.14
Filing and registration of intellectual/industry property rights

		Applications for registrations filed by:			Registrations granted to:		
		Residents	Non-residents	Total	Residents	Non-residents	Total
Trade marks	1992	..	..	967	..	..	..
	1993	..	..	957	20	513	714
	1994	303	804	1,107	159	432	591
	1995	3,641	1,164	1,525	493	1,092	1,585
	1996	323	1,072	1,395	95	830	925
	1997	..	..	..	..	..	..
Patents	1992	13	54	67	13	54	67
	1993	29	62	91	29	62	91
	1994	14	70	84	14	70	84
	1995	24	47	71	24	47	71
	1996	..	..	119	..	..	..
	1997	..	..	171	..	..	..
Industrial designs	1992	..	..	..	..	..	..
	1993	12	6	18	12	6	18
	1994	6	3	9	6	3	9
	1995	3	2	5	3	2	5
	1996	..	..	..	..	..	..
	1997	..	..	..	..	..	..

..   Not available.

Source: Government of Trinidad and Tobago; and WIPO Industrial Property Statistics.

110.   Patents can also be filed under the Patent Co-operation Treaty of which Trinidad and Tobago has recently become a member. The Treaty makes it possible to seek patent protection for an invention simultaneously in each of a large number of countries by filing an "international" patent application. In 1995, 15,468 applications were filed under the Treaty by non-residents in Trinidad and Tobago and 16 were granted.[53]

(c)   Industrial designs

111.   The Industrial Designs Act of 1996 revised the law relating to the protection of designs and repealed certain provisions in the previous Patents and Designs Act, i.e. the possibility for U.K. designs to be registered in Trinidad and Tobago within three years of registration in the United Kingdom. The 1996 Act widened the definition of "design" to include aesthetic quality while excluding features in the design engineered exclusively to obtain a technical result. The Act provides protection to designs that satisfy the requirements of universal novelty and of conformity with public order and morality. While the period of protection, five years, remains unchanged with respect to the previous Act, it may be renewed for two further five-year periods.

(d)   Copyright

112.   The Copyright Act of 1997 repealed the previous Copyright Act of 1985 which was based on the 1956 U.K. Copyright law. Literary, musical, artistic and dramatic works are protected by copyright provided that such work is original and has been written down, recorded or otherwise

---

[53]WIPO, Industrial Property Statistics (1995).

expressed in some material form. There are no formal requirements for registration of copyrights in Trinidad and Tobago. The new Act widened the definition of copyright to include specific reference to collective works, in which copyright vests in non-human authors, such as publishing houses. Computer software is now afforded protection as a derivative work. Copyright in audio-visual production made by foreign performers and foreign producers as well as neighbouring rights in a broadcast made by a foreign broadcasting organization are also protected under the Act. The duration of copyright protection was extended from 50 to 75 years for the majority of works.[54]

113.   The new legislation introduced provisions on civil and criminal proceedings against any person or organization which manufactures or imports, for sale or rental, any device that has been specifically designed to decode or circumvent another device intended to prevent or restrict reproduction of a work or production.

(e)   Trade secrets and unfair competition

114.   The Protection Against Unfair Competition Act introduced legislation for the first time in Trinidad and Tobago in 1996. Prior to this, protection of trade secrets and from unfair competition was derived from the general common law principles of contract and tort. The 1996 law provides for protection within a commercial and industrial setting. While to a large extent the Act codifies the common law principles in relation to the torts of breach of confidence and passing-off, its scope is broader. It provides a new statutory remedy to any competitor, customer or user of goods and services who is damaged or likely to be damaged by an act of unfair competition. Such acts include: damaging another's goodwill or reputation; causing confusion with respect to another's enterprise; misleading the public; discrediting another enterprise or activities; and disclosure, acquisition or use of secret information, including use of secret test or other data, submitted to a competent authority for marketing approval of pharmaceutical or agricultural chemical products utilizing new chemical entities.

(f)   Geographical indications

115.   The Geographical Indications Act of 1996 introduced protection for geographical indications in Trinidad and Tobago for the first time. The subject matter of protection goes beyond appellations of origin. It includes protection for indications that are used to designate a product that originates from a particular region and whose quality, reputation or characteristics are essentially attributable to that region. Protection is further available irrespective of registration. Criminal sanctions may be imposed upon persons who deliberately and wrongfully use geographical indications.

(g)   Layout-designs of integrated circuits

116.   The Layout-Designs (Topographies) of Integrated Circuits Act of 1996 protects layout-designs of integrated circuits against reproduction, importation, sale or other distribution in a commercial setting. The Act provides protection for designs or circuits that are original within the context of the Act, provided the layout-design is the result of the creator's own effort and is not commonplace among creators at the time of creation. The term of protection is ten years either from the date of first commercial exploitation or, if not yet commercial, from the filing date.

(h)   Plant varieties

117.   The Protection of New Plant Varieties Act of 1996 grants plant breeders' rights in respect of new plant varieties and related matters. A variety under the Act must be new, distinct, uniform and

---

[54]Article 12 of the TRIPS Agreement requires the protection period to be of at least 50 years.

stable. The Act establishes a Plant Variety Rights Office to oversee proceedings pursuant to this Act. There are three separate periods of protection relative to different species of plants ranging from 18 to 25 years.

(ix) Environmental policies

118.   The Environmental Management Authority, established by the Environmental Management Act of 1995 and reporting to the Ministry of Planning and Development, is responsible for bringing together and redrafting a patchwork of more than 40 pieces of environment-related legislation which are scattered among some 28 government agencies.[55] The Authority is also in charge of formulating a National Environmental Policy as well as specific sectoral policies, of coordinating activities with the government and with non-governmental organizations, and of establishing and monitoring compliance with environmental standards and criteria. To meet this goal, the Authority issues Certificates of Environmental Clearance. Environmental issues are also administered by other government and non-governmental organizations, including the Institute of Marine Affairs on marine-related environmental issues, and the Ministry of Planning and Development on non-marine-related issues.

119.   The Government, recognizing the need to incorporate environmental concerns in business operation and planning, has introduced environmental criteria in the investment incentive approval process. Where it is deemed necessary, investment projects are required to complete an Environmental Impact Assessment, and will in the future require a Certificate of Environmental Clearance from the Environmental Management Authority.

120.   The Ministry of Energy and Energy Industries is responsible for monitoring and ensuring that all activities in the energy sector have minimal impact on the environment, and has assumed the role of initiator and co-ordinator of oil-spill prevention and emergency-response planning in Trinidad and Tobago. In order to provide a comprehensive framework for marine pollution prevention and compensation, the Government is formulating new legislation which incorporates the provisions of international conventions.[56] The Ministry is also working closely with the Environment Management Agency in the formulation of a Code of Practice for the Prevention and Control of Pollution in the petroleum sector.

121.   Trinidad and Tobago is party to major international environmental agreements. These include the Basel Convention on the Control of Transboundary Movements of Hazardous Wastes and Their Disposal, the Convention on International Trade in Endangered Species of Wild Fauna and Flora, the Vienna Convention for the Protection of the Ozone Layer and the Montreal Protocol on Substances that Deplete the Ozone Layer. In keeping with its commitments under the Montreal Protocol, Trinidad and Tobago has implemented a programme for phasing out the use of ozone-depleting substances under the supervision of the Environmental Management Authority.[57]

---

[55]The Environmental Management Authority, http://users.carib-link.et/`ganness/aboutus.htm

[56]These conventions are administered by the International Maritime Organization, and include: the International Convention for the Prevention of Pollution from Ships (MARPOL); the Convention on the Prevention of Marine Pollution by Dumping of Waste and Other Matter; the International Convention Relating to Intervention on the High Seas in Cases of Oil Pollution Casualties; the International Convention on Oil Pollution Preparedness, Response and Co-operation; the International Convention on Civil Liability for Oil Pollution Damage; the International Convention on the Establishment of an International Fund for Compensation for Oil Pollution Damage; the Convention on Limitation of Liability for Maritime Claims.

[57]Ministry of Finance (1997).

IV. TRADE POLICIES BY SECTOR

(1) OVERVIEW

1.   The economic development of Trinidad and Tobago is dependent on oil and natural gas. While the Government has used trade policies and incentives schemes to promote non-petroleum sectors, such as manufacturing and agriculture, petroleum and petroleum-related sectors still account for over one quarter of the domestic economy and about three-quarters of exports.

2.   Agriculture was the main source of economic development before the discovery of oil. It still employs a large share of labour and the Government considers it an important source of employment. Sugar production has traditionally dominated the agricultural sector, although agro-processing has played an important role in recent years. Agriculture and food products as well as beverages are subject to higher tariffs than the average (Chart IV.1).

3.   The mining and quarrying sector is dominated by hydrocarbons. Remaining oil reserves are estimated at another 12 years of supply. Large reserves of natural gas have been discovered and they are sufficient to supply another 55 years. Due to this discovery, energy policy has shifted its focus to the development of the natural gas subsector.

4.   The services sector accounts for the largest share in both GDP and employment. Recent liberalization and reform efforts have had the greatest impact on financial services and telecommunications. In other subsectors, the Government is in the process of reviewing the legislation.

(2) AGRICULTURE AND FOOD PRODUCTS AND FISHING

5.   Agriculture was the major force of the economy until the commercialization of petroleum in the 1960s. Since then, the importance of the sector has diminished, despite the Government's attempts to offset the decline by heavily protecting activities. Agriculture remains, however, an important provider of employment: including fishing and forestry but excluding food products, it employed 9.6% of the labour force in 1996, while accounting for just 2.3% of total GDP. The production of processed agricultural goods is less labour-intensive, accounting for an additional 3% of employment and 4.2% of GDP (Chart IV.2).

6.   The cornerstone of traditional agriculture has been sugar production; sugar cane accounted for more than one third of non-processed agricultural products in 1996. Other major traditional crops include cocoa, coffee, coconut and bananas, though exports of coffee have been negligible in recent years. The main exports of processed products are beverages and prepared cereals. Trinidad and Tobago is a net importer of agricultural products, with imports about 50% larger than exports in 1993. The main imported agricultural products are cereals, dairy products, oil seeds and vegetables. In recent years, government policies have encouraged diversification into the production of non-traditional crops such as citrus, rice and vegetables.

Chart IV.1
Average tariffs by ISIC classification, 1998

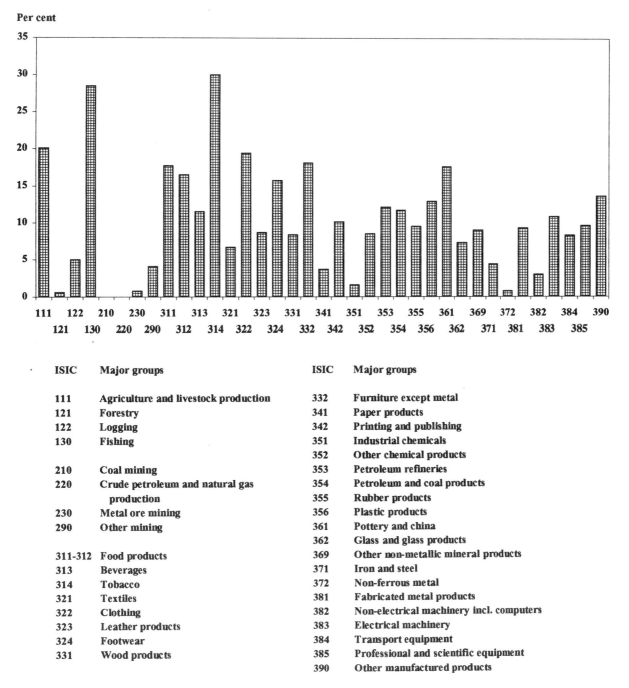

ISIC	Major groups	ISIC	Major groups
111	Agriculture and livestock production	332	Furniture except metal
121	Forestry	341	Paper products
122	Logging	342	Printing and publishing
130	Fishing	351	Industrial chemicals
		352	Other chemical products
210	Coal mining	353	Petroleum refineries
220	Crude petroleum and natural gas production	354	Petroleum and coal products
230	Metal ore mining	355	Rubber products
290	Other mining	356	Plastic products
		361	Pottery and china
311-312	Food products	362	Glass and glass products
313	Beverages	369	Other non-metallic mineral products
314	Tobacco	371	Iron and steel
321	Textiles	372	Non-ferrous metal
322	Clothing	381	Fabricated metal products
323	Leather products	382	Non-electrical machinery incl. computers
324	Footwear	383	Electrical machinery
331	Wood products	384	Transport equipment
		385	Professional and scientific equipment
		390	Other manufactured products

Source: Data provided by the authorities of Trinidad and Tobago; and estimates by the WTO Secretariat.

Chart IV.2
Agriculture GDP by sector, 1992 and 1996

Per cent

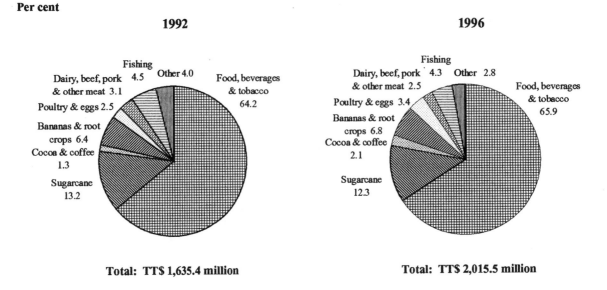

Total: TT$ 1,635.4 million   Total: TT$ 2,015.5 million

Source: Central Statistical Office.

7.   The Government considers agriculture to have great potential for income, employment growth and foreign exchange generation, and therefore plays a major role in the development of the sector. It owns more than half of the country's agricultural land, partly through state-owned enterprises. The Ministry of Agriculture, Land and Marine Resources (MALMR) formulates the overall policy framework and sector-specific policy measures, including subsidies and incentives. There are several large public enterprises operating in the sector, including Caroni, National Flour Mills, the National Agricultural Marketing and Development Company, Non Pareil Estate, National Agro-Chemicals, and the Agricultural Development Bank (Table IV.1). Until recently, some of these enterprises were granted monopoly over the purchase and import of their products. The MALMR provides policy guidelines for the state corporations and, in some cases, subsidies for their operation. The MALMR also has representation on the Boards of Directors of these enterprises.

Table IV.1
Main state enterprises in the agricultural sector

Company	Government holding	Activities
Caroni	100%	Major producer and sole processor of sugar products. Now diversified to include citrus and rice.
National Flour Mills	80%	Sole producer of flour and major producer of rice, edible oil and soybean.
National Agricultural Marketing and Development Company	100%	Provision of market information and administration of wholesale markets.
Agricultural Development Bank	100%	Provision of loans to farmers and fishermen.
Non Pareil Estate	100%	Production of cocoa.

Source: Information provided by the authorities of Trinidad and Tobago.

8. After decades of heavy protection of the agricultural sector, reforms were undertaken in the context of a comprehensive structural adjustment programme with support from the Inter-American Development Bank. Prior to these reforms, agricultural products were protected by various measures such as price supports, quantitative restrictions, tariffs, stamp duties, exchange and price controls, as well as stringent licensing requirements (for products in the Negative List). The reform programme aimed at removing or reducing distortions and at rationalizing incentives, and included measures such as the divestment of state-owned agricultural enterprises, the restructuring of the dominant sugar sector, and the diversification of agricultural production.

9. As identified by the Government, the major constraints affecting agricultural production include an inadequate water supply for dry season production, the high cost of inputs, a lack of adequate facilities, poor market organization, predial larceny, weak linkages between primary production and the agro-industrial sector and poor soil management.[1]

(i) Market access

10. There are no quantitative restrictions on the importation of agricultural products. Quantity-based measures were converted to equivalent tariffs in accordance with the Uruguay Round Agreement on Agriculture. Agricultural products, with the exception of a few items, were also removed from the licensing requirements set by the Import Negative List, and are now subject to import surcharges, some of which are to be eliminated by 1999. Licences are still required for imports of livestock, fish, crustaceans, molluscs, and oils and fats (Table III.7).

11. In the Uruguay Round, Trinidad and Tobago bound its tariffs on all agricultural products at ceiling rates of 100%, with the exception of seven items bound at higher levels; these include poultry, cabbage, lettuce and coffee (Table III.2). Other duties and charges were bound at 15%.

12. The 1998 applied MFN tariff on imports of agricultural products (HS Chapters 1-24) averaged 19.1%, with a maximum rate of 40% (Table IV.2). There is considerable dispersion of MFN rates by product groups in the agricultural sector. The highest tariffs are applied to edible fruit and nuts (33.6%), fish products (29.2%), edible vegetables (24.4%), animal and vegetable fat and oil (23.8%), meat and edible meat offal (23.4%), and live animals (21.9%), while gums and resins, and vegetable plaiting materials are granted duty-free access.

13. Several agricultural products are subject to additional import surcharges, which are subject to a phasing-out timetable. In 1998, import surcharges are applied to various parts of poultry (100%), sugar and icing sugar (60-70%), vegetables (15%) and fruit (5%). The surcharges on the latter two items are to be removed by 1999. Rates on poultry parts are to be reduced to 86% in 2004; those on sugar and icing sugar are not subject to reduction (Table III.5). Import duties on alcoholic beverages are set at specific rates, ranging from TT$4.75 per litre for beer to TT$40.00 per litre for cordials and liqueurs. Alcoholic beverages which are locally and regionally produced face excise duties (Table III.6).

(ii) Sanitary and phytosanitary regulations

14. The main sanitary and phytosanitary regulations are listed in the Animals (Diseases and Importation) Act 1954 and the Plant Protection Regulations 1953, both most recently amended in 1997. However, according to the authorities, the amendments did not address compliance with the WTO Agreement on the Application of Sanitary and Phytosanitary Measures.

---

[1]MALMR (1997).

Table IV.2
Trade and tariff data for agricultural products, 1998
(Per cent and US'000)

HS	Description	Unweighted MFN average (%)	Min. (%)	Max. (%)	Imports (US$ '000) 1996	Exports (US$ '000) 1996
01-24	**Agricultural products**	**19.1**	**0**	**40**	**302,088.2**	**203,769.6**
01	Live animals	21.9	0	40	570.6	16.7
02	Meat and edible meat offal	23.4	0	40	13,964.1	517.8
03	Fish & crustaceans, molluscs & other aquatic invertebrate	29.2	0	40	2,986.3	12,033.5
04	Dairy products; birds eggs; natural honey; edible prod. n.e.s.	19.6	0	40	46,240.6	4,453.7
05	Products of animal origin, n.e.s. or included	0.0	0	0	76.7	0.1
06	Live trees & other plants; bulbs, roots; cut flowers etc.	21.6	0	40	416.5	1,743.9
07	Edible vegetables and certain roots and tubers	24.4	0	40	20,933.8	2,124.2
08	Edible fruit and nuts; peel of citrus fruit or melons	33.6	0	40	4,542.2	1,286.2
09	Coffee, tea, mate and spices	21.7	0	40	3,196.7	1,725.0
10	Cereals	14.5	0	40	58,899.9	1,235.2
11	Prod. mill. industry; malt; starches; inulin; wheat gluten	6.4	0	40	9,730.4	600.5
12	Oil-seed, oleagi. fruit; miscell. grain, seed, fruit, etc.	2.5	0	40	33,551.4	53.4
13	Lac; gums, resins & other vegetable saps & extracts	0.0	0	0	961.7	0.8
14	Vegetable plaiting materials; vegetable products n.e.s..	0.0	0	0	114.0	0.2
15	Animal/veg. fats & oils & their cleavage products; etc.	23.8	0	40	15,386.4	9,141.0
16	Prep. of meat, fish or crustaceans, molluscs etc.	16.4	0	20	7,117.4	2,357.5
17	Sugars and sugar confectionery	21.5	0	40	17,691.7	34,014.7
18	Cocoa and cocoa preparations	9.2	0	20	3,178.3	6,942.9
19	Prep. of cereal, four, starch/milk	16.0	0	20	11,453.2	29,376.7
20	Prep. of vegetables, fruit, nuts or other parts of plants	15.9	0	40	10,441.5	8,196.6
21	Misc. edible preparations	17.0	0	20	16,630.8	9,247.2
22	Beverages, spirits and vinegar	16.5	5	20	7,668.9	60,223.8
23	Residues & waste from the food industry.; prep. animal fodder	4.4	0	20	12,076.7	16,603.3
24	Tobacco and manufactured tobacco substitutes	21.0	0	30	4,258.3	1,874.9

Source: WTO calculations based on data provided by the authorities of Trinidad and Tobago and UNSD, Comtrade database.

15.   All live animals imported into the country require an import permit, issued by the Animal Protection and Health Division of the Ministry of Agriculture, Land and Marine Resources, prior to the arrival of the animal. They are also subject to quarantine regulations, which may differ according to the country of origin of the imported animal.

16.   Imports of all plants, fruits and vegetables also need to obtain an import permit, issued by the Plant Quarantine Division of the Ministry of Agriculture, Land and Marine Resources. Import requirements vary depending on the country's pest status.

17.   Trinidad and Tobago notified the WTO in 1995 that the Ministry of Agriculture, Land and Marine Resources had introduced an emergency measure on imports of fruit and vegetables from Grenada and other islands in the Caribbean which would be subject to controls to prevent the import of mealy bug-infested vegetable material.[2]

---

[2]WTO, G/SPS/N/TTO/1, 10 October 1995

(iii)   Domestic support

18.   Incentives available to the agricultural sector are listed in the Agricultural Incentive Programme which has been in place since 1985.   The Government's domestic support policy is to provide incentives which result in minimal market distortions, and which comply with the WTO Agreement on Agriculture.[3]   Agricultural incentives in Trinidad and Tobago include price supports (e.g. guaranteed prices), and subsidies for soil conservation, equipment and machinery, agricultural vehicles and wheel tractors.   Commodities under the price support scheme include sugarcane, coffee, cocoa, milk, oranges, grapefruit, paddy, copra and sorrel (Table IV.3).   In 1996, the Government granted payments totalling TT$45.9 million for price support and TT$1.4 million for input subsidies, altogether accounting for 6.8% of agricultural GDP (Table IV.4).   According to the authorities, in 1997, the Government granted payments totalling TT$35.97 million for price support and TT$0.4 million for input subsidies.

Table IV.3
Price support programme: guaranteed prices, 1997

Commodity	Guaranteed price (TT$)
Sugarcane	153.77/tonne
Cocoa	9.55/kg.
Coffee	8.36/kg.
Milk	2.00/litre
Oranges	20.00/crate[a]
Grapefruit	12.00/crate[b]
Paddy	0.66-2.02/kg.
Copra	2.66/kg.
Sorrel	0.25/kg.

a   Crate of oranges = 40.9 kg.
b   Crate of grapefruit = 36.4 kg.

Source: Ministry of Agriculture, Land and Marine Resources.

Table IV.4
Price support programme: subsidy payments
(TT$ million)

Commodity	1992	1993	1994	1995	1996
Sugarcane	14.4	5.4	9.3	16.7	15.7
Cocoa and coffee	5.0	-	3.2	3.2	5.7
Milk	6.1	7.7	11.3	8.1	8.4
Paddy	-	-	9.0	12.7	14.7
Copra	2.5	1.9	2.9	4.7	1.1
Other input subsidies[a]	5.6	1.2	0.9	0.5	1.4
Total subsidy payments	**33.6**	**16.2**	**36.6**	**45.9**	**47.0**
Agricultural GDP	**586.2**	**607.9**	**651.4**	**627.2**	**688.1**
Subsidy as % of agricultural GDP	**5.7**	**2.7**	**5.6**	**7.3**	**6.8**

a   Includes soil conservation, equipment and machinery, vehicles, wheel tractors, and rebates.

Source: Ministry of Agriculture, Land and Marine Resources.

---

[3]The Agreement on Agriculture Article 6:4(b) allows a developing country Member to provide domestic support up to a limit not exceeding 10% of the value of its total agricultural production.

19.   Fiscal incentives available to the agricultural sector include import duty concessions and VAT exemptions. Under the Customs Act Section 56, approved agricultural enterprises, (including fishery and forestry), are exempted from import duty on a range of agricultural inputs and equipment including wheel tractors, agricultural chemicals (e.g. insecticides, herbicides, fungicides, vitamin and drug preparations), hand tools and machinery. A range of agricultural inputs and equipment is also exempted from VAT. In addition, an income tax exemption is provided for a maximum period of ten years for approved agricultural holdings of less than or equal to 40.5 hectares. The food processing, beverages and tobacco sub-sectors are eligible to apply for the same incentives available to the manufacturing sector (section II).

(iv)   Export assistance

20.   Trinidad and Tobago does not subsidize its exports of agricultural goods.

21.   Export financing is made available through the Agricultural Development Bank, which was set up in 1968 as a wholly government-owned institution. The bank lends to individuals, companies and co-operatives for a wide range of agricultural activities, including crop and livestock production, floriculture, agro-processing and commercial fishing. In 1996, total loans of TT$37.0 million were disbursed, while loan repayments amounted to TT$42.0 million. Prior to 1987, the ADB provided most of its finance at concessional rates;[4] this policy led to negative real interest rates and triggered problems of capital depletion, which made it necessary to bring rates more in line with market values. Since 1993 the interest rate for approved loans has been 12%.[5] Access to financing is also available through the Small Business Development Company, which provides a loan guarantee scheme to small businesses including agricultural and agro-processing companies.

(v)   Crop production and livestock

(a)   Sugar

22.   Sugar has been the single most important agricultural subsector, accounting for a third of non-processed agricultural GDP in 1996 and over a quarter of employment. In 1997, exports of raw sugar reached 109,300 tonnes.

Table IV.5
Sugar production and exports, 1992-97
('000 tonnes)

	1992	1993	1994	1995	1996	1997
Production						
Cane	1,292	1,210	1,398	1,327	1,404	..
Raw sugar	110.4	104.7	131.1	117.1	92.0	90.8
Refined sugar	34.3	32.9	38.0	41.9	42.0	45.9
Exports						
Raw sugar	59.2	51.4	57.1	68.1	71.5	109.3

..   Not available.

Source: Central Bank of Trinidad and Tobago.

---

[4]Loans to agricultural credit societies were made at interest rates of 1% and those to individuals at 3% and 6.5% according to the type of activity, Forde and Joseph *et al.* (1997).
    [5]Forde and Joseph *et al.* (1997).

23.   Sugar exports depend primarily on the quota arrangements with the European Union and the United States, which offer guaranteed prices above the world-market price. Trinidad and Tobago was allocated an export quota of 47,556 tons of raw sugar by the European Union under the Sugar Protocol to the Lomé Convention, and an additional 10,000 tonnes under the Special Preferential Sugar Arrangement. The United States allocated Trinidad and Tobago a quota of 14,201 tonnes of raw sugar for fiscal year 1997, of which 13,576 tonnes were exported. Prices paid by the European Union (£403 a tonne in 1997 for imports under the Protocol, and £308.5 a tonne for imports under the Special Preferential Agreement) and the United States (some US$421 a tonne) are well above world-market prices. Refined sugar is exported to other CARICOM countries.

24.   While sugar is Trinidad and Tobago's main agricultural export, it is imported when domestic production is insufficient to meet export quotas and domestic demand. This makes economic sense for Trinidad as a small supplier, since exports to the EU receive a price higher than the world price, while imports are acquired at lower prices.[6] Some 29,000 tonnes of raw sugar and 9,105 tonnes of refined sugar were imported in 1997. Imports of raw sugar are subject to a customs duty of 40%, and an additional charge of 60%. Imports of refined sugar face a 15% import tariff.

25.   The sugar industry is dominated by Caroni, the largest state-owned enterprise in Trinidad and Tobago. Caroni is also the largest employer and owner of fertile land and generates about 2% of GDP. Caroni produces about half of the country's cane, and has a de facto monopoly in refining and operations monopoly milling.[7] The company purchases sugar cane from private farmers at a guaranteed price based on production costs. The guaranteed price applies only when it is higher than the price determined by the Seemungal Formula[8], which reflects international prices. Both prices have increased since the beginning of the 1990s, but the Seemungal Formula price has exceeded the guaranteed price since 1993 (Table IV.6). There was no price support in 1996, only an input subsidy payment (TT$15.7 million). Caroni has traditionally handled all sugar exports and imports. In 1998, however, industrial manufacturers have been allowed to import sugar.

Table IV.6
Guaranteed prices, Seemungal formula prices and price support payments, 1992-96

	Guaranteed prices/tonne (TT$)	Seemungal formula price/tonne (TT$)	Price support payment (TT$ million)
1992	126	100.59	16.0
1993	126	128.94	0.0
1994	126	139.25	0.0
1995	136	161.63	0.0
1996	136	157.57	0.0

Source: Ministry of Agriculture, Land and Marine Resources.

26.   With a view to reviving the viability of Caroni, which accumulated deficits between 1977 and 1991, the Cabinet appointed a Tripartite Committee, composed of representatives of the Government, Caroni and labour, which developed a comprehensive reform programme for the sugar industry in 1992. The reform programme included: increased reliance on private cane production to reach

---

[6] According to the authorities, import prices for raw sugar in 1997 ranged between US$282.6 and US$308.4 a tonne, while prices for refined sugar range between US$380 and US$387.7 per tonne.

[7] In recent years it has diversified into the production of other crops including rice, citrus fruits, aquaculture and vegetables.

[8] The Seemungal Formula seeks to calculate two prices: (i) the price of cane purchased at factory gate; (ii) the price of cane purchased at outside purchasing points. The formula subtracts the costs of distribution and storage from average revenue obtained in the previous year, and accrues by 75% the resulting value.

60-75% of supply, modernization of capital equipment, diversification into other agricultural products, rationalization of land-holding, increased mechanization of the cane harvest, and reduction of surplus labour. Under the terms of the Tripartite Committee programme, Caroni is to reach the break-even point in 1999 or 2000, and operate at a profit thereafter. While the share of cane produced by private farmers did increase from 47.3% in 1992 to 52.2% in 1996, the implementation of the programme appears to have been difficult.[9] In 1998, the Government is to introduce a new cane pricing system based on quality, which is expected to encourage further private cane production.

(b)   Cocoa and coffee

27.   Along with sugar, cocoa and coffee have historically been exported, although in declining amounts.[10] In 1997, the production of cocoa reached 1.74 million kg., of which 1.55 million kg. were exported; the production of coffee was 1.10 million kg., mostly consumed at home. There have been virtually no exports of coffee since 1995 (Table IV.7).

Table IV.7
Production and exports of selected agricultural commodities, 1993-97
('000 kg.)

	1993	1994	1995	1996	1997
Production					
Cocoa	1,578	1,489	1,694	2,292	1740
Coffee	874	1015	830	353	1,102
Citrus	8,620	10,418	10,255	11,798	10,423
Rice	16,204	17,514	10,193	17,858	8,990
Exports					
Cocoa	1,503	1,342	1,595	1,741	1545
Coffee	445	42	3	0	0

Source: Central Bank of Trinidad and Tobago.

28.   The Cocoa and Coffee Industry Board is a state agency administered by the MALMR. There are no laws or regulations that force growers to sell their crops to the Board; however, the Board buys up some 85% of domestic production. The crops are purchased from farmers at the guaranteed prices, TT$9.55/kg. for cocoa and TT$8.36/kg. for coffee, whenever international prices fall below guaranteed levels.[11] In recent years, international prices have been higher than guaranteed prices.

(c)   Citrus fruit

29.   The production of citrus fruit has increased substantially in recent years from 8.62 million kg. in 1993 to 10.42 million kg. in 1997 (Table IV.7). All the citrus production is domestically consumed. Imports of citrus face a 40% tariff and an additional 5% import surcharge, which is to be eliminated in 1999.

---

[9]World Bank (1996).

[10]Trinidad and Tobago is a signatory to the International Cocoa Agreement and its successor agreements.

[11]A 1992 study estimated that the costs of producing one kilogram of cocoa was TT$9.41 since then production costs have increased. The Ministry of Agriculture, Land and Marine Resources is currently considering an increase in guaranteed prices, which have remained fixed for over ten years, to TT$11.55/kg. for cocoa and TT$10.36/kg. for coffee (MALMR, 1997).

30.   The Co-operative Citrus Growers' Association (CCGA), a private association, is the major local citrus purchaser and processor. Of the fruits delivered to the CCGA in 1996/97, 46% were processed into single strength juice, while the remaining 54% were used in the production of frozen concentrate in 1996/97. Caroni accounted for over 80% of total fruit delivered to the CCGA. Citrus producers who deliver to the CCGA are entitled to receive a guaranteed price of TT$20/crate (equivalent to 40.9kg.) for oranges and TT$12/crate (equivalent to 36.4kg.) for grapefruit. Guaranteed prices have been below market rates over the last ten years.[12] Direct sales to the fresh fruit market by smaller producers have been expanding since they receive higher prices than those offered by the CCGA.

(d)   Rice

31.   Rice is an important domestic staple in Trinidad and Tobago. Annual paddy production has fluctuated considerably over the period 1993-97 (Table IV.7). Local production of paddy satisfies approximately a fourth of domestic demand for rice, with the remainder being met through imports from the United States, Guyana and India. Rice imports face a tariff of 25%.

32.   Farmers currently receive guaranteed prices ranging between TT$0.66/kg. and TT$2.02/kg., depending on the grade, for paddy delivered to the majority government-owned National Flour Mills. Until recently, National Flour Mills had exclusive rights to purchase, import and distribute rice. The subsidy incorporated in the guaranteed price (calculated based on the cost of production) is: TT$1.25/kg., TT$1.06/kg., TT$0.72 and TT$0.09 for grades I, II, III and IV respectively. An average TT$10.85 million of subsidies have been paid annually by the Government since 1994 when the grading system was introduced. By providing a higher subsidy to higher quality rice, the introduction of the grading system has improved the overall quality of paddy production, with 80% of the paddy delivered to National Flour Mills falling in or above the grade II category. The share of Grade I paddy in total rice deliveries increased from 40% in 1996 to 55% in 1997.

(e)   Coconut/copra

33.   Production of copra has varied between 2,600 and 3,000 metric tonnes in the 1994-96 period. Imports of coconut/copra are subject to a licensing requirement and the maximum tariff rate of 40%.

34.   A guaranteed price of TT$2.66/kg. is paid to coconut producers. TT$2.00 is paid by the Coconut Growers Association, the major purchaser of coconut in the country, and TT$0.66 is paid by the Ministry of Trade and Industry as a subsidy. Annual payments averaged TT$2.6 million in the period 1992-96. Currently, guaranteed prices are below market prices.

(f)   Meat and dairy products

35.   Domestic meat production, excluding poultry, accounted for 35.6% of total meat supply in the period 1993-1997, with the rest being imported. While pork meat is mainly supplied by local producers, beef and sheep supplies are dependent on imports. Imports of beef and mutton face a 15% tariff, and pork and poultry face the maximum rate of 40%. While import surcharges on beef, mutton and pork were eliminated in 1998, poultry continues to be subject to a 100% import surcharge, which is to be reduced to 86% in 2004. Domestic poultry production is further protected by licensing requirements for imported poultry. Imports of milk supplied roughly 60% of domestic requirements in the 1993-95 period. The average MFN tariff for dairy products (HS04) is at 20.2%; fresh milk carries a tariff of 40%. An import surcharge of 20% on liquid milk was abolished at the beginning of 1998.

---

[12]CCGA paid TT$24.50/crate for oranges and TT$19.70/crate for grapefruit in 1997.

36.   The guaranteed price for milk is TT$2.45/kg., of which TT$0.90/kg. is paid by the Government as a subsidy and TT$1.55/kg. is paid by Nestlé, the main milk processor. An informal arrangement exists between the Government and Nestlé, by which the Government pays a subsidy to the farmers who sell their milk to Nestlé. This financial arrangement is managed by Nestlé and is not extended to any other milk processor. The Government paid annual average subsidies of TT$8.4 million in the period 1992-97.[13] Approximately 600 dairy farmers benefit from the subsidy. To benefit under the present arrangement, farmers must be registered as regular suppliers to Nestlé. Despite subsidization, supply of milk to Nestlé for processing declined from 10.2 to 9.8 million kg. in the 1992-97 period.

(g)   Beverages and tobacco

37.   Tobacco and breweries accounted for about 45% of agricultural GDP in 1997. Beverages, spirits and vinegar are by far the largest agricultural export, totalling US$75.1 million in 1997. Rum is exported to the EU market under the Lomé Convention's Rum Protocol. Specific customs duties are levied on alcoholic beverages, while excise duties are levied on local and CARICOM production. In the case of beer and wine, customs duties are higher than excise duties on local and CARICOM goods; for spirits they are generally lower. Imports of most tobacco products are subject to a 30% tariff, while local and CARICOM tobacco products are subject to excise duties (Chapter III(2)(iv) and Table III.6). A tobacco tax is applied on all tobacco products.

(vi)   **Fisheries**

38.   The fishing industry accounted for 4.3% of agricultural GDP in 1996. Exports of fish products reached US$10 million, while imports totalled about US$5.8 million in the same year. Imports of fish products face an average tariff rate 29.2%. In general, fish imported for processing purposes is duty-free, while fish imported for consumption faces tariffs between 25 to 40%

39.   The Government has provided subsides since 1977 to encourage growth in the fishing industry, which include a fuel rebate of TT$0.05/litre for gasoline and a rebate of 25% of the value up to a maximum of TT$2,500 for the construction of locally built fishing boats. Fishing activities benefit from VAT and import duty exemption. In 1996, the subsidies paid by the Government amounted to TT$0.6 million. In December 1997, a new Fishing Agreement was signed between the Republics of Venezuela and Trinidad and Tobago. Essentially, the Agreement delineated a shared fishing area where fishermen from both countries could fish without permits provided they followed the terms of the Agreement, such as flying the flag of their country or being registered in one of the countries.

(3)   **MINING AND QUARRYING**

40.   The mining and quarrying sector makes a large contribution to the economy of Trinidad and Tobago. While the sector employed only 3.8% of total labour, it produced 14.4% of GDP in 1996. The hydrocarbon subsector accounts for 99% of the sector's total output.

(i)   **Hydrocarbons**

41.   While Trinidad and Tobago is a relatively small producer of hydrocarbon products in the world market, they have played a significant role in shaping the economy since 1908, when production of crude oil started. The discovery of large reserves of crude oil in the late 1960s and

---

[13]This amount is within the TT$10 million limit negotiated between the Government of Trinidad and Tobago and the Inter-American Development Bank for the Agricultural Sector Loan (MALMR, 1997).

early 1970s allowed Trinidad and Tobago to benefit from the price rises caused by the two oil shocks. Oil production peaked at 229,500 barrels per day (b/d) in 1978. In 1997, oil production reached 123,874 b/d. Natural gas production has been increasing since 1978; in 1997, production reached 884 million cubic feet per day (mmcf/d) (Table IV.8).

Table IV.8
Crude oil[a] and natural gas production, 1993-97

	1993	1994	1995	1996	1997
Crude Oil ('000 barrels)					
Total Production	45,203	47,814	47,698	47,171	45,174
Daily Average	123.9	131.0	130.7	128.9	123.9
Imports	11,195	11,621	12,682	14,634	10,700
Exports	21,806	22,025	21,414	21,516	20,300
Natural Gas (million cubic feet/day)					
Production	684.7	744.0	773.6	874.0	884.0
Utilization	506.0	575.0	592.0	682.0	714.0
of which: Petrochemicals	287.0	334.0	335.0	416.1	407.7
TTEC	136.0	139.0	149.0	154.8	167.3

a   Also includes condensates.

Source: Central Bank of Trinidad and Tobago, Ministry of Energy and Energy Industries.

42.   Dependence on the energy sector - which, according to the definition used by the authorities of Trinidad and Tobago, consists of exploration and production, refining, marketing and distribution of petroleum products, petroleum-related services, petrochemicals, as well as asphalt - has gradually declined over time. However, the sector still accounted for 26.6% of GDP, 22% of government revenue and 73% of foreign exchange earnings in 1997 (Table IV.9). The sector also accounts for most of the foreign investment flowing into Trinidad and Tobago. Foreign investment in energy-related projects is estimated over the next four years at over US$2.5 billion, a large amount relative to the size of the economy.

Table IV.9
Contribution of the energy sector[a] to the economy, 1970-97
(Per cent)

	1970	1975	1980	1985	1990	1997
Share in GDP	21.5	41.3	42.1	26.8	31.8	26.6
Share in government revenue	23.1	69.4	58.9	42.1	40.9	22.0
Share in foreign exchange earnings	---	77.2	90.6	79.7	82.5	73.0

a   Also includes refineries, petrochemicals, and marketing and distribution of petroleum products.

Source: Ministry of Energy and Energy Industries.

43.   The Ministry of Energy and Energy Industries has overall responsibility for managing and regulating the energy sector and is also responsible for the operational and commercial aspects of the state petroleum and energy-based industries. Policy initiatives taken since 1993 include: a reduction in direct state participation in the industry; the merging and restructuring of state-owned oil companies; a review of the petroleum taxation system; increased exploration and production activities, particularly in deep waters; and development of downstream natural gas-based industries.

44.   As oil reserves are relatively limited, the focus of energy policy has been shifting from oil to natural gas. Proven oil reserves were estimated at 534 million barrels at the beginning of 1998, equivalent to 12 years of output at the current level of production. Proven reserves of natural gas have been estimated at 18 trillion cubit feet (equivalent to 3,155 million barrels of oil) in 1998, sufficient for another 55 years of output. In addition, probable and possible gas reserves are estimated at 6.37 trillion cubic feet. Natural gas is mainly used in the petrochemical industry.

45.   The Petroleum Act of 1969 established a framework for the granting of licences/contracts for the conduct of petroleum operations on land and submarine areas. The Ministry of Energy and Energy Industries is responsible for determining the areas available for exploration and production, and through prior competitive bidding, grants the rights of exploration and production of petroleum. The following types of licences/contracts are issued: (a) an exploration licence which grants the licensee the non-exclusive right to carry out the petroleum operations stated in the licence; (b) an exploration and production licence which grants the licensee the exclusive right to explore for, produce and dispose of petroleum in accordance with the terms of the licence; (c) a production-sharing contract for the conduct of petroleum operations relating to the exploration, production and disposition of petroleum within a prescribed contract area. Since 1995, production-sharing contracts have been issued on the basis of a system of three-phased competitive bidding rounds. Over the 1995-98 period, production-sharing contracts were granted for 13 offshore blocks, with a total acreage of 1,108,172 hectares.[14]

46.   The tax regime in the petroleum industry is governed by the Petroleum Act, the Petroleum Taxes Act, the Petroleum Production Levy and Subsidy Act, the Income Tax (In Aid of Industry) Act, and the Unemployment Levy Act. The regime, which was most recently revised in 1992, is based on a three-tier system consisting of two profit-based corporation taxes (the Petroleum Profits Tax (PPT) and an Unemployment Levy), of three production-based taxes (a Royalty, a Petroleum Production Levy, a Petroleum Impost) and of an income-based tax, (the Supplemental Petroleum Tax) (Table IV.10). Petroleum operations are classified into three types of businesses for taxation purposes: exploration and production, refining, and marketing. While the first two types of businesses have remained subject to the Petroleum Taxes Act, the Finance Act of 1997 removed the taxation of petroleum marketing businesses from the Act's scope and placed it under the Corporation Taxes Act. As a result, the state-owned National Petroleum Marketing Company, of Trinidad and Tobago and the National Gas Company, which have a monopoly on the marketing and distribution of petroleum products and gas, are now taxed at a rate of 35%, instead of 50%. A company engaging in more than one type of petroleum business may not offset losses incurred in one type of business against profits earned in another for the purposes of PPT.[15]

47.   Incentives and tax allowances are used to encourage investment in the energy sector. Various expenses incurred in petroleum operations may be deducted from income in computing petroleum-related taxes. Capital expenditures incurred on workovers, heavy oil projects and on a development dry hole are deductible for the computation of the PPT (Table IV.10). Additionally, capital allowances under the Income Tax (In Aid of Industry) Act are also applicable to the calculation of the PPT for petroleum production businesses. These include initial and first year allowances on plant and machinery expenditure of 20% each, and an additional annual deduction of 20% for each of the five years following the initial investment. Allowances for the computation of the Supplement Petroleum Tax include geological and geophysical allowances, up to 50%; an exploration allowance, of up to 100% of direct drilling costs; a royalty payment allowance; and an investment allowance of up to 40% of tangible and intangible drilling costs (Table IV.10). Finally,

---

[14]Ministry of Energy and Energy Industries, http://www. meei.gov.tt.
[15]TIDCO (1998).

import duty and VAT exemptions are also granted under the Customs Act and the VAT Act (Chapter III).

Table IV.10
Petroleum taxation in Trinidad and Tobago

Tax category	Content	Deduction and Allowance
Royalty	12.5% of the value of all petroleum produced	
Petroleum Profits Tax	50% of taxable profits	(i) 100% on the expenditure incurred on workovers, maintenance or repair work on completed wells and qualifying side tracks;
		(ii) 100% on capital expenditure on a heavy oil project;
		(iii) expenditure on a dry hole or a development dry hole with the Minister's approval.
Supplemental Petroleum Tax	Sliding scale of tax rates based on oil prices, ranging from 0 for crude prices under US$13.01 a barrel, to a maximum of 35% for crude prices over US$49.50 a barrel.	(i) 50% of geological and geophysical costs;
		(ii) 100% of direct cost of drilling exploration wells;
		(iii) royalty payment;
		(iv) 100% of capital expenditure incurred in the drilling of wells and the acquisition of plant and machinery for use in marine thermal recovery schemes for heavy oil;
		(v) 40% of direct intangible drilling cost and 40% of tangible costs incurred in a development activity.
Petroleum Production Levy	Up to 3% of gross income from crude oil. The levy provides the subsidy for petroleum products on the domestic market.	
Petroleum Impost	Rates based on petroleum produced in the previous year. The impost is a payment to cover administrative costs of the Ministry of Energy and Energy Industries.	
Unemployment Levy	5% of taxable profits	(i) Operating and administrative expense
		(ii) Royalty
		(iii) Petroleum Production Levy
		(iv) Supplemental Petroleum Tax

Source: Information provided by the Ministry of Energy and Energy Industries and TIDCO.

(ii) Oil

48. Since 1990 oil production has been declining at an average annual rate of 2.7%. Crude oil production recorded 123,874 b/d in 1997, 46% less than in the peak year, 1978. Over three quarters of production originated in marine operations. Proven reserves (24% of which are heavy oil reserves) are estimated to be just sufficient for another 12 years of supply at the current rate of production. While probable and possible reserves are estimated at up to 2.5 billion barrels or 50 years of supply, they are not considered to be economically recoverable under current market conditions since they are composed of heavy oil.[16]

49. Approximately 46% of the crude oil produced in the period 1993-97 was exported; the rest was refined locally. To maintain optimal refinery levels, some crude oil is also imported. In 1997, 10.7 million barrels of crude oil were imported while 20.3 million barrels were exported (Table IV.8). Imports of crude oil are duty free.

50. The production of crude oil is dominated by multinationals and state-owned enterprises. The largest producer is Amoco Trinidad Oil Company, a wholly owned subsidiary of U.S.-based Amoco

---

[16]Ministry of Energy and Energy Industries, http://www.meei.gov.tt.

Corporation, which accounted for 44% of total oil and condensate production in 1997. The majority state-owned Trinmar[17] and the wholly state-owned Petroleum Company of Trinidad and Tobago (Petrotrin) accounted for 25% and 26% of production, respectively. Petrotrin was created in 1993 as a result of the merger of two fully state-owned enterprises, Trinidad and Tobago Oil Company (Trintoc) and Trinidad and Tobago Petroleum Company (Trintopec). Petrotrin owns and operates the country's only operating refinery at Pointe-à-Pierre, which manufactures petroleum products for local consumption and for export to regional and international markets. The Government is currently considering the possible privatization of Petrotrin.[18]

(iii) Natural gas

51.   The production of natural gas reached 884 mmcf/d in 1997, of which over 90% was in the hands of multinational oil/gas producers. The state-owned Trinidad and Tobago Marine Petroleum Company (Trintomar), a joint venture between the National Gas Company (NGC) and Petrotrin, does not seem to have succeeded in reaching the goal of reducing dependence on foreign suppliers. Natural gas is not only used in the production of petrochemicals (ammonia, methanol and urea) and electricity, but also in the production of iron and steel, natural gas liquids (propane, butane and natural gas gasoline), cement, iron carbide, as well as in a number of light industries. In 1997, petrochemicals accounted for 57.1% of gas usage with power generation accounting for a further 23.4%. While it is presently not exported, liquified natural gas (LNG) is expected to become a major export once the construction of a LNG plant at Point Fortin is completed in 1999.[19]

52.   NGC is a state-owned company which has a monopoly over the purchase, transmission and sale of natural gas. It is also responsible for the development of downstream gas-based industries, and for the supervision of investment projects. NGC negotiates gas purchasing contracts with suppliers as needed and separate gas supply contracts with consumers. Pricing is set on a case-by-case basis and each contract is negotiated with the proposed user. Suppliers may obtain incentives under the Fiscal Incentives Act.

53.   Currently, there is no formal legislation nor a regulatory body governing the natural gas subsector. The Government is trying to establish a formal framework, including the establishment of a regulatory body for natural gas, the enactment of a Natural Gas Act, the standardization of royalties and fiscal incentives, the introduction of a licensing system for petrochemicals and the creation of a more transparent pricing structure.

(iv) Other minerals and quarrying

54.   Non-petroleum minerals produced for commercial use include: asphalt, andesite, argillite, clay, limestone, sand and gravel, plastering sand, silica sand, oil sand, quartzite and porcellanite. Of these, clay is the most abundant and extensively used. Other non-petroleum minerals found in Trinidad and Tobago, but not produced commercially include: magnetite (iron ore), gypsum and fluorite. There are 52 active quarries. Imports of non-petroleum minerals include course sand for use in petroleum operations, gypsum, iron ore and limestone for use in the manufacture of glass.

55.   Trinidad and Tobago has one of the largest natural deposits of asphalt in the world. The latest available figures show that asphalt production reached 15,396 tonnes and exports 12,278 tonnes in 1997.

---

[17]Trinmar is 66 2/3% owned by Petrotrin and 33 1/3% by Texaco Trinidad.
[18]Divestment Secretariat (1998).
[19]Ministry of Energy and Energy Industries (1997).

56.	There are nine separate pieces of legislation regulating the mineral and quarrying industries, each of which is administered by a different government agency. The Ministry of Energy and Energy Industries has been given the task to come up with new legislation to bring together all quarry-related legislation.

**(v)	Electricity**

57.	The prime source of energy is natural gas. Electricity generation accounts for 23.4% of total natural gas utilization; it increased from 3,852 million kilowatt hours (kWh) to 4,841 million kWh in the 1992-97 period. (Between 10-13% of total electricity generated is estimated to be lost in the transmission process.) The demand for electricity increased from 609 megawatts (MW) in 1993 to 746MW in 1997 and is expected to reach 930MW in the year 2000 (production is estimated at 5,964 million kWh).

58.	The Trinidad and Tobago Electricity Commission (TTEC), which falls under the purview of the Ministry of Public Utilities, has exclusive control over the generation, transmission, distribution and sale of electricity in Trinidad and Tobago. In 1994, the generation operations of TTEC became a separate company, the Power Generation Company of Trinidad and Tobago (PowerGen), which is 51% owned by TTEC, jointly with two private companies. The company is responsible for the operation and maintenance of the three thermal power plants which use natural gas as the principal fuel. TTEC serves some 298,000 customers, including businesses, industries and residents.

59.	Electricity rates, which are the lowest in the Caribbean[20], are set by the Public Utilities Commission, which is to be replaced by the Regulated Industries Commission. The financial difficulties of TTEC, which reported a deficit of over TT$276 million in 1996, has urged the setting up of the Regulated Industries Commission, which will operate under a price-cap system, expected to provide greater incentives for cost reduction and reduce cross-subsidization. As part of the Government's divestment programme, the private sector already participates in generation activities.

**(4)	MANUFACTURING**

60.	The manufacturing sector accounted for only 12.4% of GDP in 1996. Despite the Government's efforts to diversify production, the manufacturing sector remains heavily dependent on the oil refinery and petrochemical sub-sectors. The share of petroleum-related manufacturing increased from 41.5 to 66.4% of total manufacturing GDP in the 1992-96 period (Chart IV.3). Most the rest of the manufacturing sector consists of steel and cement, wood products, paper, printing and publishing, industrial gas, and metal building.

**(i)	Market access**

61.	The 1998 average MFN tariff on imports of industrial products (HS chapters 25-97, covering both manufacturing and mining) was seven, with a peak of 30% (HS chapters 27, 40, 71, 84, 85, 87, 91, 93) (Table IV.11). In all HS chapters, with the exception of chapters 37, 57, 74, 91, 92, 94, 96 and 97, the minimum tariff rate was zero (Chapter III(2)(iii)). The highest tariffs are applied on arms and ammunition, clocks and watches, works of art, clothing and apparel articles, carpets, furniture, toys, footwear, soap and leather goods.

---

[20]For instance, the industrial rate is 2.45 US cents per kWh in Trinidad and Tobago, 16.72 US cents per kWh in Barbados, 16.30 US cents per kWh in Grenada, and 10.67 US cents per kWh in Jamaica. (Trinidad Express, 21 July 1997)

Chart IV.3
Manufacturing GDP by activity, 1992 and 1996

Per cent

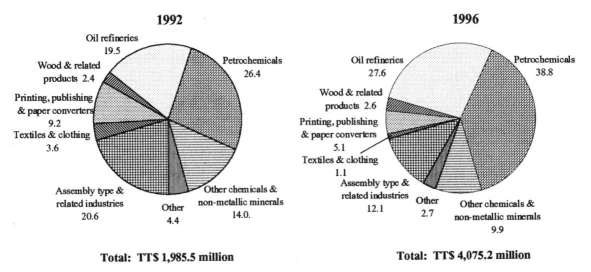

1992

Oil refineries 19.5

Wood & related products 2.4

Printing, publishing & paper converters 9.2

Textiles & clothing 3.6

Petrochemicals 26.4

Assembly type & related industries 20.6

Other 4.4

Other chemicals & non-metallic minerals 14.0.

Total: TT$ 1,985.5 million

1996

Oil refineries 27.6

Wood & related products 2.6

Printing, publishing & paper converters 5.1

Textiles & clothing 1.1

Assembly type & related industries 12.1

Petrochemicals 38.8

Other 2.7

Other chemicals & non-metallic minerals 9.9

Total: TT$ 4,075.2 million

Source: Central Statistical Office.

62.   Under its Uruguay Round commitments, Trinidad and Tobago bound virtually all of its industrial tariffs at ceiling rates of 50%; as exceptions, a few items were bound at 70%. Other duties and charges were bound at 15%.

(ii)   Incentives schemes

63.   A number of incentive schemes are available for manufacturers. The Customs Act Section 56 allows customs duty concessions of imports of machinery, equipment and materials for a wide range of approved manufacturing activities - including petroleum-related manufacturing - listed in the Third Schedule of the Act (Chapter III(2)(iii)(e)). The Fiscal Incentives Act grants tax relief from corporate tax and customs duties to approved enterprises for a period of up to ten years (Chapter III(4)(ii)). A number of free zones have been established to encourage the development of export-oriented manufacturing. In order to be eligible for free-zone status, and enjoy various tax exemptions, firms must export more than 80% of their production outside of CARICOM (Chapter III(3)(vii)). Accelerated tax depreciation is granted in the form of an initial allowance (10% of capital expenditure for general manufacturing and 20% for petrochemicals) and an annual allowance (10% of capital expenditure).

Table IV.11
Trade and tariff data for industrial products, 1998
(Per cent and US$'000)

HS	Description	Unweighted MFN average (%)	Min. (%)	Max. (%)	Import (US$ '000) 1996	Exports (US$ '000) 1996
25-97	**Industrial products**	**7.0**	**0**	**30**	**1,894,551.1**	**2,253,401.0**
25	Slat; sulphur; earth & stone; plastering mat.; lime & cem.	1.7	0	20	12,985.4	21,278.5
26	Ores, slag and ash	1.1	0	10	59,658.4	188.4
27	Mineral fuels, oils & products of their distillation; etc.	11.0	0	30	422,734.9	1,291,836.2
28	Inorg. chem; compds. of prec. met., radioact. elements, etc.	0.7	0	15	21,855.6	301,580.5
29	Organic chemicals	0.1	0	15	14,946.4	123,235.6
30	Pharmaceutical products	7.5	0	15	35,351.4	1,693.5
31	Fertilizers	0.4	0	10	2,901.9	115,601.8
32	Tanning/dyeing extract; tannins & derivs; pigm. etc.	8.0	0	25	11,721.7	6,664.5
33	Essential oils & resinoids; perf, cosmetic/toilet prep.	11.7	0	20	13,177.2	5,469.9
34	Soap, organic surface-active agents, washing prep. etc.	14.9	0	20	9,364.8	16,532.3
35	Albuminoidal subs; modified starches; glues; enzymes	3.9	0	15	2,582.9	630.8
36	Explosives; pyrotechnic prod; matches; pyrop alloy; etc.	11.2	0	20	1,479.1	770.3
37	Photographic or cinematographic goods	11.6	5	20	4,292.6	2.1
38	Miscellaneous chemical products	2.7	0	20	58,298.6	4,077.3
39	Plastics and articles thereof	7.7	0	20	78,000.6	16,760.8
40	Rubber and articles thereof	5.9	0	30	21,557.3	48.8
41	Raw hides and skins (other than furskins) and leather	0.1	0	5	523.6	-
42	Articles of leather; saddlery/harness; travel goods etc.	18.0	0	20	1,379.9	217.1
43	Furskins and artificial fur; manufactures thereof	3.0	0	20	1.4	-
44	Wood and articles of wood; wood charcoal	7.6	0	20	26,575.6	10,901.3
45	Cork and articles of cork	4.2	0	20	79.3	0.1
46	Manufactures of straw, esparto/other plaiting mat.; etc.	12.5	0	20	75.6	2.1
47	Pulp of wood/of other fibrous cellulosic mat.; waste etc.	0.0	0	0	2,051.8	1,735.2
48	Paper & paperboard; art of paper pulp, paper/paperboard	6.3	0	20	69,840.8	38,000.5
49	Printed books, newspapers, pictures & other products etc.	6.9	0	20	14,942.7	2,793.6
50	Silk	0.5	0	5	32.0	-
51	Wool, fine/coarse animal hair, horsehair yarn & fabric	0.3	0	5	164.4	-
52	Cotton	0.1	0	5	6,011.9	23.8
53	Other vegetable textile fibres; paper yarn & woven fab.	0.0	0	0	26.3	0.4
54	Man-made filaments	0.3	0	5	526.6	4.2
55	Man-made staple fibres	0.2	0	5	22,709.4	235.1
56	Wadding, felt & non-woven; yarns; twine, cordage, etc.	6.5	0	20	4,634.6	1,025.7
57	Carpets and other textile floor coverings	20.0	20	20	2,212.6	44.5
58	Special woven fab.; tufted tex. fab.; lace; tapestries etc.	0.9	0	15	5,554.8	8.1

Table IV.11 (cont'd)

HS	Description	Unweighted MFN average (%)	Min. (%)	Max. (%)	Import (US$ '000) 1996	Exports (US$ '000)
59	Impregnated, coated, cover/laminated textile fabric etc.	3.2	0	20	2,964.8	0.6
60	Knitted or crocheted fabrics	0.0	0	0	6,203.9	10.8
61	Art of apparel & clothing access, knitted or crocheted	19.9	0	20	1,910.5	4,470.3
62	Art of apparel & clothing access, not knitted/crocheted	19.8	0	20	4,254.6	5,348.1
63	Other made up textile articles; sets; worn clothing etc.	17	0	20	2,953.1	1,101.4
64	Footwear, gaiters and the like; parts of such articles	16.3	0	20	11,532.7	552.5
65	Headgear and parts thereof	14.6	0	20	536.7	250.3
66	Umbrellas, walking-sticks, seat-sticks, whips, etc.	11.4	0	20	205.4	7.1
67	Prep. feathers & down; arti.flower; articles human hair	16.3	0	20	387.1	0.7
68	Art of stone, plaster, cement, asbestos, mica/sim.mat.	10.7	0	25	4,476.2	2,244.0
69	Ceramic products	13.8	0	25	17,026.3	1,450.4
70	Glass and glassware	7	0	25	8,143.9	9,214.8
71	Natural/cultured pearls, prec.stones & metals, coins etc.	15.9	0	30	735.0	672.9
72	Iron and steel	4.6	0	15	47,521.3	209,842.6
73	Articles of iron or steel	9.7	0	25	69,926.9	11,810.4
74	Copper and articles thereof	3	5	20	7,634.1	5,914.6
75	Nickel and articles thereof	1.7	0	5	30.7	60.3
76	Aluminium and articles thereof	6.6	0	20	20,748.1	4,166.3
78	Lead and articles thereof	0.8	0	5	301.9	31.2
79	Zinc and articles thereof	0.9	0	5	279.6	8.1
80	Tin and articles thereof	0.8	0	5	186.3	-
81	Other base metals; cements; articles thereof	0.0	0	0	400.6	0.1
82	Tool, implement, cutlery, spoons & forks, of base met. etc.	6.6	0	20	9,919.9	40.8
83	Miscellaneous articles of base metal	7.7	0	20	9,598.7	1,277.8
84	Nuclear reactors, boilers, mchy. & mech. appliances; parts	2.8	0	30	346,769.7	10,928.9
85	Electrical mchy. equip. parts thereof; sound recorders etc.	10	0	30	104,196.1	9,079.7
86	Railw./tramw. locom., rolling-stock & parts thereof; etc.	0.3	0	5	716.1	7.8
87	Vehicles o/t railw./tramw. roll-stock, pts. & accessories.	10.8	0	30	113,494.7	784.5
88	Aircraft, spacecraft, and parts thereof	4.7	0	20	74,476.7	-
89	Ships, boats and floating structures	3.9	0	20	37,364.8	1,180.6
90	Optical, photo, cine, meas., checking, precision, etc.	6.4	0	25	39,659.7	2,322.3
91	Clocks and watches and parts thereof	20.1	2.5	30	759.4	9.6
92	Musical instruments; parts and access. of such articles	10.4	10	20	345.1	556.2
93	Arms and ammunition; parts and accessories thereof	21.4	0	30	522.3	-
94	Furniture; bedding, mattresses, matt. supports, cushions etc	17.3	2.5	20	10,872.3	6,497.7
95	Toys, games & sports requisites; parts & access. thereof	14.2	0	20	4,847.0	261.6
96	Miscellaneous manufactured articles	14.4	2.5	20	4,355.6	924.1
97	Works of art, collectors, pieces and antiques	20	20	20	41.2	9.9

Note: Trade data applied for 1996.

Source: WTO calculations based on data provided by the authorities of Trinidad and Tobago and UNSD, Comtrade database.

64.   The majority of petroleum-related manufacturing companies are located at the (natural-gas abundant) Point Lisas Industrial Estate, which enjoys free-zone privileges. The Industrial Estate is managed by the majority state-owned Point Lisas Industrial Port Development Corporation (PLIPDECO).[21] The Trinidad and Tobago Free Zones Act was amended in 1995 to expand the definition of free-zone activities and to include petroleum-related manufacturing (Chapter III(3)(vii)). Petrochemical companies, as well as steel plants and medium-sized manufacturers, located in the Industrial Estate, enjoy exemptions from customs duties, income and corporate taxes, business levies, withholding taxes on remittance of profits, dividends and other distributions, and land and building taxes. The Industrial Estate is also equipped with the second largest port in Trinidad and Tobago, Port Point Lisas, which specializes in industrial cargo, including petrochemicals, iron and steel products.

(iii)   Petroleum-related manufacturing

65.   The petroleum-related manufacturing subsector consists of one refinery, thirteen petrochemical plants, a natural gas liquid recovery plant and electricity power plants. In recent years, the abundance of natural gas reserves has attracted a large number of investment in gas utilization projects including petrochemicals and liquified natural gas. In 1997, the production of petrochemicals (fertilizer, methanol) accounted for 57% of gas utilization (Chart IV.4). The construction of a liquified natural gas (LNG) plant, to be completed in 1999, will increase utilization of natural gas by another 450 mcf/d, and LNG is expected to become a major export.[22] The development of downstream natural gas sub-sectors altogether will increase gas utilization from the current 900 mcf/d to 1400 mcf/d in the year 2000.[23]

(a)   Crude oil refining

66.   Trinidad and Tobago has an important oil refining industry which manufactures petroleum products such as motor gasoline, gas/diesel oil, fuel oil, kerosene, and aviation turbine fuel. Refinery capacity, which attained 450,000 b/d, in the1960s, declined to 100,000 b/d in the early 1990s, before increasing to 160,000 b/d in 1998, after the completion of a project which upgraded the only operating refinery at Point-à-Pierre.[24] Refinery output is expected to average 125,000 b/d in 1998, increasing to 160,000 b/d in 2000.

67.   The Pointe-à-Pierre refinery, owned by the state-controlled Petrotrin, has access to 75,000 b/d of low-cost indigenous crude oil, with the rest of its refining capacity met by imported oil. In the 1993-96 period, an annual average 12.5 million barrels were imported. Petrotrin has a processing agreement with Venezuela under which Venezuela provides crude oil for Petrotrin's surplus refinery capacity. In 1996, 58% of crude oil was imported under the agreement. All imports of crude oil enter duty free. In 1996, Trinidad and Tobago produced 41 million barrels of various petroleum products and exported 28.2 million barrels to regional and international markets (Table IV.12).

---

[21]PLIPDECO is 43% owned by the Government, 8% by Caroni (100% government-owned agricultural enterprise), with the rest of the shares traded on the stock exchange. It also manages the Port of Point Lisas, the second largest port, which specializes in industrial cargo including petrochemicals, iron and steel products.

[22]In 1993, a project of the construction of a LNG plant at Point Fortin was agreed by five partners, NGC and four multinationals. It is the single largest investment in downstream industries in the country with a cost estimated at US$1 billion. LNG is expected to start being delivered to the United States and Spain in 1999.

[23]The Ministry of Energy and Energy Industries (1997).

[24]The second refinery, Point Fortin, is at present idle. The Government is trying to privatize it, so far unsuccessfully.

Chart IV. 4
Utilization of natural gas, 1997

Per cent

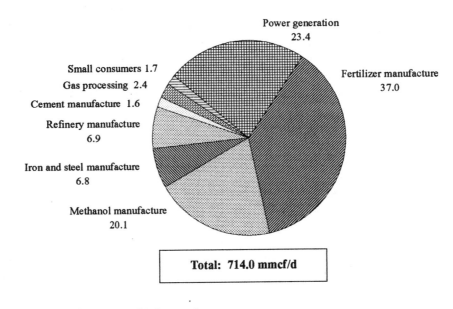

Power generation
23.4

Fertilizer manufacture
37.0

Small consumers 1.7
Gas processing 2.4
Cement manufacture 1.6
Refinery manufacture
6.9
Iron and steel manufacture
6.8
Methanol manufacture
20.1

Total: 714.0 mmcf/d

Note: Mmcf/d stands for million cubic feet per day.
Source: Ministry of Energy and Energy Industries.

Table IV.12
Oil refinery output and exports, 1993-97
('000 barrels)

		1993	1994	1995	1996	1997
Refinery throughput		38,229.3	37,839.3	37,001.9	40,249.3	34,263.8
Refinery output		37,269	36,227	34,391	41,067	..
Of which:	Motor gasoline	6,466.9	6,983.0	7,799.7	5,708.3	7,547.2
	Gas/diesel oil	6,397.4	6,780.5	7,489.5	7,793.0	8,338.4
	Fuel oil	19,640.1	17,909.1	14,774.4	17,008.9	14,271.4
	Kerosene and aviation turbine fuel	3,629.1	4,452.9	3,660.0	4,068.9	3,287.2
Refinery exports		23,899	27,179	31,877	28,203	..

..   Not available.

Source: Central Bank of Trinidad and Tobago.

68.   For refining operations, a refinery throughput tax is levied at US$0.05/barrel for full refining and US$0.02 for light refining.[25]

69.   The domestic distribution of petroleum products is handled by the National Petroleum Marketing Company, a state-owned company which had a monopoly right until recently. In 1997, its monopoly status was eliminated; distribution activities are now open for entry, initially by domestic companies only.

---

[25]The refinery throughput tax is deductible when computing the profits of a refining business for the purpose of the PPT.

(b)   Petrochemicals (including fertilizers)

70.   The production of petrochemicals increased from TT$523.4 million in 1992 to TT$1580.1 million in 1996. The hub of the country's petrochemical industry is located at the Point Lisas Industrial Estate, which is governed by the Point Lisas Industrial Port Development Corporation (PLIPDECO).

71.   Trinidad and Tobago is the world's second largest producer of ammonia and the third largest producer of urea. There are eight ammonia plants and one urea plant, with total capacities of 3.54 million tonnes per year for ammonia and 0.58 million tonnes per year for urea. Fertilizer production, combining production of ammonia and urea together, amounted to 2.7 million tonnes in 1997, with exports reaching 2.3 million tonnes (Table IV.13). An ongoing construction project of a new ammonia plant with a production capacity of 620,000 tonnes per year will further enhance capacity for fertilizer production.

Table IV.13
Petroleum-related production and exports, 1993-97

	1993	1994	1995	1996	1997
Production					
Fertilizers ('000 tonnes)	2,292	2,453	2,631	2,674	2,691
Methanol ('000 tonnes)	493	1,020	963	1,355	1,520
Natural gas liquids[a] ('000 barrels)	3,257	3,485	3,750	4,460	4,111
Exports					
Fertilizers ('000 tonnes)	1,946	2,185	2,268	2,336	2,292
Methanol ('000 tonnes)	456	1,009	963	1,317	1,580
Natural gas liquids ('000 barrels)	2,315	2,718	3,715	4,310	4,145

a   Natural gas liquids include propane, butane and natural gasoline.

Source: Central Bank of Trinidad and Tobago.

72.   There are four methanol plants, with a production capacity of 2.9 million tonnes per annum (up from 0.45 million tonnes in 1991). In 1997, methanol production amounted to 1.52 million tonnes and exports to 1.58 million tonnes. A fifth methanol plant with a capacity of 0.86 million tonnes per annum is presently under construction.

73.   State involvement in the petrochemicals sub-sector has declined since the beginning of the decade, when the Government held 100% of the Trinidad and Tobago Urea Company (TTUC) and the Trinidad and Tobago Methanol Company (TTMC) and 51% of Fertilizers of Trinidad and Tobago, Ltd. (Fertrin). As part of a divestment exercise, TTUC and Fertrin were sold to foreign investors in 1993, and TTMC to a consortium comprising local and foreign investors in 1997.

(c)   Natural gas liquids

74.   A natural gas liquid recovery plant, Phoenix Park Gas Processors Limited (PPGPL), jointly owned by NGC (49%) and two other partners (Comoco, 41% and Pan West Constructors 10%), extracts propane, butane and natural gas gasoline from local natural gas production.[26] The production of natural gas liquids commenced in 1991 and has been growing since. In 1997, some 4.1 million tonnes of gas extracts were produced and all exported (Table IV.13). A new PPGPL facility, which is

---

[26]Propane and butane are used as inputs in the manufacture of petrochemicals, plastics and textiles while natural gas is used as a gasoline blending product and chemical feedstock.

to be completed by the end of 1998, will increase gas processing capacity from the existing 750 mmcf/d to 1,350 mmcf/d.

(iv) Non-petroleum manufacturing

(a) Cement

75.   Production of cement increased from 527,200 tonnes to 652,500 tonnes in 1993-97 period. Exports of cement, mainly to CARICOM member states, reached 282,200 tonnes in 1997 (Table IV.14).

Table IV.14
Production and exports of selected manufacturing, 1993-97
('000 tonnes)

	1993	1994	1995	1996	1997
Production					
Steel Products					
Direct reduced iron	714.5	946.7	1,039.9	954.5	1,133.8
Billets	492.1	630.3	676.1	643.6	747.0
Wire rods	413.0	521.1	594.4	575.4	668.0
Cement	527.2	582.9	558.5	617.1	652.5
Exports					
Steel					
Direct reduced iron	223.9	292.3	270.5	272.9	344.9
Billets	15.7	12.6	21.0	8.2	12.7
Wire rods	357.8	495.2	564.3	551.9	603.7
Cement	297.5	334.0	296.0	323.2	298.3

Source: Central Bank of Trinidad and Tobago.

76.   Trinidad Cement Limited (TCL) is the sole producer of cement in Trinidad and Tobago. The Government acquired the company in 1976, and retained 100% ownership until 1989 when it was partly divested. The Government kept the price of cement affordable to the population, often at a price below the cost of production, and thus TCL experienced large financial losses. After three phases of divestment between 1989 and 1994, the Government at present holds 9.1% of the shares in the company, which is also expected to be sold in 1998. In 1994, TCL purchased the assets of Arawak Cement Company which was jointly established by the Governments of Barbados and Trinidad and Tobago (51% and 49%, respectively) in 1981.

(b) Iron and steel

77.   Production as well as exports of steel products have increased in the 1992-97 period (Table IV.14).

78.   The Iron and Steel Company of Trinidad and Tobago (ISCOTT) was established by the Government in 1981 to undertake the production and marketing of steel products, including direct reduced iron, billets and wire. In 1989, after years of financial losses, ISCOTT was leased to a foreign operator at a rental of US$10.84 million a year for a period of ten years. In 1994, the lease operator, Caribbean Ispat Limited, purchased the assets of ISCOTT and agreed to sell 40% of its share capital to nationals of Trinidad and Tobago within three years. The company, now called Caribbean Ispat, is the tenth largest steel producer in the world.

79.   Trinidad and Tobago has become the only exporter of iron carbide in the world. Its first iron carbide production plant with 1,000 tonnes per day was built in the Point Lisas Industrial Estate in 1993. The plant produces iron carbide by processing iron ore from Brazil with locally available natural gas. The first shipment was delivered to the United States in 1995. Three additional plants are expected to be built.

(5)   SERVICES

(i)   Overview

80.   The services sector accounted for 61% of GDP and 75% of total employment in 1996.

81.   Under the General Agreement on Trade in Services (GATS), Trinidad and Tobago's Schedule provides for horizontal commitments on two modes of supply: commercial presence and the presence of natural persons. With respect to "commercial presence", the acquisition of over 30% of the equity of publicly-traded companies is subject to approval, as is foreign purchase of over five acres of land for commercial and residential purposes. In the case of the "presence of natural persons", the employment of a foreigner, including a CARICOM national, in excess of thirty days is subject to the obtention of a work permit, which is granted on a case-by-case basis.[27]

82.   In the Uruguay Round, Trinidad and Tobago made sector-specific commitments with respect to business services (professional services, computer and related services, research and development services, other business services); communication services (telecommunications services); educational services; financial services (insurance); health-related services; tourism and travel related services; recreational, cultural and sporting services; and transport services (maritime transport services).[28]

(ii)   Financial services

83.   Financial services, including real estate and business services, accounted for 11.5% of GDP and 8.2% of total employment in 1997. The financial system comprises various financial institutions, including commercial banks, non-banking financial institutions, the stock exchange and insurance companies (Table IV.15). Total assets in the system amounted to TT$47 billion in 1996. A number of liberalization measures taken in 1993, including the removal of the Trinidad and Tobago dollar from its peg to the US dollar and of exchange restrictions on current and capital transactions, have set the stage for the local financial services sector to interact with global financial markets. At the same time, a new piece of legislation, the Financial Institutions Act, was introduced to modernize and strengthen prudential regulations.

84.   Under the WTO negotiations on Financial Services, Trinidad and Tobago made commitments in reinsurance, but not in other sub-sectors.

(a)   Banking

85.   At the end of 1997 there were five commercial banks with 120 branches operating in Trinidad and Tobago. Since the beginning of the 1990s, market consolidation has taken place in banking as the number of banks decreased from eight in 1992 to five in 1997. Out of the five commercial banks, four are either wholly or majority locally owned and one wholly foreign owned. Collectively, the five commercial banks held assets of TT$23 billion in 1996, accounting for about half the financial sector's total assets. The three largest institutions held almost two thirds of the banking system's

---

[27]GATS/SC/86, 15 April 1994.
[28]GATS/SC/86, 15 April 1994, GATS/SC/86/Suppl.1, 11 April 1997.

assets.[29] Total deposits grew from TT$8.6 million in 1992 to TT$12.4 million in 1996, mainly due to the rise in foreign currency deposits as a result of the removal of foreign exchange controls in 1993. The share of foreign currency deposits in total deposits increased from zero in early 1993 to 24% in 1996.

Table IV.15
The financial system in Trinidad and Tobago, 1996

Institutions	Number of institutions (Branches)	Total assets[a] (TTS million)
Central Bank	1	8,418
Commercial Banks	6 (121)	22,960
Financial Companies & Merchant Banks	10 (13)	2,204
Trust & Mortgage Financial Companies	6 (10)	4,452
Thrift Institutions[b]	3	80
Development Banks[c]	2	993
Unit Trust Corporation	1	1,352
Credit Unions	1	2,000
National Insurance Board	1	3,588
Insurance Companies	34	[...]
Development Insurance Corporation	1	229
Home Mortgage Bank	1	777
Trinidad and Tobago Stock Exchange	1	11
Total	**68**	**47,064**

a   Provisional.
b   Include the Post Office Savings Bank and three Building Societies.
c   Include the Agricultural Development Bank and the Trinidad and Tobago Mortgage Finance Company.

Source: Central Bank of Trinidad and Tobago.

86.   The legislative framework governing the banking sector is the Financial Institutions Act of 1993. The Act repealed and replaced the Banking Act of 1964 and the Financial Institutions (Non-Banking) Act of 1979 that had separately governed commercial banks and deposit-taking non-bank financial institutions.[30] The two types of financial institutions were brought for the first time under a single legislative umbrella which granted them greater freedom to offer a wider range of financial services. While commercial banks may engage in all types of financial activities, non-bank financial institutions can carry out only the businesses specified in their licences (Table IV.16). The Central Bank is responsible for the examination of applications for licences for both commercial banks and non-bank financial institutions.[31] If a non-bank financial institution wishes to vary or increase its activities, it must first obtain the approval of the Central Bank which may require the

---

[29]Forde and Joseph et al. (1997).

[30]According to the definition used by the Central Bank of Trinidad and Tobago, non-bank financial institutions include finance companies and merchant banks, and trust and mortgage financial companies. The major distinctions between commercial banks and non-bank financial institutions under the previous Acts were that non-bank financial institutions were not allowed to take demand deposits or to provide loans with repayment periods of less than one year, and that their licences specified the types of financial services they could offer.

[31]Under the previous legislation, these tasks were handled by the Ministry of Finance.

licensee to increase its paid-up capital above the stipulated minimum. Under the Financial Institutions Act, all financial institutions are required to have a minimum paid-up capital of TT$15 million to carry out financial business specified in the Act.

Table IV.16
Types of licences and activities covered by the Financial Institutions Act

Type of license	Activities
Business of banking (Commercial banks)	Receiving deposits of money from the public which may be withdrawn on demand, by cheque, draft, order or notice; and the making of loans, or the granting of credit facilities, and generally the undertaking of any business pertaining to the business of commercial banking.
Business of a financial nature (Non-bank financial institutions)	
1. Confirming house or acceptance house	Confirming, accepting or financing import and export bills.
2. Finance house or finance company	Hire purchase and instalment credit; trade and inventory financing; factoring; block financing.
3. Leasing corporation	Lease financing.
4. Merchant bank	Floating and undertaking stocks, shares and bonds; loans syndication; dealing in gold; providing consultancy and investment management services and corporate advisory services; project development; lease financing; foreign exchange dealing; inter-bank financing.
5. Mortgage institutions	Mortgage lending.
6. Trust company	Managing trust funds; performing duties of trustees, executor or administrator and attorney.
7. Union trust	Providing facilities for the participation by persons as beneficiaries under a trust or other schemes, in profits or income arising from the acquisition, holding, management or disposal of securities or any other property whatever.
8. Credit card business	Issuing payment, credit or charge credit cards and, in cooperation with others including other financial institutions, operating a payment, credit or charge card plan.
9. Financial services	Providing financial services relating to future and contingent liabilities in relation to foreign exchange and commodities.

Source: Financial Institutions Act, 1993.

87.   The Financial Institutions Act of 1993, together with the Financial Institutions (Prudential Criteria) Regulations of 1994, was legislated to enhance prudential standards in an increasingly liberal economic environment. The 8% capital adequacy ratio was established as the minimum, with a recommendation of 12% or more. The ceiling on unsecured loans to a single borrower was lowered from 10 to 5% of total bank capital, while such ceiling on secured loans was lifted from 10 to 25% for a single person or to 32% for a single borrowing group, including related parties. The Act required that banks hold reserves in a fixed ratio to their deposits liabilities. For local currency deposits, the reserve-requirement ratio is 24%, held in a non-interest-bearing account at the Central Bank; another 5% of deposits must be held in government bonds. For foreign currency deposits, there is a liquidity requirement ratio of 25%.[32]   The Act also established minimum accounting standards as well as criteria for analysing loan performance, asset classification, interest on non-performing loans, treatment of foreign exchange losses, dividend payments, loan provisioning and disclosure requirements. The enforcement of these prudential standards is monitored by the Central Bank whose supervisory power was strengthened by the Financial Institutions Act and the Central Bank (Amendment) Act of 1994. The Central Bank may impose conditions or restrictions and use the form of 'cease and desist' orders to curb conduct that is in violation of prudential standards. Overall assessment of the financial sector reform has been positive. The International Monetary Fund (IMF)

---

[32]Liquid reserves comprise selected foreign government securities of up to six-month maturity, bank deposits and cash.

reported that commercial bank performance was overall healthy, with a very high average ratio of capital to assets, low non-performing loans and adequate provisioning (Table IV.7).[33]

Table IV.17
Commercial bank performance indicators, 1993-96
(Per cent at end of period)

	1993	1994	1995	1996
Profitability ratio				
Ratios to average total assets				
Total operating income	12.4	10.9	10.2	10.9
Interest Income	9.4	8.4	8.0	8.4
Non-interest income	3.1	2.4	2.2	2.4
Net interest margin	4.2	3.8	3.6	3.3
Net profits after tax	1.2	1.0	1.1	1.3
Ratios to equity capital				
Net profits before tax				
Net profits after tax	15.5	13.4	15.3	17.1
Assets quality ratio				
Ratios to average total loans				
Non-performing loans	13.2	10.0	9.7	9.5
Accumulated loan loss provision	6.7	5.2	5.4	4.8
Liquidity ratio				
Ratios to average total deposits				
Total loans	81.3	69.7	61.5	61.6
Total liquid assets	23.5	27.7	27.6	26.7
Capital adequacy ratio				
Ratios to average total assets[a]	14.0	14.7	15.7	..

..   Not available.
a   Ratio of qualifying capital to total risk-adjusted assets.

Source: Central Bank of Trinidad and Tobago.

88.   On the other hand, the IMF has also argued that the local commercial banks were operating with a high degree of monopolistic power.[34] Large bank profits, which more than doubled from TT$123 million in 1992 to TT$ 279 million in 1996, the report said, were achieved by large interest rate spreads of seven to eight percentage points that could not be explained solely by high reserve requirements (Chart IV.5).[35] While none of the commercial banks was large enough to exercise monopoly power, their relatively small number and lack of new entrants over many years suggested a capacity for monopolistic pricing. Local bankers argued that the report did not take into consideration the banks' high administrative and other costs, as well as critical high-risk lending. These considerations would, they argued, reduce effective spreads to between 4% and 5%.[36]

---

[33]IMF (1997).

[34]IMF (1997).

[35]The IMF report identified two major factors that may contribute to a wide spread of interest rates. One is a high statutory reserve requirement. In recent years, the statutory reserve requirement in Trinidad and Tobago has been between 21 and 24%. The other factor is a high level of non-performing loans. In Trinidad and Tobago, however, the share of non-performing loans in total loans has declined from 14.2% in 1992 to 9.5% in 1996.

[36]EIU (1997).

Chart IV.5
Commercial bank interest rates in Trinidad and Tobago, 1992-96

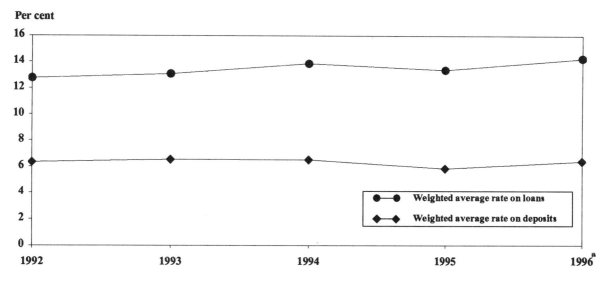

a   Estimates

<u>Source</u>: Data provided by the authorities of Trinidad and Tobago.

89.   Despite the predominance of commercial banks, non-bank financial institutions have also played a role in the financial sector. At the end of 1997, there were ten financial companies and merchant banks and six trust and mortgage finance companies. Their total assets amounted to TT$7.9 million in 1997, up from TT$3.4 million in 1992. In 1997, non-bank financial institutions granted 26% of loans and managed 20% of the deposits in the banking sector. In comparison with commercial banks, non-bank financial institutions offer lower lending rates and higher deposit rates, and thus smaller interest rate spreads. This is partly because non-bank financial institutions face lower reserve ratio requirements than commercial banks; an 8% reserve requirement currently operates for non-bank financial institutions in contrast to the 23% for commercial banks. The difference also reflects greater public confidence in the solvency of commercial banks, a larger range of services provided, and easier access to services (more bank branches).[37]

(b)   Securities trading

90.   The Stock Exchange of Trinidad and Tobago was established under the provision of the Securities Industry Act of 1981 and began operating under the auspices of the Ministry of Finance. At the end of 1997, there were 25 companies listed on the Exchange, with a total market capitalization of TT$19.64 billion, up from TT$2.85 billion at the end of 1993. Trading has increased from 34.2 million shares valued at TT$94.6 million in 1993 to 100.7 million shares valued at TT$846.1 million in 1997. Equities in the banking industry tend to be the most active in terms of volume and value, followed by the conglomerates and then the manufacturing sector.

91.   The Securities Industry Act of 1995, which repealed and replaced the obsolete Securities Industry Act of 1981, governs securities trading in Trinidad and Tobago. In addition to stipulating the conditions for the issue and listing of securities on the stock exchange, the Act established a Securities and Exchange Commission which assumed the authority "to maintain surveillance over the securities

---

[37]IMF (1997).

market and ensure orderly, fair and equitable dealings in securities."[38] All market actors, i.e. issuers, underwriters, investment advisers, stockbrokers and dealers, must register with the Commission which is responsible for controlling and supervising their activities. The Commission is equipped with investigative and dispute settlement powers to enforce rules and regulations.

92.   Cross-border trading among three regional stock exchanges - Jamaica, Barbados and Trinidad and Tobago - started in 1991. Despite initial enthusiasm, trading remains insignificant. In 1996, Trinidad and Tobago investors bought 25,000 shares valued at J$587,500 on the Jamaican stock market, while Barbados investors purchased 3,062 shares valued at TT$18,372 on the Trinidad and Tobago Stock Exchange.

(c)   Insurance

93.   At the beginning of 1998, the insurance industry was comprised of 43 firms, 36 of which were locally owned and seven of which were foreign-owned; 25 of these companies handled non-life insurance. The local insurance industry is heavily concentrated: in 1996, the six largest life insurance firms accounted for 93.1% of total assets in the life insurance sub-sector, and the ten largest firms accounted for 86.1% of total assets in the non-life sub-sector.[39] Gross premium income in the insurance sector increased from TT$1,155 million in 1992 to TT$1,571.4 million in 1996. Long-term insurance amounted to TT$841.4 million; motor-vehicle insurance to TT$216 million; property insurance to TT$307 million, and other insurance to TT$207 million.

94.   In recent years, cross-ownership in banking and insurance has been rising.[40] Neither the Insurance Act nor the Financial Institutions Act prohibit cross-ownership, but approval from the Central Bank is required. A bank may not acquire any part of the share of an insurance company in excess of 100% of its capital base, and shareholding must not exceed 25% of the bank's paid-up share capital and statutory reserve.

95.   There are no limitations on national treatment and market access for foreign companies wishing to carry out insurance business in Trinidad and Tobago, though a foreign company must incorporate locally and establish itself as a subsidiary. In the Uruguay Round negotiations, Trinidad and Tobago only bound commitments in the reinsurance sector. The country's only reinsurance company, Reinsurance Company of Trinidad and Tobago, partly owned by the Government until 1995 when it became foreign-controlled, has ceased to offer reinsurance and now offers only long-term and general insurance services. The reinsurance market is now totally foreign-controlled. There are no restrictions on the purchase of insurance abroad by local residents. Nor does the Government impose any obligation on traders to buy freight insurance locally.

96.   The main regulatory framework governing the insurance sector is the Insurance Act of 1980. The registration of insurance companies and intermediaries is the responsibility of the Supervisor of Insurance at the Ministry of Finance. The principal criteria for approval include minimum capital requirements - TT$3 million for life insurance and TT$1 million for non-life insurance - and

---

[38]Trinidad and Tobago Stock Exchange, http://stockex.co.tt.

[39]Price Waterhouse (1997).

[40] The country's largest insurance company, Colonial Insurance Company (CLICO), owns 34% of the shares of the largest bank, Republic Bank. Royal Bank, the second largest, owns 29% of Guardian Holdings, which is the owner of Guardian Life, CLICO's main competitor in the local insurance market, and 10% of Republic Bank. In turn, Guardian Holdings owns 20% of Royal Bank. These developments have led to the Government's fear of over-concentration of ownership in financial services. (EIU, 1997).

assessment of insurance policies and financial health in terms of solvency.[41] All insurance companies, including foreign-owned ones, must hold at least 80% of their investment assets locally. All insurers are required to arrange adequate reinsurance. In addition, life and motor insurers must maintain statutory funds to support policy holders' liabilities, and all general insurance business must maintain statutory deposits. The Supervisor of Insurance reviews annual returns which are submitted by insurance companies to assess compliance with these statutory requirements. The Minister of Finance has the power under the Insurance Act to prescribe minimum rates of premium in respect of motor vehicle insurance business.

97. According to the authorities, changes leading to stricter rules on the operations of insurance companies are envisaged for 1998. Proposed changes include increasing the level of minimum paid-up capital to TT$10 million for life insurance and non-life insurance companies, and to TT$20 million for composite insurance companies.

(iii) Telecommunications

98. The telecommunications subsector has grown in line with economic development in the last several years: between 1990 and 1995, value added grew from US$122 million to US$163 million, investment from US$19 million to US$37 million, equipment imports from US$0.9 million to US$1.4 million, and equipment exports from US$4.9 million to US$28.7 million.[42] At the end of 1997, there were 208,927 telephone lines in service, of which 92% were digital.[43] Telecommunications value added accounted for 3.1% of GDP in 1997 (Table IV.18).

Table IV.18
Telecommunications value added, 1993-97
(TT$ '000)

	1993	1994	1995	1996	1997
Telecommunications Value Added	758.1	815.6	925.3	1,035.9	1,111.2
Share in GDP (per cent)	3.1	2.8	2.9	3.0	3.1

Source: Government of Trinidad and Tobago.

99. The telecommunications system is operated by the Telecommunication Services of Trinidad and Tobago Limited (TSTT), at present 51% owned by the Government.[44] In 1989, TSTT was granted an exclusive license by the Government for 20 years to provide both local and international telecommunication services. TSTT's monopoly is *de facto*, not *de jure*, i.e. it is not granted by any domestic legislation.

100. The legislation governing the telecommunications sector is the Telecommunications Act of 1991, amending the preceding Trinidad and Tobago Telephone Act. The 1991 Act was approved by Parliament, however, it is not in effect since it has yet to be assented to by the President.[45] The law is currently under revision including changes necessary to meet GATS obligations. The Telecommunications Act proposes the establishment of the Trinidad and Tobago Telecommunications Authority which is to be responsible for the formulation of telecommunications policies, development

---

[41] Solvency requirements only apply to general insurance companies. The margin of solvency is the greater of 20% of the general premium income of the company. With TT$250,000 respect to life insurance companies, an actuarial certificate is provided annually by the actuary of the company.

[42] ITU (1997).

[43] http://www.ttst.net.tt.

[44] Cable & Wireless of the West Indies holds the remaining 49%.

[45] The main reason for the delay in assent by the President is said to be the change in the Government leadership in December 1991 (McCormick, 1994).

and implementation of national telecommunications standards and regulations, the setting of tariffs for both internal and external communication services, and for issuing of licences and the granting of concessions. Since the Act has not received the President's assent, the Authority is not yet in place. At present, the regulatory authority is the Telecommunications Division in the Office of the Prime Minister. Rates for the provision of domestic communications services are established through the regulating authority, the Public Utilities Commission, under the Ministry of Public Utilities, while international rates are set by the Telephone Act, Section 16. Regulations governing the setting of rates for domestic services are based on the Wireless Telegraphy Ordinance of 1959. Relative costs of telecommunications for international services include accounting rates, overhead coverage, sales, adjustments for fluctuations in the exchange rate, etc.

101.   While basic telecommunications services are in the hands of TSTT, there are no restrictions on the provisions of value-added services using the network of the exclusive service provider. Such services include on-line information and data base retrieval, electronic data interchange, enhanced facsimile services, code and protocol conversion, and on-line data processing. Currently, paging services are being provided by a number of operators other than TSTT, who must apply for a licence from TSTT. The criteria used for granting licences, *inter alia*, are technical compatibility with existing systems and availability of frequencies. Currently there are 12 companies providing these services. Cellular mobile telephone service was introduced by TSTT in 1991 and TSTT is still the single operator, serving 13,000 customers as of July 1998. Private networks are allowed on self-provided or leased facilities for a company's own use and are not normally permitted to connect to the public network (i.e. no interconnection or resale). There are no restrictions on the sale, rental, connection, maintenance and repairs of customer-premised equipment but previous approval is required.

102.   The Government of Trinidad and Tobago participated in the GATS negotiations on Basic Telecommunications. Trinidad and Tobago bound full competition in value-added services, using TSTT's network, full competition on satellite-based mobile services and fixed satellite services for public use. Those who wish to provide the public terrestrial-based mobile services, internet and internet access and teleconferencing for private use through cross-border and commercial-presence modes must negotiate with TSTT. Trinidad and Tobago bound full competition in telecommunications equipment sales, rental, maintenance, connection, repair and consulting services, as noted above. Finally, as additional commitment under GATS Article XVIII, Trinidad and Tobago agreed to abide by all the regulatory principles described in the Reference Paper.[46]

103.   In 1997, a Telecommunications Policy Committee was established with representatives from both the public and private sectors to prepare a national policy for telecommunications. The policy is intended to provide a framework to create a competitive environment in the industry. A Working Group, appointed in June 1997 by the Cabinet, submitted recommendations for the establishment of a National Policy on Telecommunications. Some of these include: amendments to the Telecommunications Authority Act 1991 prior to proclamation; the creation of a new regulatory body, the Telecommunications Authority; the establishment of an appropriate telecommunications regulatory framework; the development of a policy on divestment and competition; identification of the requirements for optimum network expansion; and the provision of universal service.

(iv)   Maritime transport

104.   The ports of Port of Spain in Trinidad, and Scarborough in Tobago, are owned and administered by the state-owned Port Authority of Trinidad and Tobago. The Port Authority was set

---

[46]The Reference Paper outlines a set of pro-competitive regulatory principles such as competition safeguards, interconnection guarantees, transparent licensing processes, and the independence of regulators.

up in 1961 to manage ports as well as to provide cargo-handling services, towage and dredging services, and inter-island ferry services. Port of Spain, the country's largest, Port of Spain, handles all major dry cargoes, containers and general cargo, break bulk cargo, liquid bulk cargo and passenger traffic, and in recent years it has increasingly become a major regional hub for transhipment. The country's second largest port, Point Lisas, is managed by PLIPDECO, which also manages the Point Lisas Industrial Estate and Free Trade Zone.[47] Point Lisas specializes in industrial cargo including steel, ammonia, methanol, urea, iron carbide and iron ore.[48] The third largest port, Scarborough, is used mainly for inter-island passenger and cargo transport, and international cruise ships. Approval from the Port Authority is required to discharge and load general cargo at any port in the country, other than Point Lisas.

105.   The Shipping Act of 1987 governs the registration and licensing of ships. The Maritime Services Division was set up within the Ministry of Works and Transport to administrate and enforce all the provisions of the law. The Act limits registration to ships owned by nationals of Trinidad and Tobago and other CARICOM member States, by foreigners engaged in bareboat charters and in joint venture shipping arrangements with Trinidad and Tobago nationals. Local shipowners are not required to fly the national flag; nor is there much incentive to do so: in 1997, only 42 vessels registered in Trinidad and Tobago. One reason why locally owned oil and gas carriers do not register locally is the Government's failure to ratify the Marpol Convention, the international marine pollution treaty. However, according to the authorities, legislation to give effect to MARPOL and other major pollution prevention, liability and compensation treaties have been prepared and should be promulgated by the end of 1998. The Government is currently reviewing the Act with a view to improving shipping legislation and regulatory mechanisms[49], and providing new incentives to legislation.

106.   There are no restrictions on the entry of ships into the waters of Trinidad and Tobago. Vessels are, however, expected to comply with applicable standards of safety and pollution prevention. However, inter-island routes between Trinidad and Tobago are protected by a cabotage policy and are operated by the Port Authority. Vessels wishing to engage in coastal trade between the islands of Trinidad and Tobago are required to obtain a licence; this requirement is applied to both local and foreign operators.

107.   The geographical location of Trinidad and Tobago - 15km off the coast of Venezuela - has made its ports attractive as container transhipment centres between North America/Europe and South America. In Port of Spain, transhipment container traffic increased by 261% between 1992 and 1997. In 1997, 49% of the 209,530 TEU (twenty-foot equivalent unit) container cargo entering the port was in transit. Transshipment container handling charges of US$74 a box are the lowest in the region with a 21-day free storage period.[50]

108.   After decades of losses, the Port Authority's operations have been profitable since 1994, recording TT$40 million in operating profits in 1997. Plans are under way to commercialize operations, which will involve setting up separate companies for cargo-handing and marine services. The Port Authority would initially hold 100% of the shares, which would subsequently be sold to local and foreign investors.

---

[47]The Point Lisas Port Development Company manages the Container Examination Stations (CES) on behalf of the Customs and Excise Department.

[48]In recent years, Point Lisas has also handled containers and general cargo.

[49]Ministry of Finance (1997).

[50] Lloyd's List, 28 August 1996.

109.   Trinidad and Tobago's commitments on maritime transport services under the GATS include: no limitations on any of the four modes of supply regarding dry docking/ship repairs, boat building and ship management/freight and transportation; no limitations on navigation aid and communications/meteorological services (for maritime purposes); no limitations on commercial presence and presence of natural persons for ship surveys, subject to registration and certification requirements.

(v)   **Civil aviation**

110.   There are two international airports, the Piarco Airport in Trinidad and the Crown Point Airport in Tobago, which are owned and managed by the Government-controlled Airport Authority of Trinidad and Tobago. A US$80 million project to upgrade the Piarco Airport is under way, including the construction of a new terminal and facilities, and improvements of air cargo handling, storage, aircraft maintenance and airline catering. The airport's capacity is expected to increase up to 1,500 passengers per hour as a result of the upgrading project.[51]

111.   The Trinidad and Tobago Airways Corporation (BWIA International), the national carrier, was partly divested in February 1995, after incurring losses of TT$1.9 billion over the period 1980-94.[52] With a view to improving BWIA's financial performance, 51% of the shares were sold to private investors, while the Government retained 33.5% and allocated 15.5% to the airline's employees.[53] BWIA is a member of the International Air Transport Association (IATA).

112.   The regulatory framework governing the civil aviation sector is embodied in the Civil Aviation Order of 1995. With the issuance of the Act, Trinidad and Tobago meets the requirements of the International Civil Aviation Organization. The registration of aircraft is handled by the Civil Aviation Division within the Ministry of Works and Transport, which issues aircraft operating certificates. The principal criteria for the registration is safety. Those aircraft which are registered abroad and hold operating certificates simply need clearance from the Division. In September 1997, there were 45 locally-registered aircraft and two foreign-registered aircraft based and operating in Trinidad and Tobago. The country has bilateral air services agreements with 17 countries and 17 airlines are registered to operate in Trinidad and Tobago.[54] Only four operators carry passengers on international routes (excluding regional routes). Inter-island traffic is protected by a cabotage policy and operated by a domestic privately owned airline, Air Caribbean, and by BWIA.

113.   Air cargo handling services are in the hands of private sector companies, both foreign and domestic. Airline facilities and repair services are open to foreigners but there is no actual foreign presence; these services are provided by BWIA and Air Caribbean.

114.   A CARICOM Multilateral Air Services Agreement has been finalized and signed by most of the member States, except the Bahamas, Jamaica and Montserrat.[55] The Agreement allows those CARICOM designated air carriers to offer all types of air services within the Community. Domestic traffic, however, would be reserved for national carriers. The Agreement also establishes guidelines

---

[51]Recently it was reported that the project was temporally halted (EIU, 1997).

[52]Ministry of Finance (1995).

[53]BWIA was bought by the Government from the British Overseas Airways Corporation (BOAC) in 1961. In 1980, BWIA was transformed into Trinidad and Tobago Airways Corporation, by Parliament Act.

[54]Trinidad and Tobago has bilateral aviation agreements with: Aruba, Antigua and Barbuda, Barbados, Belgium, Canada, Cuba, Denmark, France, Jamaica, the Netherlands, Poland, St. Lucia, St. Kitt and Nevis, Sweden, Switzerland, the United Kingdom, the United States.

[55] The Governments of the Bahamas and Jamaica have indicated their wish not to be parties to the Agreement at this time.

on competition, fares and security. Furthermore, CARICOM and the United States at the 1997 CARICOM-United States Summit agreed to set up a regional aviation system including the establishment of safety standards and other regulations. CARICOM is pursuing the establishment of a Regional Aviation Safety Oversight mechanism. The objective is to provide for the utilization by all participating members of Flight Operations and Airworthiness Inspectors employed by individual states, so as to make available their services in a manner consistent with the Standards of Safety set by the International Civil Aviation Organization.

(vi) Tourism

115.   Although the tourism sector in Trinidad and Tobago makes a relatively small contribution to the economy in comparison with other Caribbean islands, the Government recognizes that it has considerable potential to generate employment as well as foreign exchange. The sector accounted for 1.0% of GDP and 1.5% of total employment in 1997. Tourist arrivals increased from 219,836 in 1991 to 324,293 in 1997, during the same period, the number of rooms increased from 2,141 to 3,652.

116.   With a view to encouraging the development of the hotel industry, the Hotel Development Act was enacted in 1963 and subsequently amended to provide incentives to hotel owners and operators. These incentives include: a tax holiday for a period of five to ten years; an accelerated depreciation for equipment owned by the hotelier; a capital allowance in respect of approved capital expenditure; carry-over of losses incurred by owners and/or operators during the tax holiday period; and tax exemption on dividends accruing to the owner/operator. Customs and excise duty exemptions are also granted on building materials and articles of hotel equipment used in connection with the construction and equipping of a hotel project. To be eligible for the incentives, any hotel project with a minimum ten guestrooms, must be approved by the Ministry of Tourism, which grants approval on a discretionary basis depending on the size of the project. The Ministry is responsible for overall tourism policy formulation, monitoring and regulation. TIDCO is responsible for the overall coordination and marketing of Trinidad and Tobago as an international tourist destination, as well as the promotion of investment opportunities and private sector participation.

117.   With a view to promoting the tourism industry as a whole, including the hotel industry, a Tourism Development Bill, repealing the Hotel Development Act, is to be implemented in the latter half of 1998, extending investment incentives to a wide range of activities in the tourism industry. The activities include land and marine transportation, historical site development, production of feature films and international artistic and sports events, marina, diving, water sports and charterboat cruise developments as well as the operation of restaurants, night-clubs and other entertainment facilities that cater mainly to tourists.

REFERENCES

Central Bank of Trinidad and Tobago (1997a), Annual Economic Survey, 1996. Port of Spain.

Central Bank of Trinidad and Tobago (1997b), Quarterly Economic Bulletin, Vol. XXII, No. 4, Port of Spain.

Clarke, L and H. Leon, eds. (1996), Liquidity Management in Liberalizing Economies: Some Experiences from the Caribbean, Caribbean Center for Monetary Studies, University of the West Indies, Trinidad and Tobago.

Divestment Secretariat (1998), Memorandum on Status of Divestment Secretariat, Port of Spain

Economist Intelligence Unit, (1997), Country Report: Trinidad and Tobago, Suriname, Netherlands Antilles, Aruba, London.

Forde, P. and A. Joseph *et al.* (1997), "The Evolution of the Financial Sector in Trinidad and Tobago", in L. Clarke and D. Danns, ed. The Financial Evolution of the Caribbean Community 1970-1996, Caribbean Centre for Monetary Studies, University of the West Indies, Trinidad and Tobago.

International Monetary Fund (1997), "Trinidad and Tobago: Selected Issues", IMF Staff Country Reports No. 97/41, Washington, D.C.

ITU (1997), Telecommunications Development Indicators, International Telecommunications Union, Geneva.

Lloyd's List, various issues.

McCormick (1994), "Caribbean Telecommunications: Privatization and Regulation in the Information Age", Bulletin of East Caribbean Affairs, September 1994, pp.17-27.

MALMR (1997), Agricultural Incentive Progamme - Proposed, Ministry of Agriculture, Land and Marine Resources, Port of Spain.

Ministry of Energy and Energy Industries (1997), Energy Policy Green Paper, Port of Spain.

Ministry of Finance (1995), Executive Report: Divestment of Trinidad and Tobago (BWIA) Airways Corporation, Port of Spain.

Ministry of Finance (1997), Medium Term Policy Framework 1998-2000, Port of Spain.

Ministry of Trade and Industry (1996), Industrial Policy 1996-2000, A Vision for the Industrial Development of Trinidad and Tobago, Port of Spain.

Ministry of Trade and Industry (1997), Trade Policy for Trinidad and Tobago, 1997-2001, Port of Spain.

Price Waterhouse (1997), Trinidad and Tobago Insurance Industry Review 1996, Port of Spain.

Small Business Development Company (1997), Annual Report 1996, Port of Spain.

APPENDIX TABLES

Table AI.1
Exports by groups of products, 1991-96
(US$ million and per cent)

Commodity	1991	1992	1993	1994	1995	1996
Total (US$ million)	1,985.0	1,868.9	1,662.1	1,954.3	2,467.0	2,456.4
Total primary products	71.4	70.0	65.7	56.1	55.2	61.3
Agriculture	6.0	6.3	7.9	6.8	7.2	8.4
Food	5.9	6.2	7.8	6.7	7.1	8.2
1110 Non-alcoholic beverages n.e.s.	0.4	0.5	0.7	0.8	1.4	1.4
0611 Raw beet and cane sugar	1.6	1.8	1.6	1.4	1.7	1.1
1124 Distilled alcoholic beverages	0.5	0.6	0.6	0.6	0.3	0.7
0484 Bread, biscuit, cake, etc.	0.4	0.5	0.4	0.0	0.0	0.6
0813 Vegetable oil residues	0.6	0.4	0.6	0.5	0.3	0.5
Agricultural raw material	0.1	0.1	0.1	0.1	0.1	0.2
Mining	65.4	63.7	57.7	49.2	48.1	52.9
Ores and other minerals	0.1	0.1	0.1	0.1	0.1	0.1
Non-ferrous metals	0.0	0.0	0.0	0.0	0.1	0.2
Fuels	65.3	63.6	57.6	49.2	47.9	52.6
3310 Crude petroleum, etc.	30.7	23.6	21.8	18.1	15.9	17.9
3324 Residual fuel oils	14.2	17.3	13.8	17.5	19.4	13.1
3323 Distillate fuels	7.4	9.8	7.9	0.2	0.2	9.6
3321 Motor spirit, gasoline	5.4	5.3	6.8	5.6	5.4	4.8
3322 White spirit, kerosene	5.5	4.0	4.0	4.0	3.4	3.5
3411 Gas natural	1.0	2.3	2.2	1.7	2.5	2.1
3325 Lubricating oils, greases	0.5	1.2	0.9	1.8	0.8	1.3
Manufactures	28.5	29.9	34.3	24.8	25.6	38.7
Iron & steel	6.5	7.9	8.6	1.4	2.2	8.6
6731 Iron, steel wire rod	4.7	6.1	6.7	0.0	0.0	6.8
6713 Iron, steel powder, shot, etc.	0.8	0.7	0.9	1.2	1.6	1.1
6732 Iron, steel bars, etc.	0.8	0.9	0.7	0.2	0.2	0.5
Chemicals	16.8	15.8	16.8	16.1	15.7	23.6
5136 Inorganic bases etc. n.e.s..	9.1	8.4	8.9	11.8	10.6	12.2
5122 Alcohols, phenols, etc.	3.1	2.3	2.4	0.0	0.0	5.0
5611 Chemical nitrogenous fertilizer	3.4	3.2	3.5	3.0	3.8	4.7
5542 Washing preparations etc.	0.3	0.4	0.5	0.5	0.4	0.5
Other semi-manufactures	2.7	2.8	3.7	3.6	3.6	3.8
6612 Cement	0.7	0.8	1.0	0.8	0.7	0.8
6429 Paper etc. articles n.e.s.	0.4	0.5	0.8	0.9	0.7	0.8
Machinery and transport equipment	1.0	1.3	2.8	1.5	2.1	0.9
Power generating machines	0.0	0.0	0.1	0.0	0.0	0.0
Other non-electrical machinery	0.2	0.4	0.4	0.7	0.7	0.4
Agricultural machinery and tractors	0.0	0.0	0.0	0.0	0.0	0.0
Office machines & telecom. equipment	0.2	0.2	0.5	0.2	0.1	0.1
Other electrical machines	0.4	0.5	0.7	0.2	0.4	0.3
Automotive products	0.1	0.1	0.1	0.1	0.0	0.0
Other transport equipment	0.1	0.1	1.0	0.3	0.8	0.0
Textiles	0.1	0.2	0.3	0.3	0.3	0.1
Clothing	0.3	0.4	0.5	0.5	0.5	0.4
Other consumer goods	1.1	1.5	1.6	1.2	1.4	1.3
Other	0.1	0.1	0.1	19.2	19.1	0.0

Source: UNSD, Comtrade database (SITC Rev.1).

Table AI.2
Imports by groups of products, 1991-96
(US$ million and per cent)

Commodity	1991	1992	1993	1994	1995	1996
Total (US$ million)	**1,667.0**	**1,435.6**	**1,462.9**	**1,133.3**	**1,723.0**	**2,204.5**
Total primary products	**35.8**	**31.8**	**34.6**	**22.8**	**18.6**	**37.8**
Agriculture	17.0	18.6	16.3	16.6	13.5	14.5
Food	15.6	17.5	15.4	16.3	13.2	13.5
Agricultural raw material	1.3	1.2	1.0	0.3	0.3	0.9
Mining	18.9	13.2	18.2	6.2	5.1	23.3
Ores and other minerals	3.0	3.1	1.5	5.3	4.2	3.2
2813 Iron ore, etc. excl. pyrites	2.2	2.3	1.0	4.9	3.8	2.7
Non-ferrous metals	1.2	1.1	0.9	0.3	0.3	0.9
Fuels	14.7	9.0	15.9	0.6	0.5	19.2
3310 Crude petroleum, etc.	12.9	8.2	15.5	0.0	0.0	18.4
Manufactures	63.5	67.5	65.2	53.4	59.0	61.8
Iron & steel	4.1	4.4	3.4	2.8	4.6	3.8
6783 Iron, steel tube, pipe, n.e.s.	1.0	1.2	1.2	0.9	2.1	1.0
Chemicals	12.5	12.5	10.9	6.8	6.4	9.9
5812 Prod. of polymerising etc.	2.0	1.6	1.4	0.1	0.1	1.6
5999 Chemical prods., preps., n.e.s.	1.3	1.2	1.1	0.2	0.2	1.4
5417 Medicaments	2.0	2.1	1.9	2.3	1.5	1.4
Other semi-manufactures	10.7	10.9	9.2	9.5	7.5	9.1
6419 Other paper etc. n.e.s. bulk	0.8	0.9	0.9	1.0	0.8	0.9
Machinery and transport equipment	26.3	29.2	33.1	25.6	32.9	30.8
Power generating machines	1.1	2.4	0.8	1.8	1.2	1.2
Other non-electrical machinery	10.4	10.4	16.9	9.8	16.5	11.7
7191 Heating, cooling, equipment	1.6	1.0	7.2	3.7	10.4	4.2
7199 Machine parts, accessories n.e.s.	2.2	2.1	2.0	0.1	0.1	1.5
7192 Pumps, centrifuges	1.7	1.8	2.5	1.9	1.4	1.4
7193 Mechanical handling equipment.	0.7	1.1	0.9	1.3	1.3	1.2
Agricultural machinery and tractors	0.2	0.4	0.1	0.2	0.2	0.1
Office machines & telecom. equipment	3.0	4.4	3.2	4.0	4.3	3.3
7143 Statistical machines	0.7	0.9	0.8	1.3	1.2	1.2
7249 Telecomm. equipment n.e.s.	1.1	2.1	1.5	1.8	1.9	1.0
Other electrical machines	3.9	4.3	3.1	4.4	3.9	3.6
Automotive products	6.0	6.1	3.8	4.4	4.2	5.5
7321 Pass. motor vehicles. exc. buses	2.5	3.2	2.0	2.3	2.5	3.2
Other transport equipment	1.8	1.6	5.5	1.1	2.9	5.5
7341 Aircraft heavier than air ...	0.1	0.2	1.3	0.2	0.1	3.2
7359 Ships and boats n.e.s.	0.0	0.4	3.5	0.1	1.8	1.6
Textiles	3.3	3.7	3.1	2.5	1.8	2.4
Clothing	0.5	0.2	0.2	0.2	0.4	0.4
Other consumer goods	6.1	6.5	5.2	6.0	5.4	5.5
8930 Articles of plastic n.e.s.	1.2	1.3	1.2	1.5	1.4	1.2
8619 Measuring, controlling instr.	1.3	1.1	0.6	0.8	0.7	1.0
Other	0.7	0.7	0.3	23.7	22.4	0.4

Source: UNSD, Comtrade database (SITC Rev.1).

Table AI.3
Exports by destinations, 1991-96
(US$ million and per cent)

	1991	1992	1993	1994	1995	1996
Total (US$ million)	**1,985.0**	**1,868.9**	**1,662.1**	**1,954.3**	**2,467.0**	**2,456.4**
CARICOM	14.8	16.1	22.2	20.2	22.1	24.8
America	84.8	88.1	88.6	87.5	86.0	88.4
USA	50.0	48.6	47.7	46.4	42.9	48.3
Canada	1.8	1.8	2.0	3.8	1.9	2.2
Other America	33.1	37.7	38.9	37.2	41.2	37.8
Jamaica	2.1	1.7	4.3	6.1	8.4	8.9
Barbados	3.3	3.4	4.4	3.6	3.5	3.6
Guyana	1.5	2.3	3.6	3.1	3.3	3.4
Suriname	1.9	2.2	2.2	1.9	2.0	2.7
Dominican Rep.	0.5	1.8	1.9	1.2	2.2	1.9
St Lucia	1.5	1.6	1.9	1.7	1.5	1.6
Venezuela	2.7	1.7	0.9	1.6	1.2	1.5
Mexico	0.3	1.4	1.1	1.5	1.8	1.5
Grenada	1.1	1.1	1.7	1.3	1.3	1.4
Colombia	1.6	1.8	1.9	2.7	2.4	1.4
Netherlands Antilles	4.2	6.5	3.2	1.5	1.5	1.3
Cuba	0.2	0.6	0.5	0.3	0.8	1.1
St Vincent and the Grenadines	0.9	1.0	1.3	0.0	0.0	1.0
Brazil	2.0	1.0	0.2	0.8	1.6	1.0
Chile	0.4	0.3	0.5	0.9	0.7	0.7
Antigua and Barbuda	0.4	0.8	0.9	1.1	0.7	0.6
Dominica	0.5	0.6	0.6	0.6	0.6	0.6
St Kitts and Nevis	0.6	0.8	0.9	0.5	0.6	0.6
Europe	9.6	5.9	5.1	8.0	10.6	9.9
EU15	9.5	5.8	4.8	7.7	10.1	9.9
France	1.4	1.9	1.5	2.8	2.9	5.5
United Kingdom	2.2	1.7	2.0	1.9	2.5	1.9
Netherlands	1.9	0.5	0.1	1.5	1.7	0.7
EFTA	0.0	0.1	0.2	0.1	0.1	0.0
East Europe	0.0	0.0	0.0	0.0	0.0	0.0
Former USSR	0.0	0.0	0.0	0.0	0.0	0.0
Other Europe	0.0	0.0	0.0	0.3	0.3	0.0
Asia	3.2	2.3	3.1	2.6	1.7	0.4
Middle East	0.1	0.1	0.0	1.2	1.0	0.0
East Asia	2.7	2.1	3.1	1.4	0.5	0.3
South Asia	0.4	0.1	0.0	0.1	0.2	0.1
Oceania	0.0	0.3	0.1	0.0	0.1	0.1
Africa	1.0	1.8	1.7	0.9	0.6	0.3
Sub-Saharan Africa	0.1	1.7	1.5	0.4	0.6	0.3
Other Africa	0.8	0.1	0.2	0.5	0.0	0.0
Other	1.4	1.6	1.3	0.9	1.0	0.9

Source: UNSD, Comtrade database (SITC Rev.3).

Table AI.4
Imports by origin, 1991-96
(US$ million and per cent)

	1991	1992	1993	1994	1995	1996
Total (US$ million)	**1,667.0**	**1,435.6**	**1,462.9**	**1,133.7**	**1,723.7**	**2,204.5**
CARICOM	5.2	5.6	4.1	4.6	3.1	3.8
America	69.8	68.6	69.3	69.4	68.4	70.5
USA	39.6	42.1	39.6	48.3	50.6	38.1
Canada	4.9	5.1	4.9	5.8	5.1	3.6
Other America	25.2	21.3	24.8	15.4	12.7	28.8
Venezuela	13.9	9.7	16.8	2.9	2.9	12.2
Colombia	0.3	0.3	0.3	0.3	0.4	7.0
Brazil	3.8	3.4	2.2	5.3	4.1	3.3
Suriname	0.3	0.3	0.3	0.0	0.0	1.1
Mexico	0.4	0.5	0.3	0.8	0.8	0.9
Jamaica	2.1	2.2	1.4	1.8	1.2	0.9
Barbados	1.5	1.4	1.3	1.6	0.9	0.8
Guyana	0.4	0.5	0.5	0.6	0.6	0.6
Europe	17.2	18.3	20.9	17.7	21.0	18.6
EU15	15.7	16.6	20.0	16.2	19.1	17.2
United Kingdom	7.4	7.8	8.1	8.3	7.2	6.0
Germany	1.9	2.6	6.6	2.1	5.9	5.0
Netherlands	1.8	1.4	1.1	1.4	1.4	1.9
France	1.1	1.2	1.4	0.9	0.9	0.9
Italy	0.8	0.8	0.5	0.8	1.0	0.8
Ireland	0.7	1.0	0.9	0.9	0.6	0.7
Spain	0.3	0.2	0.2	0.3	0.4	0.5
EFTA	0.8	1.2	0.7	1.1	1.2	0.7
Switzerland	0.6	1.1	0.5	1.0	0.8	0.5
East Europe	0.5	0.3	0.1	0.3	0.5	0.6
Former USSR	0.3	0.0	0.0	0.0	0.1	0.0
Other Europe	0.2	0.1	0.1	0.1	0.1	0.1
Asia	10.1	11.5	8.5	11.1	9.1	9.3
Middle East	0.1	0.1	0.1	0.2	0.3	0.1
East Asia	9.8	11.2	8.2	10.5	8.5	8.8
Japan	5.6	6.7	3.8	4.6	3.2	4.0
Korea, Rep. of	0.7	1.1	1.1	1.5	1.9	1.6
China	1.0	1.0	1.1	1.6	1.3	1.4
Chinese Taipei	1.5	1.2	1.1	1.1	0.8	0.8
South Asia	0.2	0.2	0.3	0.4	0.4	0.4
Oceania	1.3	1.3	1.1	1.2	0.8	0.7
Africa	1.2	0.2	0.1	0.2	0.4	0.8
Sub-Saharan Africa	0.9	0.1	0.0	0.0	0.0	0.6
Nigeria	0.6	0.0	0.0	0.0	0.0	0.6
Other Africa	0.3	0.1	0.0	0.1	0.4	0.2
Other	0.5	0.2	0.2	0.3	0.3	0.1

Source: UNSD, Comtrade database (SITC Rev.3).

Table AIII.1
Items on CARICOM List A (exeptions to CET), 1997
(Per cent)

HS No.	Description	Negotiated tariff rate	CET
0201	MEAT OF BOVINE ANIMALS, FRESH OR CHILLED		
020110	Carcasses and half-carcasses	15	40
0201201	Other cuts with bone in: brisket	15	40
0201209	Other cuts with bone in: other	15	40
0201301	Boneless: tenderloin	15	40
0201302	Boneless: sirloin	15	40
0201303	Boneless: minced (ground)	15	40
0201309	Boneless: other		40
0202	MEAT OF BOVINE ANIMALS, FROZEN		
020210	Carcasses and half-carcasses	15	40
0202201	Other cuts with bone in: brisket	15	40
0202209	Other cuts with bone in: other	15	40
0202301	Boneless: tenderloin	15	40
0202302	Boneless: sirloin	15	40
0202303	Boneless: minced (ground)	15	40
0202309	Boneless: other	15	40
0203	MEAT OF SWINE, FRESH, CHILLED OR FROZEN		
020311	Fresh or chilled: carcasses and half-carcasses	40	40
020312	Fresh or chilled: hams, shoulders and cuts thereof, with bone in	40	40
020319	Fresh or chilled: other	40	40
020321	Frozen: carcasses and half-carcasses	40	40
020322	Frozen: hams, shoulders and cuts thereof, with bone in	40	40
020329	Frozen: other	40	40
0204	MEAT OF SHEEP OR GOATS, FRESH, CHILLED OR FROZEN		
020410	Carcasses and half-carcasses of lamb, fresh or chilled	15	40
020421	Other meat of sheep, fresh or chilled: carcasses and half-carcasses	15	40
020422	Other meat of sheep, fresh or chilled: other cuts with bone in	15	40
020423	Other meat of sheep, fresh or chilled: boneless	15	40
020430	Carcasses and half-carcasses of lamb, frozen	15	40
020441	Other meat of sheep, frozen: carcasses and half-carcasses	15	40
020442	Other meat of sheep, frozen: other cuts with bone in	15	40
020443	Other meat of sheep, frozen: boneless	15	40
020450	Meat of goats	15	40
0207	MEAT AND EDIBLE OFFAL, OF THE POULTRY OF HDG #01.05 (...)		
020711	Of fowls (...): not cut in pieces, fresh or chilled	40	40
020712	Of fowls (...): not cut in pieces, frozen	40	40
020713	Of fowls (...): cuts and offal, fresh or chilled	40	40
0207141	Of fowls (...): cuts and offal, frozen: back and necks	40	40
0207142	Of fowls (...): cuts and offal, frozen: wings	40	40
0207143	Of fowls (...): cuts and offal, frozen: livers	40	40
0207149	Of fowls (...): cuts and offal, frozen: other	40	40
020724	Of turkeys: not cut in pieces, fresh or chilled	40	40
020725	Of turkeys: not cut in pieces, frozen	40	40
020726	Of turkeys: cuts and offal, fresh or chilled	40	40
0207271	Of turkeys: cuts and offal, frozen: backs, necks and wings	40	40

Table AIII.1 (cont'd)

HS No.	Description	Negotiated tariff rate	CET
0207279	Of turkeys: cuts and offal, frozen: other	40	40
020732	Of ducks (...): not cut in pieces, fresh or chilled	40	40
020733	Of ducks (...): not cut in pieces, frozen	40	40
020734	Of ducks (...): fatty livers, fresh or chilled	40	40
020735	Of ducks (...): other, fresh or chilled	40	40
020736	Of ducks (...): other, frozen		
0305	FISH, DRIED, SALTED OR IN BRINE; SMOKED FISH, (...)		
030542	Smoked fish incl. fillets: herrings	0	30-35
0305491	Smoked fish incl. fillets: other: cod, mackerel and alewives	30	30-35
030551	Dried fish (...) not smoked: cod	30	30-35
0305591	Dried fish (...) not smoked: other: mackerel	0	30-35
0305592	Dried fish (...) not smoked: other: herrings, alewives, saithe, pollock, haddock and hake	0	30-35
0305610	Fish Salted (...): herrings	0	30-35
0305620	Fish Salted (...): cod	0	30-35
0305691	Fish Salted (...): other: mackerel	25	30-35
0305692	Fish Salted (...): other: herrings, alewives, saithe, pollock, haddock and hake	25	30-35
0401	MILK AND CREAM NOT CONCENTRATED NOR CONTAINING ADDED (...)		
040110	Of a fat content, by weight, not exceeding 1%	40	40
040120	Of a fat content, by weight, exceeding 1% but not exceeding 6%	40	40
040130	Of a fat content, by weight, exceeding 6%	40	40
0402	MILK AND CREAM, CONCENTRATED OR CONTAINING ADDED SUGAR (...)		
040210	In powder, granules or other solid forms, of a fat content by weight, not exceeding 1.5%	5	30-35
040220	In powder, granules (...) exceeding 1.5%: Not containing added sugar or other sweetening matter	5	30-35
040229	In powder, granules (...) exceeding 1.5%: other	5	30-35
042091	Other: not containing added sugar or other sweetening matter	25	30-35
0402991	Other: condensed milk	25	30-35
0407	BIRDS' EGGS, IN SHELL, FRESH, PRESERVED OR COOKED		
0407002	Hatching eggs, not for breeder flock	25	40
0701	POTATOES, FRESH OR CHILLED		
070190	Other, not including seed potatoes	0	40
0703	ONIONS, SHALLOTS, GARLIC, LEEKS AND OTHER ALLIAC (...)		
0703101	Onions	0	40
0710	VEGETABLES (UNCOOKED OR COOKED BY STEAMING OR (...), FROZEN		
071010	Potatoes	0	40
1005	MAIZE (CORN)		
100590	Other, not seed corn	0	40
1201009	Soya beans, whether or not broken: other not for sowing	0	5
1701	CANE OR BEET SUGAR AND CHEMICALLY PURE SUCROSE IN SOLID FOR		
1701991	Icing sugar	25	25
1701999	Other sugar (excl. raw sugar and sugar containing added flavouring or colouring matter)	40	40

Table AIII.1 (cont'd)

HS No.	Description	Negotiated tariff rate	CET
2710	PETROLEUM OILS AND OILS OBTAINED FROM BITUMINOUS MINERALS, (...)		
2710221	Illuminating kerosene: exported under the processing agreement	30	35
2710229	Illuminating kerosene: other	30	35
2804	HYDROGEN, RARE GASES AND OTHER NON-METALS		
280421	Rare gases: Argon	10	10
3215	PRINTING INK, WRITING OR DRAWING INK AND OTHER INKS, WHETHER OR NOT (...)		
3215909	Other: Other inks, not including writing or drawing ink	25	25
3923	ARTICLES FOR THE CONVEYANCE OR PACKING OF GOODS, OF PLASTIC; STOPPERS (...)		
3923109	Boxes (...): other, not including egg boxes	15	25
3923901	Other: cups	15	25
4819	CARTONS, BOXES, CASES, BAGS, AND OTHER PACKING CONTAINERS OF PAPER, (...)		
4819409	Other sacks and bags, including cones: other, printed	10	25
6908	GLAZED CERAMIC FLAGS AND PAVING, HEARTH OR WALL TILES; (...)		
6908101	Tiles (...)	25	25
6910	CERAMIC SINKS, WASH BASINS, WASH BASIN PEDESTALS, BATHS, BIDETS, WATER (...)		
6910101	Of porcelain or china: sinks	25	25
6910102	Of porcelain or china: wash basins and wash basin pedestals	25	25
6910103	Of porcelain or china: baths	25	25
6910104	Of porcelain or china: bidets	25	25
6910105	Of porcelain or china: water closet pans (lavatory bowls)	25	25
6910106	Of porcelain or china: flushing cisterns (tanks)	25	25
6910107	Of porcelain or china: urinals	25	25
6910108	Of porcelain or china: complete lavatory sets	25	25
6910109	Of porcelain or china: other	25	25
691090	Other	25	25
8450	HOUSEHOLD OR LAUNDRY-TYPE WASHING MACHINES, INCL. MACHINES (...)		
8450111	Household or laundry-type washing machines: full automatic: for domestic use	30	30-35
8450121	Household or laundry-type washing machines: other machines(...): for domestic use	30	30-35
8450191	Household or laundry-type washing machines: other: for domestic use	30	30-35

Source: Data provided by the authorities and CARICOM Secretariat.

Table AIII.2

Items on CARICOM List C, 1997

(Per cent)

HS No.	Description	Negotiated tariff rate	CET
0101	LIVE HORSES, ASSES, MULES AND HINNES		
0101192	Other: Race horses, not for breeding	2.5	0
2106	FOOD PREPARATIONS NOT ELSEWHERE SPECIFIED OR INCLUDED		
2106908	Other: Preparations (…) of types used in the manufacture of beverages with an alcoholic (…)	$35.00/l	20
2203	BEER MADE FROM MALT		
2203001	Beer	$4.75/l	35
2203002	Stout	$5/l	35
2203009	Other	$5/l	35
2204	WINE OR FRESH GRAPES, INCLUDING FORTIFIED WINES, GRAPE MUST (EXCEPT 2009)		
220410	Sparkling wine	$40.00/l	20
220421	Other wine; grape must (...): in containers holding 2 litres or less	5	20
2204291	Grape must with fermentation prevented/arrested by the addition of alcohol	5	5
2204299	Other wine	$25.00/l	20
220430	Other grape must	5	. 5
2205	VERMOUTH AND OTHER WINE OF FRESH GRAPES FLAVOURED W/ PLANTS (…)		
220510	In containers holding 2 litres or less	$30.00/l	20
220590	Other	$30.00/l	20
2206001	Other fermented beverages (for example, cider, perry, mead) (…):shandy	$20.00/l	20
2206009	Other fermented beverages (for example, cider, perry, mead) (…): other	$20.00/l	20
2207	UNDENATURED ETHYL ALCOHOL OF AN ALCOHOLIC STRENGTH (>80%)		
220710	Undenatured ethyl alcohol of an alcoholic strength by vol. of 80% vol. or higher	$14.30/l	20
220720	Ethyl alcohol and other spirit (...): Methylated spirits (…)	$1.32/l	20
2208	UNDENATURED ETHYL ALCOHOL (<80%), COMPOUND ALCOHOLIC PREPARATIONS (…)		
2208201	Spirits obtained by distilling grape wine/grape marc: brandy, in bottles of a strength <=46% vol.	$35.00/l	20
2208209	Spirits obtained by distilling grape wine/grape marc: other	$35.00/l[a]	20
2208301	Whiskies: In bottles of a strength not exceeding 46% vol.	$35.00/l	20
2208309	Whiskies: other	$35.00/l[a]	20
2208401	Rum and tafia: in bottles of strength not exceeding 46% vol.	$35.00/l	35
2208409	Rum and tafia: other	$35.00/l[a]	35
2208501	Gin and Geneva: in bottles of strength not exceeding 46% vol.	$35.00/l	20
2208509	Gin and Geneva: other	$35.00/l[a]	20
220860	Vodka	$40.00/l	20
220870	Liqueurs and cordials	$40.00/l	20
2208901	Other: aromatic bitters used as a flavouring agent for food and beverages	$1.10/l	35
2208902	Other: other aromatic bitters	$14.30/l	20
2208909	Other: other	$14.30/l	20
2402	CIGARS, CHEROOTS, CIGARILLOS AND CIGARETTES, OF TOBACCO (...)		
240210	Cigars, cheroots and cigarillos containing tobacco	30	25
240220	Cigarettes containing tobacco	30	35
240290	Other	30	35
2403	OTHER MANUFACTURED TOBACCO AND MANUFACTURED TOBACCO SUBSTITUTE; (...)		
240310	Smoking tobacco, whether or not containing tobacco substitutes in any proportion	30	25
240391	Other: homogenised or "reconstituted" tobacco	30	25
2403991	Other: other: snuff	30	25
2403999	Other: other: other	30	25
2710	PETROLEUM OILS AND OILS OBTAINED FROM BITUMINOUS MINERALS, OTHER THAN (…)		
2710131	Motor spirit (gasolene): exported under the processing agreement	30	10

Table AIII.2 (cont'd)

HS No.	Description	Negotiated tariff rate	CET
2710139	Motor spirit (gasolene): other	30	10
2710231	Vaporising oil or white spirit: exported under the processing agreement	30	10
2710239	Vaporising oil or white spirit: other	30	10
2710311	Gas oils: diesel oils: exported under the processing agreement	30	10
2710319	Gas oils: diesel oils: other	30	10
2710391	Other: exported under the processing agreement	30	10
2710399	Other: other	30	10
2710421	Fuel oils, n.e.s.: bunker "C" grade fuel oil: exported under the processing agreement	30	10
2710429	Fuel oils, n.e.s.: bunker "C" grade fuel oil: other	30	10
2710491	Other fuel oils: exported under the processing agreement	30	10
2710499	Other fuel oils: other	30	10
271092	Lubricating oils	30	25
271093	Lubricating greases	30	25
2713	PETROLEUM COKE, PETROLEUM BITUMEN AND OTHER RESIDUES OF PETROLEUM (...)		
271320	Petroleum bitumen	30	10
271390	Other residues of petroleum oils or of oils obtained from bituminous minerals	30	10
2714	BITUMEN AND ASPHALT, NATURAL; BITUMINOUS OR OIL SHALE AND TAR SANDS, (...)		
271410	Bituminous or oil shale and tar sands	30	10
2714901	Other: natural bitumen	30	10
2714903	Other: asphalites and asphaltic rocks	30	10
2715	BITUMINOUS MIXTURES BASED ON NATURAL ASPHALT, ON NATURAL BITUMEN, (...)		
2715001	Cut-backs	30	10
2715009	Other	30	10
3706	CINEMATOGRAPH FILM, EXPOSED AND DEVELOPED, WHETHER OR NOT (...)		
370610	Of a width of 35mm or more	$3.00/100m	0
370690	Other	$3.00/100m	0
4011	NEW PNEUMATIC TYRES, OR RUBBER		
401110	Of a kind used on motor cars (including station wagons and racing cars)	30	25
4012	RETREADED OR USED PNEUMATIC TYRES OF RUBBER; SOLID OR CUSHION TYRES, (...)		
4012101	Retreaded tyres: Of a kind used on motor cars (including stations wagons and racing cars)	30	25
4012102	Retreaded tyres: of a kind used on buses or lorries	30	25
4013	INNER TUBES OF RUBBER		
4013101	Of a kind used on motor cars (including station wagons and racing cars)	10	5
4013102	Of a kind used on buses or lorries	10	5
6813	FRICTION MATERIAL & ARTICLES THEREOF (FOR EX., SHEETS, ROLLS, STRIPS, (...))		
681310	Brake linings and pads	25	5
7007	SAFETY GLASS, CONSISTING OF TOUGHENED (TEMPERED) OR LAMINATED GLASS		
7007111	Motor car windscreens	20	5
7007211	Motor car windscreens	20	5
7009	GLASS MIRRORS, WHETHER OR NOT FRAMED, INCLUDING REAR-VIEW MIRROR		
700910	Glass mirrors, whether or not framed: rear-view mirrors for vehicles	20	5
7013	GLASS WARE OF A KIND USED FOR TABLE, KITCHEN, TOILET, OFFICE, INDOOR (...)		
70132100	Glassware: drinking glasses other than of glass-ceramics: of lead crystal	25	10
70133100	Glassware of a kind used for table or kitchen purposes other than of glass-ceramics: of lead crystal	25	10
7014	SIGNALLING GLASSWARE & OPTICAL ELEMENTS OF GLASS (...) NOT OPTICALLY WORKED		
7014001	Signalling glassware & optical elements of glass, for road motor vehicles	20	5
7101	PEARLS, NATURAL OR CULTURED, WHETHER OR NOT WORKED OR GRADED BUT (...)		
7101101	Natural pearls: temporarily strung for convenience of transport	30	25
7101109	Natural pearls: other	30	25

Table AIII.2 (cont'd)

HS No.	Description	Negotiated tariff rate	CET
7101211	Cultured pearls: unworked: temporarily strung for convenience of transport	30	25
7101219	Cultured pearls: unworked: other	30	25
7101221	Cultured pearls: worked: temporarily strung for convenience of transport	30	25
7101229	Cultured pearls: worked: other	30	25
7102	DIAMONDS, WHETHER OR NOT WORKED, BUT NOT MOUNTED OR SET		
710210	Unsorted	30	25
710221	Industrial: unworked or simply sawn, cleaved or bruted	30	25
710229	Industrial: other	30	25
710231	Non-industrial: unworked or simply sawn, cleaved or bruted	30	25
710239	Non-industrial: other	30	25
7103	PRECIOUS STONES (OTHER THAN DIAMONDS) AND SEMI-PRECIOUS STONES, WHETHER (…)		
7103101	Unworked or simply sawn or roughly shaped: temporarily strung for convenience of transport	30	25
7103109	Unworked or simply sawn or roughly shaped: other	30	25
7103911	Otherwise worked: Rubies, sapphires and emeralds: temp. strung for convenience of transport	30	25
7103919	Otherwise worked: rubies, sapphires and emeralds: other	30	25
7103991	Other: temporarily strung for convenience of transport	30	25
7103999	Other: other	30	25
7104	SYNTHETIC OR RECONSTRUCTED PRECIOUS OR SEMI-PRECIOUS STONES, WHETHER (…)		
710410	Piezo-electric quartz	30	25
710420	Other, unworked or simply sawn or roughly shaped	30	25
710490	Other	30	25
7113	ARTICLES OF JEWELLERY AND PARTS THEREOF, OF PRECIOUS METAL OR OF METAL (…)		
711311	Of silver whether or not plated or clad with other precious metal	30	10
7113191	Of other precious metal, whether or not plated or clad with precious metal: gold	30	10
7113199	Of other precious metal, whether or not plated or clad with precious metal: gther	30	10
711320	Of base metal clad with precious metal	30	10
7114	ARTICLES OF GOLDSMITHS' OR SILVERSMITHS' WARES AND PARTS THEREOF, OF (…)		
711411	Of silver whether or not plated or clad with other precious metal	30	10
711419	Of other precious metal, whether or not plated or clad with precious metal	30	10
711420	Of base metal clad with precious metal	30	10
7116	ARTICLES OF NATURAL OR CULTURED PEARLS, PRECIOUS OR SEMI-PRECIOUS STONES (...)		
711610	Of natural or cultured pearls	30	10
711620	Of precious or semi-precious stones (natural, synthetic or reconstructed)	30	10
7117	IMITATION JEWELLERY		
711711	Of base metal, whether or not plated with precious metal: cuff-links and studs	30	10
711719	Of base metal, whether or not plated with precious metal: other	30	10
711790	Other	30	10
7320	SPRINGS AND LEAVES FOR SPRINGS, OF IRON OR STEEL		
7320101	Leaf-springs and leaves therefor: For road motor vehicles	20	5
7320201	Helical springs: For road motor vehicles	20	5
7320901	Other: for road motor vehicles	20	5
8302	BASE METAL MOUNTINGS, FITTINGS & SIMILAR ARTICLES SUITABLE FOR FURNITURE, (...)		
830230	Other mountings, fittings and similar articles suitable for motor vehicles	20	5
8407	SPARK-IGNITION RECIPROCATING OR ROTARY INTERNAL COMBUSTION PISTON ENGINES		
840733	Of a cylinder capacity exceeding 250 cc but not exceeding 1000 cc	30	5
840734	Of a cylinder capacity exceeding 1000 cc	30	5
8408	COMPRESSION-IGNITION INTERNAL COMBUSTION PISTON ENGINES (...)		
840820	Engines of a kind used for the propulsion of vehicles of Chapter 87	30	5

Table AIII.2 (cont'd)

HS No.	Description	Negotiated tariff rate	CET
8409	PARTS SUITABLE FOR USE SOLELY OR PRINCIPALLY WITH THE ENGINES OF (..)		
8409911	Suitable for use solely or principally with sparkignition internal (…): for road motor vehicles	20	5
8409991	Other: for road motor vehicles	20	5
8413	PUMPS FOR LIQUIDS, WHETHER OR NOT FILLED WITH A MEASURING DEVICE; (...)		
841330	Fuel, lubricating or cooling medium pumps for internal combustion piston engines	20	5
8421	CENTRIFUGES, INCL. CENTRIFUGAL DRYERS; FILTERING OR PURIFYING (...)		
8421231	Oil filters	30	25
8421232	Petrol filters	30	25
842131	Intake air filters for internal combustion engines	30	25
8483	TRANSMISSION SHAFTS (...) AND CRANKS; BEARING HOUSING & PLAIN SHAFT (...)		
8483101	Transmission shafts (…) and cranks: For road motor vehicle engines	20	5
8483201	Bearing housings, incorporating ball or roller bearings: for road motor vehicle engines	20	5
8483301	Bearing housing, not incorporating ball or roller bearings; plain shaft bearings: for road motor vehicle engines	20	5
8483401	Gears and gearing, other than toothed wheels (…): for road motor vehicle engines	20	5
8483501	Flywheel and pulleys, including pulley blocks: for road motor vehicle engines	20	5
8483901	Parts: for road motor vehicle engines	20	5
8511	ELECTRICAL IGNITION OR STARTING EQUIPMENT OF A KIND USED FOR (…)		
851110	Sparking plugs	10	5
851120	Ignition magnetos; magneto-dynamos; magnetic flywheels	20	5
851130	Distributors; ignition coils	20	5
851140	Starter motors and dual purpose starter-generators	20	5
851150	Other generators	20	5
851180	Other equipment	20	5
851190	Parts	10	5
8512	ELECTRICAL LIGHTING OF SIGNALLING EQUIPMENT (...), WIND-SCREEN WIPERS, (...)		
851220	Other lighting or visual signalling equipment	25	25
851230	Sound signalling equipment	25	25
851240	Windscreen wipers, defrosters and demisters	25	25
8518	MICROPHONES AND STANDS THEREFOR; LOUD-SPEAKERS, WHETHER OR NOT (...)		
851840	Audio-frequency electric amplifiers	30	25
851910	Coin or disc-operated record players	30	25
8521	VIDEO RECORDING OR REPRODUCING APPARATUS		
852110	Magnetic tape-type	30	25
852190	Other	30	25
8524	RECORDS, TAPES AND OTHER RECORDED MEDIA FOR SOUND OR OTHER SIMILARLY (...)		
8524991	Other: audio compact discs	30	25
8524992	Other: other compact discs	30	25
8539	ELECTRIC FILAMENT OR DISCHARGE LAMPS, INCL. SEALED BEAM LAMP (...)		
853910	Sealed beam lamp units	30	25
8543	ELECTRICAL MACHINES AND APPARATUS, HAVING INDIVIDUAL FUNCTIONS (...)		
8543891	Sound mixing units (equalizers) for domestic use	30	25
8702	PUBLIC-TRANSPORT TYPE PASSENGER MOTOR VEHICLES		
870210	With compression-ignition internal combustion piston engine (diesel or semi-diesel)		
8702102	Other coaches, buses and mini-buses, of a seating capacity not exceeding 21 persons	10	5
8702104	Other coaches, buses and mini-buses, of a seating capacity >21 persons but <= 29 persons	10	5
8702106	Other coaches, buses and mini-buses, of a seating capacity exceeding 29 persons	10	5
8702109	Other	10	5
8702902	Other: other coaches, buses and mini-buses, of a seating capacity <21 persons	10	5
8702904	Other: other coaches, buses and mini-buses, of a seating capacity >21 but <=29 persons	10	5

Table AIII.2 (cont'd)

HS No.	Description	Negotiated tariff rate	CET
8702906	Other: other coaches, buses and mini-buses, of a seating capacity >29 persons	10	5
8702909	Other: other	10	5
8703	MOTOR CARS AND OTHER MOTOR VEHICLES PRINCIPALLY DESIGNED FOR THE (...)		
8703219	Other vehicles, with spark-ignition (...): of a cylinder capacity not exceeding 1,000cc: other	20	25
8703229	Other vehicles, with spark-ignition (...): of a cylinder capacity >1,000cc but <=1,500cc: other	20	25
8703232	Other vehicles, with spark-ignition (...): of a cylinder capacity >1,500cc but <=1,800cc	20	25
8703233	Other vehicles, with spark-ignition (...): of a cylinder capacity >1,800cc but <=2,000cc	25	25
8703234	Other vehicles, with spark-ignition (...): of a cylinder capacity >2,000cc but <=3,000cc	30	25
8703249	Of a cylinder capacity exceeding 3,000cc: other	30	25
8703319	Other vehicles, with compression-ignition (...): of a cylinder capacity <=1,500cc: other	30	25
8703322	Other vehicles, with compression-ignition (...): of a cylinder capacity >1,500cc but <=2,000cc: other	30	25
8703324	Other vehicles, with compression-ignition (...): of a cylinder capacity >2,000cc but <=2,500cc: other	30	25
8703339	Other vehicles, with compression-ignition (...): of a cylinder capacity >2,500cc: other	30	25
870390	Other	30	25
8704	MOTOR VEHICLES FOR THE TRANSPORT OF GOODS		
870410	Dumpers designed for off-highway use	10	5
8704219	Other (...compression-ignition): <=5 tonnes: other	10	5
8704229	Other (...compression-ignition): >5 tonnes but <=20 tonnes: other	10	5
8704319	Other (...spark-ignition): <=5 tonnes: other	10	5
8704329	Other (...spark-ignition): >5 tonnes: other	10	5
870490	Other	10	5
8708	PARTS AND ACCESSORIES OF THE MOTOR VEHICLES OF HEADING 87.01 TO 87.05		
870810	Bumpers and parts thereof	30	25
870821	Other parts and accessories (...): safety seat belts	30	25
870829	Other parts and accessories (...): other	30	25
8708319	Brakes and servo-brakes (...): mounted brake linings: other	30	25
8708399	Brakes and servo-brakes (...): other: other	30	25
8708409	Gear boxes: other	30	25
8708509	Drive-axles with differential, whether or not provided with other transmission components: other	30	25
8708609	Non-driving axles and parts thereof: other	30	25
8708709	Road wheels and parts and accessories thereof: other	30	25
8708809	Suspension shock-absorbers: other	30	25
8708919	Other parts and accessories: radiators: other	30	25
8708929	Other parts and accessories: silencers and exhaust pipes: other	30	25
8708939	Other parts and accessories: clutches and parts thereof: other	30	25
8708949	Other parts and accessories: steering wheels, steering columns and steering boxes: other	30	25
8708999	Other parts and accessories: other: other	30	25
9006	PHOTOGRAPHIC (...) CAMERAS; PHOTOGRAPHIC FLASHLIGHT APPARATUS (...)		
900640	Instant print cameras	25	25
900651	Other cameras: with a through-the-lens view-finder (...), for roll film of a width <=35mm	25	25
900652	Other cameras: other, for roll film of a width <35mm	25	25
900653	Other cameras: other, for roll film of a width of 35mm	25	25
900659	Other cameras: other	25	25
9101	WRIST-WATCHES, POCKET-WATCHES AND OTHER WATCHES, INCL. STOP- (...)		25
910111	Wrist-watches (...): with mechanical display only	30	25
910112	Wrist-watches (...): with opto-electronic display only	30	25
910119	Wrist-watches (...): other	30	25
910121	Other wrist-watches (...): with automatic winding	30	25
910129	Other wrist-watches (...): other	30	25
910191	Other: electrically operated	30	25
9102	WRIST-WATCHES, POCKET-WATCHES AND OTHER WATCHES, INCL. STOP-(...)		
910211	Wrist-watches (...): With mechanical display only	30	25
910212	Wrist-watches (...): with opto-electronic display only	30	25

Table AIII.2 (cont'd)

HS No.	Description	Negotiated tariff rate	CET
910219	Wrist-watches (...): other	30	25
910221	Other wrist-watches (...): with automatic winding	30	25
910229	Other wrist-watches (...): other	30	25
910291	Other wrist-watches (...): electrically operated	30	25
910299	Other	30	25
9103	CLOCKS WITH WATCH MOVEMENTS, EXCL. CLOCKS OF HEADING 91.04		
910310	Electrically operated	30	25
910390	Other	30	25
910400	Instrument panel clocks and clocks of a similar type for vehicles, aircraft, spacecraft or vessels	30	25
9105	OTHER CLOCKS		
910511	Alarm clocks: Electrically operated	30	25
910519	Alarm clocks: other	30	25
910521	Wall clocks: electrically operated	30	25
910529	Wall clocks: other	30	25
910591	Other: electrically operated	30	25
910599	Other: other	30	25
9108	WATCH MOVEMENTS, COMPLETE AND ASSEMBLED		
910811	Electrically operated: with mechanical display only or with a device to which a mechanical (...)	30	25
910812	Electrically operated: with opto-electronic display only	30	25
910819	Electrically operated: other	30	25
910820	With automatic winding	30	25
910891	Other: measuring 33.8mm or less	30	25
910899	Other: other	30	25
9110	COMPLETE WATCH OR CLOCK MOVEMENTS, UNASSEMBLED OR PARTLY (...)		
911011	Of watches: complete movements, unassembled or partly assembled (movements sets)	30	25
911012	Of watches: incomplete movements, assembled	30	25
911019	Of watches: rough movements	30	25
9113	WATCH STRAPS, WATCH BANDS AND WATCH BRACELETS, AND PARTS THEREOF		
911310	Of precious metal or of metal clad with precious metal	30	25
930200	Revolvers and pistols, other than those of Heading No. 93.03 or 9304.00	30	25
9303	OTHER FIREARM AND SIMILAR DEVICES WHICH OPERATE BY THE FIRING OF AN (...)		25
930310	Muzzle-loading firearms	30	25
930320	Other sporting, hunting or target-shooting shotguns, including combination shotgun-rifles	30	25
930330	Other sporting, hunting or target-shooting rifles	30	25
9303909	Other: other		
930400	Other arms (for example, spring, air or gas guns ...),excl. Heading 93.07	30	25
9305	PARTS AND ACCESSORIES OF ARTICLES OF HEADING 93.01 TO 93.04		
930510	Of revolvers or pistols	30	25
930521	Of shotguns or rifles of Heading 93.03: shotgun barrels	30	25
930529	Of shotguns or rifles of Heading 93.03: other	30	25
930590	Other	30	25

a   Of alcohol by volume.

Source: Data provided by the authorities and CARICOM Secretariat.

Table AIII.3
Conditional duty exemptions for approved industries (Third Schedule of the Customs Act)

I.	For approved industry
1.	Processing, canning and packaging food products
2.	Manufacture and packaging of beverages
3.	Manufacture and packaging of wax, wax products and candles
4.	Manufacture of soap
5.	Manufacture of textiles, textiles fabrics including finishing and printing; and garments and other textiles manufactures
6.	Manufacture of building products
7.	Manufacture of leather and leather products
8.	Manufacture and packaging of headgear
9.	Manufacture of footwear
10.	Manufacture of telephonic and telegraphic materials
11.	Manufacture of electrical goods, electrical and electronic equipment, applicants and apparatus.
12.	Manufacture of non-electrical stoves, ranges, heaters and refrigerators
13.	Manufacture and packaging drugs, pharmaceutical and medical preparations
14.	Manufacture, processing, packaging, storing and transporting of petroleum and petroleum products and petrochemicals
15.	Manufacture and packaging or drinking straws
16.	Manufacture of rope, twine and cordage
17.	Manufacture of mirrors
18.	Manufacture of containers for compressed or liquified gas
19.	Manufacture of welding electrodes
20.	Manufacture of jewellery
21.	Printing and engraving industry including blank lithographic sheets
22.	Manufacture of pens, pencils, chalk and crayon
23.	Manufacture of rubbing compound
24.	Manufacture of cleansing compound
25.	Manufacture of travel goods
26.	Manufacture of glass and glass products
27.	Manufacture of hoisting tackle
28.	Manufacture of spectacles and spectacle frames.
29.	Manufacture of ceramics and ceramic products
30.	Manufacture of crown corks and bottle closures
31.	Boat and ship building and repairs industry
32.	Manufacture of industrial chemicals including brake fluids
33.	Manufacture of stock feed
34.	Manufacture of alumina, aluminium and aluminium products
35.	Manufacture of stock feed
36.	Manufacture of fertilizers
37.	Production and packaging of wood and wood products
38.	Treatment (including impregnation and preservation) of wood
39.	Manufacture of anti-corrosion products
40.	Manufacture of packaging of matches
41.	Manufacture or repair of containers and other packaging materials and parts for packaging
42.	Manufacture of tyres and tubes and recapping. remoulding and retreading of tyres
43.	Manufacture of detergents and other cleansing and sanitising agents
44.	Manufacture and packaging of furniture
45.	Manufacture of toys
46.	Manufacture of packaging of paints, enamels, varnishes, lacquers, synthetic resins and related goods
47.	Manufacture of plastics and plastic products
48.	Manufacture of gramophone records and other sound or similar recordings
49.	Manufacture and assembly of plants and organs
50.	Manufacture of wire products
51.	Manufacture and packaging of cosmetics, perfumery and toilet preparations
52.	Manufacture of hosiery
53.	Manufacture of umbrellas
54.	Assembly and /or manufacture of motor vehicles or parts thereof

Table AIII.3 (cont'd)

55.	Manufacture and packaging of paper and paper products
56.	Manufacture of tobacco and tobacco products
57.	Manufacture (including blending) of vegetable oils
58.	Manufacture of adhesives
59.	Manufacture of adhesive tapes
60.	Manufacture of basketwork
61.	Manufacture of polishes, cremes and other products for polishing/preserving floors, furniture, metal, footwear and like goods
62.	Manufacture of brooms and brushes
63.	Manufacture of slide fasteners
64.	Manufacture of artificial flowers
65.	Manufacture of cutlery including razor blades
66.	Manufacture of foams and foams products
67.	Manufacture and processing of iron and steel products
68.	Manufacture of products made from non-ferrous metals
69.	Manufacture of disinfectants, insecticides, fungicides, weed killers and similar products
70.	Building materials for first installation or approved extension in approved industrial enterprises
71.	Polishing diamonds
72.	Printing of colour films
73.	Production of motion pictures
74.	Manufacture and repair of machinery
75.	Manufacture of printing ink
76.	Manufacture of gramophones and cassette and cassette tape recorders
77.	Manufacture of asphalt-based products
78.	Manufacture of essential oils and oleo-resins
79.	Manufacture of carbon and carbon-passed products
80.	Information services and processing
81.	Production of items using bio-technology
82.	Manufacture of products utilizing local wastes and industry by-products
83.	Manufacture of handicraft
II.	**For approved agriculture, forestry and fisheries**
1.	Agricultural machinery, equipment, implements and tools (including poultry farming equipment)
2.	Medicines and minerals supplement for livestock
3.	Machinery and equipment for irrigation and drainage purposes
4.	Incubators and other poultry farming equipment and such other goods as are intended solely for use in the breeding and rearing of poultry
5.	Bee hives and bee-keeping apparatus
6.	Vats, tanks and parts for water storage
7.	Fish, crustacea, mollusc caught by boats operating out of national countries
8.	Textiles for protecting agricultural products
9.	Eggs for hatching, semen for artificial semination imported in accordance with a permit issued by the proper authorities
10.	Boats, and boat equipment and fuels for fishing
11.	Other goods intended solely for use in approved agriculture, livestock, forestry and fisheries
12.	Pipes having an internal diameter exceeding 50mm and pipe fittings, except plastic pipes
III.	**For approved hotels**
1.	Building materials for first installation or approved extension and renovations
2.	Equipment and appliances for equipping hotels initially or for approved extensions and renovations
IV.	**For approved mining purposes**
1.	Machinery, equipment and materials for exploration and extraction of minerals, including natural gas
2.	Machinery, equipment and materials for mining, quarrying and finishing stone products
3.	Machinery, equipment and materials for the liquefaction and transportation of natural gas
V.	**For other approved purposes**
1.	Boats, boats and navigation equipment, marine engines for approved services
2.	Equipment for use in sports and recreational activities for the tourism industry
3.	Public transport-type passenger vehicles (including coaches and mini-buses for the tourism industry).

Source: Customs Act, Third Schedule.

PART C

REPORT BY THE GOVERNMENT

CONTENTS

I. INTRODUCTION

1. Trinidad and Tobago prior to the 1980's pursued an industrialization policy based on import substitution, which involved a strategy of utilizing relatively cheap labour combined with both local and foreign investment, implementation of a regime of fiscal incentives including tax holidays and duty concessions, and a system of quantitative restrictions in the form of a Negative List. Although this strategy produced some measure of growth in the productive capacity of the country, the meaningful diversification or transformation of the country's production base was not realized.

2. Consequently, in the 1980's, with the accrual of substantial windfall earnings from the increase in the price of petroleum on the international market, the focus of industrialization policy shifted to economic diversification and transformation largely through investment in the energy-based sector. Policy initiatives were also taken to stimulate development of the non-oil manufacturing sector, with a focus on exports.

3. These initiatives to develop the non-oil manufacturing sector via a trade liberalization regime were intensified largely through a Structural Adjustment Programme (SAP) which was embarked upon by the Government of Trinidad and Tobago in 1990. Within the context of the SAP, the Trade Reform Programme has been specifically geared to foster improved efficiency in the operations of local companies, expansion in export-oriented production in the manufacturing, services, tourism and agricultural sectors, enhanced international competitiveness and increased export earnings, all of which would contribute to sustained growth, increased generation of employment and an overall improvement in the standard of living in Trinidad and Tobago.

4. The Trade Reform Programme essentially seeks to transform the trade regime from one which was inward-looking to one which is outward-looking, based on the principle of export-led growth and the development of an investment regime with an improved legal, regulatory and institutional framework, aimed at rendering the economy more attractive to export-led investment both local and foreign.

5. Within the policy reform environment, the private sector is expected to become the prime generator of economic growth and development. The role of the Government, on the other hand, has been redefined as a promoter and catalyst of trade and industrial development.

6. The Trade Reform Programme can be categorized into six major areas of activity, namely trade liberalization, enhanced competitiveness, sectoral programmes, market access opportunities, the Free Zones Programme and institutional support measures and facilities.

7. These trade policy measures have been supplemented by a substantive reform of the financial, fiscal and investment legislation, including the removal of foreign exchange controls and the flotation of the local currency.

II. ECONOMIC POLICY AND ENVIRONMENT

8. The Government of Trinidad and Tobago has implemented a comprehensive economic programme since 1989, aimed at restructuring the economy and restoring a path of self sustaining, non inflationary growth. Monetary, fiscal, trade and investment policies have all been directed towards stabilising and diversifying the economy.

9. Fiscal policy has been conducted within the context of a comprehensive macro-economic structural adjustment programme. The Government of Trinidad and Tobago continues to maintain a prudent fiscal strategy. This strategy together with administrative restructuring of the revenue

collecting agencies have resulted in an overall decrease in the fiscal deficit. The current account balance of the central government has recorded a surplus in the last five years contributing to improved national savings and a reduction in the investment/savings gap.

10. Monetary policy is being pursued with the priority objective of maintaining exchange rate stability, and the enhancement of the country's foreign reserves. The foreign exchange rate was liberalized in 1993, since then Trinidad and Tobago adopted a floating exchange rate followed by the removal of exchange controls on the current and capital accounts. The Central Bank currently relies on the managing of liquidity and interest rate policy to achieve its main objective of a stable and low rate of inflation. The monetary authorities are increasingly adopting the use of open market operations as a tool for liquidity management, and reducing the dependence on the cash reserve requirement. It is expected that the use of open market operations will lower the cost of financial intermediation and therefore the cost of borrowing.

11. These initiatives have been accompanied by legislative and institutional reforms in the financial sector which were designed to facilitate the transformation of the domestic capital market. The following pieces of financial legislation have been revised and amended:

(i)   The Central Bank Amendment Act;

(ii)   The Financial Institutions Act;

(iii)   The Securities Industry Act;

(iv)   The Companies Act.

12. Consequently, the Securities and Exchange Commission was established in April, 1997 to supervise and regulate the authorities of the domestic stock exchange and to foster the use of this facility as a source of start-up capital for business ventures.

13. Government has also focused on the provision of capital for the development of the small business sector. The development of the small business sector is an essential prerequisite for the balanced development of the local economy. It is evident that this sector will continue to be the foundation for the Trinidad and Tobago economy by providing products and services and most importantly, opportunities which would permit the small investor to gain a foothold in the local market.

14. In keeping with these objectives, Government has improved the range of fiscal incentives which are available to the small business sector. These incentives were outlined in the 1998 budget presentation and include:

(i)   an increase in the loan guarantee ceiling available for small business financing;

(ii)   the asset value threshold for qualification as a small business at the Small Business Development Company (SBDC) has been increased from $500,000 to $1.5 million;

(iii)   Government's annual financial grant to the SBDC has been increased to $8 million.

15. These initiatives have immediately borne fruit, based on figures supplied by the SBDC which indicate that loan applications have increased by 30% between January to March, 1998 when compared to the same period in 1997. In fact, a total of $5 million in loan guarantees have already been processed in 1998.

16.   The recently introduced Venture Capital Act will also serve to enhance the sector's ability to obtain much needed financial inflows. The Venture Capital Act is designed to promote the injection of equity capital into small and medium sized enterprises, without the burden of excessive financial charges which are usually associated with debt financing.

17.   Based on the above factors, it is obvious that Government's economic policies are specifically designed to foster private sector growth and development by providing a favourable climate for investment and commercial activities. The role of the Government has therefore been transformed to that of a promoter and catalyst of trade and industrial development.

18.   The implementation of the programme of structural reforms has impacted favourably on the economy. In 1997, Trinidad and Tobago's economy recorded its fourth consecutive year of economic growth. Real output has been positively growing by an average of 3% since 1994 (Table 1). This growth has been propelled by increased exploration and production activity in the Petroleum Sector as well as expansion in the output of the non-oil sector. In 1997, strong performances were recorded in the manufacturing, construction, distribution and transport sub-sectors, while the tourism sector displayed increased vibrancy. Such improved performance highlights the continued success of government's policy towards diversification of the economy.

19.   The growth in the economy has impacted positively on both the unemployment and inflation rates. The annual average rate of inflation has been on the decline, from 11.4% in 1993 to 3.7% in 1997. The reduced rate of inflation was partly due to the reduction or removal of import surcharges on several categories of capital and consumer goods.

20.   The rate of unemployment has also reflected a significant contraction, from 22.4% of the labour force in 1989 to 15% in 1997. Overall the economy is reflecting a positive trend.

Table 1
Macro-economic indicators of the economy of Trinidad and Tobago, 1989 – 1997
(MN$TT and per cent)

	1989	1990	1991	1992	1993	1994	1995	1996	1997
GDP 1985 Constant prices	15,894.90	16,134.4	16,567.3	16,294.4	16,057.5	16,630.3	17,265.2	17,872.6	18,450.8
Growth rate	-0.8	1.5	2.7	-1.7	-1.5	3.6	3.8	3.5	3.2
Unemployment rate	22.4	20	18.5	19.6	19.8	18.4	17.2	16.3	15.0
Imports	5,188.0	5,370.4	7,084.8	6,101.1	7,495.3	7,811.7	11,363.3	12,989.1	18,705.9
Exports	6,695.4	8,850.9	8,436.4	7,943.0	8,800.9	11,575.4	14,512.1	15,028.9	15,887.6
Foreign reserves	-434.3	187.5	3.4	-36.7	206.3	514.5	406.2	701.1	854.1
Rate of inflation	11.4	11	3.8	6.5	10.8	9.4	5.4	3.3	3.7
Direct investment	148.9	109.4	144.1	171.0	372.6	521.0	295.7	402.4	999.6

Source: Central Bank of Trinidad and Tobago & Central Statistical Office.

III.   TRADE AND INVESTMENT POLICY - A REVIEW

21.   The Trade Policy of Trinidad and Tobago is outlined in the document entitled "Trade Policy for the Republic of Trinidad and Tobago 1997 - 2001". As mentioned before, since 1991, the Government of Trinidad and Tobago has undertaken a number of measures in order to diversify the economy and promote sustainable export led growth and development. These programmes were

undertaken within the context of the global trend towards trade liberalization and the growing preponderance of mega trading blocs.

22.   The basic elements of the Trade Reform Programme include:

    (i)   The elimination of the Import Negative List;

    (ii)   The reduction of the Common External Tariff on imported goods;

    (iii)   The removal of price controls;

    (iv)   The removal of stamp duty on imported goods;

    (v)   The computerisation of Customs import and export procedures.

23.   The Trade Reform Programme is closely linked to initiatives to attract foreign investment and to facilitate the development of the domestic industrial base. It is obvious that an essential pre-requisite for the take-off of the economy is a substantial pool of capital, which would be utilised to fuel investment in the private sector. Such capital could be derived from both domestic and foreign sources.

24.   It is acknowledged that foreign investors and to some extent local investors can invest their funds anywhere in the world especially through the electronic networks. In this context, it is imperative that Trinidad and Tobago develops an environment that is conducive to investment, in particular to devise an appropriate incentive framework.

25.   Therefore, Trinidad and Tobago's investment thrust is characterised as follows:

    (i)   The creation of a more investor-friendly climate in the local economy. Therefore Government will seek to highlight the recent reforms which have been undertaken so that foreign investors will become aware of these efforts. To this end, the Foreign Investment Act will be amended to ensure that it is more promotional and less regulatory in nature. In this regard a draft bill, the Investment Promotion Bill, has been prepared by the Chief Parliamentary Counsel, and is at present being reviewed by an Inter-ministerial Committee following which it will be reviewed by the Legislative Review Committee before being tabled in Parliament. If approved, the Bill will become the Investment Promotion Act and replace the present Foreign Investment Act.

    (ii)   The continued effort on the part of Government to reduce the number and complexity of the bureaucratic procedures involved in investment and business transactions. The objective is to make these procedures as simple and transparent as possible.

    (iii)   Finally, Government will utilize the resources of its overseas missions and other related agencies to market the country as an attractive location for investment.

26.   In keeping with these guidelines some of the major pieces of legislation which impinge on investment have been either revised or amended. These include the Fiscal Incentives Act and the Value Added Tax Act.

27.   The Government of Trinidad and Tobago has also introduced an enhanced investment incentive framework. The basic incentives to investors are:

- tax holiday or partial holiday under the Fiscal Incentives Act to approved industrial projects;
- exemption from corporation tax on profits, and dividends (under the Fiscal Incentives Act and Hotel Development Act);
- loss write-off provisions;
- training subsidies for developing new skills;
- provision of industrial sites and developed industrial accommodation;
- export allowances and promotional and developmental assistance;
- export credit insurance;
- double taxation relief;
- exemption from Value Added Tax on inputs for companies exporting 100% of production.

28.   Government has also reduced the maximum level of corporation tax from 40% to 35% in a bid to reduce the cost of doing business.

Free Zones Programme

29.   Another key element in the quest to attract foreign investors is the Free Zones Programme. This Programme is intended to attract export-oriented firms which would not otherwise have located operations in Trinidad and Tobago. Some of the advantages which are derived from locating in a Free Zone include:

- total exemption from customs duties on capital goods, spare parts, raw materials, etc., for use in the construction and equipping of the premises and in connection with the approved activity;
- no import or export licensing requirements;
- no land and building taxes;
- no foreign currency or property ownership restrictions;
- exemption from corporation and withholding taxes in respect of profits or gains from approved free zone activities and business levy on sales;
- no VAT on goods supplied to a Free Zone.

30.   The Free Zones Programme in Trinidad and Tobago has developed quite differently from other Caribbean Programmes and in the process, has created a vehicle for economic development with particular features including the fact that all infrastructure is currently provided by private investors and the jobs that are created are generally of a high quality. The Programme is gradually becoming self sufficient and is expected eventually to reduce substantially its dependency on the Treasury. The Free Zones approach will continue to be one of the main planks of the country's export strategy.

31.   These efforts will be complemented by a series of key strategies and measures among which would be the procurement of enhanced market access opportunities for locally produced goods and services, mainly through the process of negotiations, to the markets of targeted countries.

IV.   CURRENT INDUSTRIAL POLICY

32.   Trinidad and Tobago's Industrial Policy focuses mainly on the development of the non-oil manufacturing , non-financial services and small business sectors. The Policy is designed to create an expanded, diversified export oriented non-oil business sector. The Policy objectives are to:

- generate sustained economic growth and balanced, integrated development;
- encourage increased investment flows into export-oriented production;

- expand the range of business activity in the non-oil business sector;
- generate permanent employment opportunities;
- increase the export earnings of the non-oil business sector;
- ensure that economic development takes place in harmony with national environmental consideration;
- mitigate the consequences of business failures;
- assist in the attainment of the country's food security objective.

33.   In support of this programme several strategies and measures will be implemented in order to assist the business sector in its restructuring efforts, and therefore enabling the non-oil sector to become more export-oriented.   These strategies and measures address the following areas: investment; human resource development; financing; business information; institutional and regulatory reform.

V.   AGRICULTURAL POLICY

34.   In keeping with the objective of trade liberalisation in all sectors of the economy, Government has implemented a number of reform measures in the agricultural sector. These include:

(i)   conversion of non-tariff import measures (negative list, government monopoly) to a tariff equivalent system, consistent with the GATT 1994 Agreement on Agriculture and to extend and strengthen trade and price liberalization in the agricultural sector;

(ii)   phased reduction of the dispersion among tariff rates and their average level in order to improve the incentives facing agriculture consistent with comparative advantage and attaining benefits for consumers from improved market access and lower food costs;

(iii)   within the framework of establishing tariff structures, maintenance of an open and transparent trade regime for agriculture with a minimum of government intervention;

(iv)   containment of direct support payments and subsidies to producers consistent with the GATT 1994 Agreement and prudent domestic fiscal management; and

(v)   restructuring and divestment of State-owned enterprises. Caroni (1975) Ltd. is a state-owned enterprise and the only producer of sugar in the country. A major goal of the GORTT is to make this company financially viable. Caroni (1975) Limited is to be reorganized to make its management and operations more efficient. The company is committed to implementing changes to reduce its costs through labour reduction, increased reliance on the supply of privately cultivated cane, improved cane production and greater factory efficiency.

VI.   EXTERNAL TRADE DEVELOPMENT – NEGOTIATIONS, ETC.

35.   One of the major objectives of the Trade Reform Programme which has been implemented by the Government of Trinidad and Tobago is the creation of an expanded, diversified export oriented production base in the non-oil sector of the economy. This initiative will be complemented by a series of key strategies and measures prime among which would be the procurement of enhanced market access opportunities for locally produced goods and services mainly through the process of negotiation to the markets of targeted countries.

36.   Therefore, Trinidad and Tobago's market access strategies will undoubtedly be influenced by the ongoing process of liberalization and globalization of the world economy. Such developments in the world economy have led to the configuration of the international economy into economic

mega-blocs. These developments have made it imperative that countries like Trinidad and Tobago should learn the rules of the game in order to effectively exploit the numerous opportunities that are available to local exporters now that tariff and other traditional trade barriers have been significantly reduced.

37.   The proliferation of these various trade blocs has forced Trinidad and Tobago to accelerate the pace of integration or face the prospect of being marginalized by the sheer volume of trade and investment flows which could be directed to these trade blocs, at the expense of local producers.

38.   In this regard, it is significant to note that Trinidad and Tobago's traditional markets are located within the EU and Western hemisphere, in addition to CARICOM. Non-traditional country markets are located in economic blocs such as MERCOSUR, the Andean Community, the Central American Common Market and the Association of South East Asian nations, among others. Against this background, it is imperative for Trinidad and Tobago to expand its export production in a bid to effectively compete on the international market. Therefore, Trinidad and Tobago has adopted a dual approach in order to maximize market access opportunities. Consequently, efforts would be directed towards expanding market share for non-traditional products in traditional markets, particularly where preferential market access arrangements are available, such as Lomé, the Caribbean Basin Initiative (CBI) and CARIBCAN albeit over the short to medium term while seeking to penetrate non-traditional markets in a sustained and aggressive manner.

39.   It would therefore be important to note that although the Government of Trinidad and Tobago is actively seeking to ensure that the national trade policy objectives are achieved, the realities of the configuration of the global economy may dictate, in most instances, that the negotiation of terms and conditions of access to markets be undertaken on an inter-regional or bloc to bloc basis. This has in fact been the case even in the pre-Uruguay Round scenario with respect to the Lomé, CBI and Caribbean arrangements which were negotiated with the CARICOM group of countries and similarly with the current agreements between CARICOM, Venezuela, the Dominican Republic and Colombia and the ongoing Free Trade Area of the Americas negotiations. The necessity for inter-bloc negotiations in the current post-Uruguay Round environment may become more pronounced with the passage of time.

Trinidad and Tobago Negotiations with Third Countries

40.   Trinidad and Tobago's relations with Third Countries is based on the recognition of its limited size and openness of its domestic and CARICOM Markets and the principle that the growth and expansion of the local productive base can only be realised by the penetration of foreign markets.

41.   As was mentioned above, Trinidad and Tobago is a Member State of the CARICOM grouping. CARICOM's focus is the conclusion of reciprocal free trade agreements with the Latin American countries and those of the extra CARICOM Caribbean.

42.   Trinidad and Tobago's policy objective to undertake negotiations with third countries has been guided by the following considerations:

  (i)   the enhanced efficiency and productivity capabilities of local producers would enable them to seize export opportunities in Latin American markets;

  (ii)   the physical proximity of Latin American markets and those in the extra-CARICOM Caribbean to Trinidad and Tobago;

(iii)   the proposed negotiated reciprocal market access arrangements will provide a wider range of export possibilities into the Latin American and extra-CARICOM Caribbean markets for local exporters;

(iv)   the size of some of the Latin American countries and the diverse economic segments could provide niche market possibilities for local products;

(v)   the possibility of co-production and joint venture arrangements with Latin American and extra-CARICOM Caribbean entrepreneurs utilizing Trinidad and Tobago as a production platform to access markets, particularly those provided under the CBI, Caribbean and Lomé preferential arrangements;

(vi)   the cost-effective sourcing of raw materials by local enterprises which would contribute to the competitiveness of local products in both the domestic and export markets;

(vii)   opportunities for exploring the potential for the development of export trade in services to Latin America and the extra-CARICOM Caribbean.

43.   In addition, Trinidad and Tobago has joined its CARICOM partners in entering into reciprocal free trade agreements with Colombia and the Dominican Republic and will be seeking to enter into similar agreements with the Andean, Central American, and Mercosur regional groupings. This country will shortly initiate direct bilateral free trade negotiations with certain countries such as Mexico, Costa Rica and Panama.

Trinidad and Tobago's Role in the CARICOM Single Market

44.   Trinidad and Tobago is actively involved in CARICOM's efforts to create a Single Market, a project which has been accelerated as a direct consequence of international developments such as the proposed establishment of the Free Trade Area of the Americas and other globalization trends.

45.   A single market will allow CARICOM to optimise its limited financial and economic resources in a bid to enhance its market leverage in the external trade negotiation process.

NAFTA/CBI and CARIBCAN Agreements

46.   Trinidad and Tobago is a beneficiary of the CBI and CARIBCAN preferential agreements. The CBI Agreement offers duty free access to exports of selected Caribbean and Central American countries into the market of the USA. CARIBCAN offers a similar facility for Caribbean exports into the Canadian market. A number of products are excluded from preferential treatment. Methanol and Lube Oil were included under the CARIBCAN in 1998. These products are of vital interest to Trinidad and Tobago.

47.   It is important to note that with the creation of the North American Free Trade Agreement (NAFTA) the preferential access enjoyed by Mexico into the markets of Canada and the United States in respect of these products which have been excluded from the CBI and CARIBCAN could erode the overall benefits which Trinidad and Tobago and other beneficiaries presently enjoy under these agreements.

48.   In addition, it is quite possible that foreign investors presently located in Trinidad and Tobago and engaged in the manufacture of the products excluded under the CBI and CARIBCAN might seek to locate in Mexico in order to enjoy the benefits of NAFTA market access. This element of investment diversion has already been evident by the re-location of some foreign operations from the CARIBCAN to Mexico.

49.   The result of such trade and investment diversion could be a loss of employment, and to some degree of economic dislocation.   In the context of its production capability, Trinidad and Tobago is not currently affected in any substantial manner as some other CBI and CARIBCAN beneficiary countries.

50.   In order to alleviate the possible adverse effect of the relative advantage enjoyed by Mexico from its membership in NAFTA, Trinidad and Tobago has joined its CARICOM partners in seeking to obtain "NAFTA Parity" or enhancement of the CBI in particular to include those products which are presently excluded with the aim of levelling the playing field for CARICOM exporters vis-à-vis their Mexican counterparts.

Free Trade Area of the Americas (FTAA)

51.   Consistent with its trade policy, the Government of Trinidad and Tobago has actively participated in the FTAA process at the Ministerial, Vice Ministerial and Working Group levels during the preparatory phase.   It is prepared to participate in the second negotiating phase in a more focused manner, as part of a co-ordinated CARICOM effort, in order to ensure that its interest and that of the regional grouping is served, particularly as smaller economies, in the negotiating process. This country's negotiating effort will be reinforced by the fact that it has been nominated to hold the post of Vice Chairman of the FTAA negotiating group on Competition Policy.

The Lomé IV Convention

52.   Trinidad and Tobago has benefitted from the preferential duty free access granted to local products under the provisions of the Lomé Convention.   Negotiations are currently underway between the EU and the ACP countries including Trinidad and Tobago with respect to a successor arrangement to the Lomé IV Agreement.

53.   This country has attended the recent launch of negotiations for a successor agreement to the Lomé IV. At this meeting, Trinidad and Tobago participated with other ACP States in preparing a negotiation strategy which stressed the following elements:

> (i)   ACP States should continue to negotiate the successor agreement as part of a unified bloc;
>
> (ii)   the need to recognise that certain ACP States are smaller and more vulnerable and should be granted differential treatment;
>
> (iii)   the extension of preferential access arrangements for the entry of ACP products into the European market;
>
> (iv)   removal or reduction of restrictive or non-tariff barriers in the EU as they relate to Rules of Origin, technical restrictions to trade and phytosanitary measures.

Trade Supportive Agreements

54.   One of the major planks of Trinidad and Tobago's trade policy initiative is the negotiation of Foreign Investment Protection Agreements, referred to as Bilateral Investment Treaties, which have been concluded with several countries in an effort to maximize the benefits which could be derived from its trade and investment links with extra-regional trading partners. Trinidad and Tobago has concluded Bilateral Investment Treaties with Canada, the United Kingdom, France and the United States of America. Agreements with Germany, Venezuela, and Argentina, are currently being negotiated.

55.   An Intellectual Property Rights Agreement has been concluded with the United States and consideration is being given to entering into similar agreements with other countries.   These agreements will provide a measure of security to potential investors and technology providers, and thereby improve the attractiveness of Trinidad and Tobago as a location for investment.

56.   Trinidad and Tobago have entered into Double Taxation treaties with Canada, Denmark, France, Italy, Norway, Sweden, Switzerland, the United Kingdom, the United States, Venezuela and the Federal Republic of Germany.

Future Policy Directions

57.   Although the Trade Reform Programme and other trade related policy reform measures are already at an advanced stage of implementation, in seeking to determine the way forward, the Government of Trinidad and Tobago will continue to monitor developments in the international trading system and seek to create economic space for our domestic manufacturers/exporters.

58.   In cognisance of the fact that the conduct of successful External Negotiations requires considerable human, institutional and financial resources, the Government of Trinidad and Tobago has established a National External Trade Negotiating Mechanism, the main element of which is a Technical Coordinating Committee comprised of public/private sector officials which conduct preparatory consultations with a view to making recommendations to the Government on the positions and strategies to be adopted by the national negotiating teams in various fora. A number of possible plans have already been identified for the continued enforcement of this country's external trade policy. These include:

(i)   The continued negotiation of an extension of existing preferential trade agreements, such as the CBI and CARIBCAN;

(ii)   continued negotiation of NAFTA parity for countries of the CBI;

(iii)   determination of the priority to be afforded to relations with Europe in light of the fact that the new successor arrangement to Lomé IV will be based on reciprocity;

(iv)   pursuing integration efforts within the Wider Caribbean in an effort to use their bargaining leverage in external negotiations, particularly in the FTAA;

(v)   the development of strategies to maximise the benefits of small market size while developing a competitive edge on the international market.

Export Promotional Programme and Initiatives

59.   In this regard, the Government proposes to organize and co-ordinate a number of promotional exercises.

60.   These initiatives will be facilitated by:

(i)   the organisation of visits by Trinidad and Tobago producers and entrepreneurs to specific markets abroad;

(ii)   the mounting of exhibitions by Trinidad and Tobago producers in the target markets;

(iii)   the participation by Trinidad and Tobago producers in specific or general fairs and exhibitions in foreign countries;

     (iv)   the posting of commercial officers in Trinidad and Tobago's Government Missions abroad;

Far Eastern Countries

61.   Trinidad and Tobago has for many years been a net importer from many countries in the Far East including India, Japan, Singapore, Hong Kong, China and Korea. These countries are members of the proposed Asia Pacific Economic Cooperation trading bloc. In view of this fact, the Government has identified the Far Eastern countries as potential niche markets for non-traditional products and for the expansion of market share with respect to its current exports. More particularly, these countries have been targeted as potential sources of investment into the Trinidad and Tobago economy.

Other Countries

62.   The Republic of South Africa is prime among the countries in Africa and the Middle East which in the future may be targeted in the implementation of Trinidad and Tobago's trade policy. In addition to the possible export opportunities, joint venture investments in these markets by Trinidad and Tobago's entrepreneurs might be a feasible approach to gaining market share in those countries.

VII.   CONCLUSION

63.   The Government of Trinidad and Tobago has formulated a plan of action which is designed to facilitate the meaningful integration of the local economy into the globalized trading environment. This plan of action which is expressed in the domestic trade and industrial policies will be supported by an aggressive negotiation process which will target specific countries and the multilateral forum such as the WTO and FTAA.

64.   The basic objectives will be the generation of enhanced investment, employment and trade flows between Trinidad and Tobago and its trading partners. Trinidad and Tobago is determined to become an active player in the globalized trading environment

PART D

MINUTES OF THE TPRB MEETING

CONTENTS

The Concluding Remarks by the Chairperson of the
Trade Policy Review Body are reproduced in Part A.

I.   INTRODUCTORY REMARKS BY THE CHAIRPERSON

1.   The first Trade Policy Review of Trinidad and Tobago was held on 12 and 13 November 1998.   The Chairperson welcomed the delegation of Trinidad and Tobago, led by the Honourable Mervyn Assam, Minister of Trade and Industry, as well as Chargé d'affaires Richards, and the discussants, Mr. Andrew L. Stoler (United States) and Ms. Claudia Orozco Jaramillo (Colombia).   As usual, both discussants would speak in their personal capacities and not as representatives of their countries.   In accordance with the established procedures, the discussants had made available, in advance, an outline of the main issues they intended to raise.

2.   The Chairperson recalled the purpose of the Trade Policy Reviews and the main elements of the procedures for the meeting.   The report by the Government of Trinidad and Tobago was contained in document WT/TPR/G/49 and that of the WTO Secretariat in document WT/TPR/S/49;   the main issues to be raised by the discussants were contained in document WT/TPR/D/27.   Copies of advance written questions, submitted by five delegations (Canada;   the European Union;   Hong Kong, China;   Japan;   and the United States) had been transmitted to the delegation of Trinidad and Tobago (Annex I).   Written responses by Trinidad and Tobago are reproduced in Annex II.   If full replies could not be provided during the meeting, supplementary written replies could be provided later.

II.   OPENING STATEMENT BY THE REPRESENTATIVE OF TRINIDAD AND TOBAGO

3.   The representative of Trinidad and Tobago expressed his satisfaction regarding the review of his country's trade policies. The review provided an ideal opportunity to assess the effectiveness of these policies, particularly in the wider context of the globalized economy, and to explain some of the domestic imperatives which had informed those policies. Trinidad and Tobago had become a contracting party to the General Agreement on Tariffs and Trade on 23 October 1962, and had participated in every round of multilateral trade negotiations since that date. Since 1990, within the context of a Structural Adjustment Programme, and independently of the Uruguay Round negotiations, Trinidad and Tobago had pursued a trade liberalization regime aimed at diversifying the economy and promoting improved efficiency in the operations of local companies, expansion in export-oriented production in the manufacturing, services, tourism and agricultural sectors, enhanced international competitiveness and increased export earnings.

4.   Trinidad and Tobago's trade reform programme had been closely linked to initiatives to attract foreign investment and facilitate the development of the domestic industrial base. Within this policy reform environment, the role of the Government had been redefined to that of a promoter and catalyst for trade and industrial development while the private sector was to become the prime generator of economic growth and development. In pursuit of this goal, the development of the small business sector was acknowledged to be an essential prerequisite for the balanced development of the local economy. Regarding market access, Trinidad and Tobago had adopted a dual approach directed towards the expansion of its market share for non-traditional products in traditional markets, particularly where preferential market access arrangements were available, while seeking to penetrate non-traditional markets.

5.   The implementation of the programme of structural reform had impacted favourably on the economy. In 1997, the economy had recorded its fourth consecutive year of economic growth. Real output had grown by an average of 3% since 1994 propelled by increased exploration and production activity in the petroleum sector as well as expansion in the non-oil sector.   In 1997 strong performances had been recorded in the manufacturing, construction, distribution and transport sub-sectors, while the tourism industry had displayed increased vibrancy.

6.   Trinidad and Tobago remained firmly committed to a rules-based multilateral trading system. Within the context of the Uruguay Round, it had willingly assumed obligations disproportionate to its size and assumed commitments in all areas including the services sector (financial services, telecommunications, educational services, maritime services, professional services, medical services, etc.).   Trinidad and Tobago had also done a great deal within the last three years to bring its intellectual property laws into compliance with the TRIPS Agreement.

7.   The importance and success of the WTO/GATT was reflected in the fact that membership had increased from 23 countries in 1947 to 132 countries in 1998, and average tariffs had been reduced to one tenth of the levels of 50 years ago. However, the Organization would in the future be confronted with a number of challenges including the widening gap between industrial and developing countries. The WTO needed to address the particular interests and needs of developing country Members and to ensure that sustained efforts were made towards balancing the obligations assumed by these states and the benefits they derive from the system. Against this background the WTO should formulate appropriate mechanisms designed to minimize any distorting effects of trade policies.

8.   The WTO had ushered in a regime of stricter enforcement of trade regulations.   The tightening of these regulations had to some extent restored the confidence of Member States as exemplified by the fact that in the period 1995-1998 the WTO Dispute Settlement Body had considered 132 complaints, compared to a total of 300 complaints in the 47 years of existence of the GATT.   However, it was necessary to be aware of the effect that strict enforcement devoid of socio-economic considerations could have on small economies with limited development options. The banana dispute was a case in point.   A number of small Caribbean countries with a long history of democratic and stable governance now saw their prospects for development jeopardized by a legalistic approach to trade conflicts.

9.   The ongoing global financial crisis presented another challenge to the WTO.   A key lesson to be learned from this crisis was the importance of appropriately regulated financial sectors.   This was all the more critical in a world in which an increasing amount of capital was being intermediated through private capital markets.   In order to avoid, in the future, a substantial negative fallout from similar crises, it was important that countries put in place mechanisms to strengthen their domestic financial infrastructure to allow them to: (a) exploit effectively the benefits of open capital accounts; and (b) minimize the risks associated with the high degree of volatility in capital flows.

10.   The advent of electronic commerce would have a significant impact on world trade and some countries had pressed for its inclusion in the agenda of the WTO.   Some experts had reached the conclusion that developing countries had much to gain from advances in electronic business and financial transactions.   However, at this point in time the majority of developing countries were not equipped to benefit fully from this new development. The international community had an obligation to ensure that these countries became part of this technological revolution in a manner which would be beneficial for their societies.

11.   In addition, developing countries had been subject to various trade actions such as anti-dumping and safeguard measures applied by developed countries. He reiterated the issue raised by him at the Ministerial Conference in Geneva in May 1998, that the WTO should ensure that the playing field and the rules of the game were not detrimental to the majority of players. He wondered whether the WTO was equipped to have Members rights recognized in the context of an equitable multilateral trading system without always having to resort to the dispute settlement mechanism. It was imperative that new and imaginative approaches be devised for dealing with the issue of special and differential treatment within the WTO context.

12.   He drew attention to the issue of small economies introduced by the delegation of Mauritius and co-authored by a number of countries including Trinidad and Tobago. As a small developing island, Trinidad and Tobago fully supported the initiatives undertaken within a number of international bodies and fora (Commonwealth, UNCTAD and FTAA) to address the issue of the vulnerability of small states and to identify measures aimed at facilitating their integration into the global economy.   This group of countries was more adversely affected by environmental factors including natural disasters, as witnessed by the devastation wrought on the Central American countries by Hurricane Mitch and on St Kitts/Nevis and Antigua and Barbuda by Hurricane George, deserved the special attention and support of the international community.

13.   New and imaginative approaches should be based on the need for a total package of assistance and support to developing countries and should *inter alia* include: (a) the provision of technical assistance for instituting the necessary macro-economic and trade policy reforms essential for their effective and meaningful participation in world trade; and (b) the development of

mechanisms designed to promote the transfer of technology and flows of investment into developing countries. Developing countries should examine the feasibility of establishing avenues of mutual cooperation in areas such as technology sharing, joint utilization of human and material resources and joint industrial and developmental projects. Seeking methods to expand trade and investment flows among developing countries might prove to be another avenue for the development of these countries.

14.   His Government was firmly committed to trade liberalization and had implemented a wide range of measures including virtual elimination of the Import Negative List in conjunction with the reduction of the Common External Tariff, removal of foreign exchange controls and improvement in Customs procedures. These were all detailed in the documentation presented.

15.   He had been honoured to present Trinidad and Tobago's trade policies for review and expressed his country's commitment to the principles and objectives of the WTO, which were geared towards the enhancement of economic growth and the improvement of living standards.

III. STATEMENT BY THE FIRST DISCUSSANT

16. The first discussant Mr. Andrew L. Stoler stated that the Government of Trinidad and Tobago, like many other Governments which had found themselves the beneficiaries of unexpectedly large sources of revenue in the days before oil prices collapsed, sought to build an economy with strong State intervention where the State owned the lion's share of the country's economic assets. The temptation to embark on such policies was widespread in those years and was entirely understandable, particularly in the case of a small island country. What came across in this review very clearly was that the changed macroeconomic environment had brought on the need to change those earlier policies and the Government had both recognized and embraced that need.

17. When the balloon had burst in the early 1980s, much of what had been achieved in the strong growth years had been lost and in 1988 the Government had introduced an important structural reform and liberalization programme. For a variety of reasons, the positive impact of the programme had taken some time in coming and the Secretariat's report suggested that the period of higher growth in the post 1994 period was probably directly related to the greater degree of openness in the economy in this period.

18. Most recently, higher growth rates spurred in part by increases in foreign direct investment, had also engendered a big rise in imports. After consistently having realized trade surpluses in every year since 1989, the trade account for 1997 had gone into a sizeable deficit as a result of a big increase in imports from the United States. The discussant had so far been unable to locate reliable statistics on the composition of trade by destination and source for 1997, so he could not say whether the increased imports were capital goods perhaps destined for the energy sector, or consumer goods encouraged by rising incomes. If the visiting government team from Trinidad and Tobago could shed some light on the nature of the 44% growth in imports in 1997, it would make an important contribution to his understanding of the current macroeconomic context.

19. While the trade balance had swung into a large deficit in 1997, other macroeconomic indicators were in pretty good shape. Net foreign exchange reserves had grown steadily since 1992. Inflation had fallen to only 3.7% in 1997. There had been a big increase in the percentage of GDP accounted for by private consumption and a fall in government consumption as a percentage of GDP. The economy overall had grown steadily at a rate of more than 3% in recent years and for a variety of the right reasons, the Government had been able to post a budget surplus since 1995.

20. In line with the other structural reforms introduced since 1988, it was clear that the Trinidad and Tobago Government had re-thought the role of the State in the economy. The Government report stated that it had redefined its role as a promoter and catalyst of trade and industrial development, while it now saw the private sector as the prime generator of economic growth and development. That seemed to be reflected in the big increase in private consumption as a percentage of GDP.

21. There had been a programme of privatization ongoing in Trinidad and Tobago now since the late 1980s. Both the Secretariat report and the Government submission detailed the divestment policies followed by the Government of Trinidad and Tobago. Government ownership in enterprises was much reduced from what it had been at the beginning of the decade; however, the Government of Trinidad and Tobago's commitment to divestiture seemed to be tempered by a desire to maintain effective management control of many of the enterprises where private investment had now been permitted. He wondered whether it was really either necessary or desirable for the Government of Trinidad and Tobago to maintain a controlling interest in so many commercial enterprises such as the

Iron and Steel Company and the National Flour Mills. He asked whether the Government would proceed to divest its interest in Caroni, the only producer of sugar in the country, after reorganizing its management and operations.

22.   From both the Government submission and the report prepared by the Secretariat, he got the strong feeling that the Government of Trinidad and Tobago was interested in encouraging important changes in the structure of the economy. However, for a variety of good reasons, it would seem that the desired changes were not going to be easy to bring about.

23.   He described the agricultural sector as the smallest and least "healthy" sector of the domestic economy, accounting for only 3% of GDP and dominated by the sugar industry where the Government was the owner of the monopoly enterprise, Caroni, which had accumulated sizeable deficits over the years. International trade in sugar had created circumstances in which exports of the product provided an important international subsidy to the islands' economy. Sugar sales to the European Union and the United States at quota prices well above world market prices were so important that sugar was actually imported into Trinidad and Tobago when domestic production was insufficient to meet both export quotas and domestic demand. It seemed curious that a Government-owned and operated enterprise would act to satisfy export quotas before satisfying domestic demand and still would lose large amounts of money in the process.

24.   The Secretariat report indicated that the Government of Trinidad and Tobago saw "great potential for income, employment and foreign exchange generations in the agricultural sector". He wondered how realistic such aspirations were when farmers and growers in nearly every agricultural subsector sold their production at Government guaranteed prices and where identified constraints to production included inadequate water supply, high cost of inputs, inadequate facilities, poor market organization and poor soil management. He asked the Trinidad and Tobago delegation to comment on how it would reconcile the apparent inconsistencies between its declared objectives for the agriculture sector and the evident problems facing this sector.

25.   Three quarters of the Trinidad and Tobago's labour force worked in the services sector, which accounted for 61% of GDP. More than twice as many people worked in the financial services industry than in the hydrocarbons sub-sector. So far, only one 1% of GDP was generated by the tourism industry, so this seemed to be an area of potential growth. Given the limited reserves of hydrocarbons, it would seem that the services sector was destined to increase in importance. The financial services sector, accounting for 11.5% of GDP and employing over 8% of the labour force, was the most important services sector. He worried about the long-term health of the financial services sector in the globalizing economy as the Secretariat report indicated that there could be a capacity for monopolistic pricing that had created larger than expected profits. He noted that if the growth of the sector and its relative importance in the economy had come about through a lack of effective competition then the sectors long term prospects might not be too good.

26.   The documents provided for this review indicated that the Government of Trinidad and Tobago was considering adopting a competition policy framework as part of a proposed "Fair Trading Act". He asked the delegation whether the introduction of competition policy was in part motivated by the prevailing situation in the financial services sector.

27.   The energy sector (oil and gas production) dominated goods production and was the principal reason for the important inflows of foreign investment. The Government was rightly concerned about over-reliance on this sector, particularly given the finite reserves of oil and gas. In its submission, the Government indicated that its industrial policy was focussed mainly on the development of the non-

oil manufacturing sector with a view to diversify economic activity. He wondered why, notwithstanding the introduction of diversification strategies, the share of petroleum-related manufacturing had increased from 41.5 % to 66.4 % of total manufacturing GDP in the 1992-96 period.

28.   The Government of Trinidad and Tobago appeared to have embarked on a significant modernization of economic policy-making. Starting with the 1988 policy reforms and including the more recent moves to divest State interests in commercial enterprises, Trinidad and Tobago was clearly bringing its economy more into line with the market-oriented policies that were at the base of the WTO Agreements. Other areas deserving mention and study by participants in this review included reduced reliance on price controls, the establishment of a venture capital fund and special measures to assist small businesses, and the establishment in April 1997 of the Securities and Exchange Commission. He felt that the Government of Trinidad and Tobago should be encouraged to move forward with the planned Fair Trading Act as a way of guaranteeing that the economy developed in a competitive manner.

29.   He invited WTO Members to congratulate the Government of Trinidad and Tobago on these initiatives, all of which had pointed Trinidad and Tobago in a healthy direction for the future. He would be interested in learning of the fruits of these efforts when Trinidad and Tobago next came before WTO's Trade Policy Review Mechanism.

IV.   STATEMENT BY THE SECOND DISCUSSANT

30.   The second discussant (Ms. Claudia Orozco Jaramillo) commended Trinidad and Tobago for its positive implementation of its WTO commitments, evidence of an open trade policy. Applied tariffs were below bound levels, with an average of 7% for industrial products, and 19% for agricultural goods. She noted that the TRIPS Agreement had been implemented and incorporated in domestic legislation. Commitments undertaken in various services sub-sectors were being implemented. She would like to have the delegation of Trinidad and Tobago's view on the contribution of the implementation of the WTO agreements to the modernization and diversification effort undertaken by the Government.

31.   In parallel to its participation in the WTO, Trinidad and Tobago was an active member of CARICOM, had signed bilateral agreements with Colombia and Venezuela and participated in regional agreements negotiations. Trinidad and Tobago accounted for 20% of CARICOM trade flows; exports to other CARICOM members represented a quarter of total exports. Trinidad and Tobago was also the beneficiary of various schemes of preferences. Both the European Union and the United States granted preferential treatment to their imports of sugar from Trinidad and Tobago. Notwithstanding this, it was noted that Trinidad and Tobago had to import sugar to fully utilize its quota under both preferential arrangements. She would like to know what the reasons were for this deficit in domestic production.

32.   It was clear from both the Government and the Secretariat's reports that Trinidad and Tobago was seeking to complement its trade policy with an adequate investment policy. To this end, Trinidad and Tobago had signed international agreements for the protection of investment, both at the bilateral and at the multilateral level, and was in the process of reviewing its domestic legislation to enhance the transparency of its decision-making process and of its system of incentives. The main goal was to attract foreign investment in order to enhance economic diversification and shift production to export markets. This was already the case in the natural gas sector. She cautioned, however, against the wide array of fiscal incentives for investments in tourism and petrochemical products, and against the extensive use of free zones.

33.   Trinidad and Tobago's implementation of its WTO commitments was, in general terms, satisfactory. She was concerned, however, about the level and coverage of surcharges applied on certain agricultural imports. Although levels had come down, they were still high. Moreover, certain products were subject to quantitative restrictions, and others to non-automatic import licensing. She wondered whether the delegation of Trinidad and Tobago could explain the need for the use of the previously mentioned measures, especially since applied tariff levels were below bound levels, and whether it could provide information regarding their use in the future.

34.   Noting that exports of certain agricultural products, such as coffee and cocoa, had declined, she sought clarification regarding the reasons for this decline. Regarding services, she would be interested in knowing why tourism had not contributed more to the sector's development. She noted the efforts displayed by the Government to diversify production and exports through free zones, investment promotion, promotion of small and medium-size enterprises, and a redefinition of the role of the State. However, programmes to attract investment included an array of fiscal incentives, including tax exemptions for a period of up to ten years, import duty concessions, and tax credits for expenses. She wondered if the delegation of Trinidad and Tobago could elaborate on the possible effects of these incentives on government revenue and on whether it thought they might be hindering the public sector investment needed to create an adequate framework for private investment.

V.   STATEMENTS BY MEMBERS OF THE TRADE POLICY REVIEW BODY

35.   Members appreciated Trinidad and Tobago's strong commitment to the WTO, its continuing efforts to diversify and open its economy, and to improve the investment climate, particularly in view of the recent crisis in its financial sector.

36.   The representative of <u>Hong, Kong, China</u> noted that the bilateral trade between Hong Kong, China and Trinidad and Tobago had amounted to US$15.8 million in 1997, and had observed an increasing trend in recent years.   In the first 8 months of 1998, total bilateral trade had increased by 18.6% over the same period in 1997.   Goods exported from Hong Kong, China had included textile yarn, fabrics, makeup articles, food products, apparels and machinery, while imported products from Trinidad and Tobago had included fish, cotton, wood, textile yarn, fabrics amd makeup articles. Hong Kong, China appreciated Trinidad and Tobago's recent effort to liberalize and encouraged it to continue its efforts, especially in diversifying its product base and opening up its services sector. Hong Kong, China had submitted written questions on tariffs and additional duties, standards and technical regulations, services, including financial services, telecommunications services, maritime transport and civil aviation services.

37.   The representative of <u>Canada</u> noted that Trinidad and Tobago and Canada enjoyed a longstanding and multi-faceted bilateral relationship with a strong tradition of cooperation. Trade between Canada and Trinidad and Tobago could be traced back nearly 400 years.   In 1997, two-way merchandise trade had totalled Can$129 million, excluding trade in services.   Canada also had significant investment interests in Trinidad and Tobago, particularly in the energy and banking sectors, which stood now at over Can$1 billion.

38.   Under CARIBCAN, Trinidad and Tobago enjoyed preferential access to the Canadian market for most products.   Under legislation passed by Canada earlier this year, the list of duty-exempt products under CARIBCAN had been expanded and now included travel bags, methanol, and lubricating oils; the latter two products were of particular importance to Trinidad and Tobago.

39.   In Canada's view, Trinidad and Tobago had been a solid proponent and player in efforts to liberalize international trade and commercial exchanges, had played a leadership role in the formation and evolution of CARICOM, including the implementation of the CET, and was an active participant in initiatives to develop a FTAA.   The Government of Trinidad and Tobago was to be commended for the very considerable progress achieved over the past decade in liberalizing its trade policies and import regime to bring them into conformity with its CARICOM and WTO commitments.

40.   Canada encouraged the ongoing efforts of Trinidad and Tobago to create "a more investor-friendly climate in the local economy" and trusted that, in amending its Foreign Investment Act. the Government would not reduce its protection of foreign investors.   Canada also welcomed Trinidad and Tobago's continued efforts "to reduce the number and complexity of bureaucratic procedures involved in investment and business transactions" and its stated objective of making these procedures "as simple and transparent as possible.   Canada encouraged the Government to set a more transparent pricing structure in the natural gas sub-sector, which would make it even more attractive to foreign investors.

41.   Another area where more consistency and transparency would enhance Trinidad and Tobago's attractiveness to Canadian and foreign investors was in the issuance of work permits.   While Canada appreciated that Trinidad and Tobago wished to ensure high quality employment for its many well-trained workers, the uncertainty surrounding the issuance and renewal of work permits, and the lack

of a mechanism to appeal negative decisions, presented great difficulties for foreign investors. Canada would also welcome more transparency regarding quantitative restrictions applied to the import of live poultry, both at the level of relevant WTO notifications and at the level of public dissemination of trade regulations.

42.   Canada encouraged Trinidad and Tobago to update and streamline its legal, regulatory and administrative framework with respect to trade and investment, and to increase transparency in the procedures and practices of certain government ministries and agencies.

43.   Canada welcomed the important steps taken by Trinidad and Tobago to liberalize its trade and investment regimes in recent years, which were reflected in the sustained current economic growth, and strongly encouraged Trinidad and Tobago to continue the process of privatization and of public sector modernization and reform. Canada believed that these initiatives would make an important contribution to maintaining Trinidad and Tobago's continuing drive towards full market liberalization and long-term economic growth.

44.   The representative of the United States noted that trading relations between the United States and Trinidad and Tobago were rich in tradition and extensive due in part to the geographical proximity of the two nations. The United States was Trinidad and Tobago's largest trading partner, importing almost half of its exports, while supplying more than one-third of its imports. The investment relationship between the two countries was equally close: the United States was the largest investor in Trinidad and Tobago with extensive U.S. private sector investment in hydrocarbons and related downstream industries. Trinidad and Tobago was second only to Canada in the hemisphere in per capita U.S. direct foreign investment.

45.   The United States congratulated Trinidad and Tobago's efforts in the process of liberalization and deregulation, which had produced sustained growth with low inflation in recent years. Growth had continued to accelerate largely because of investment in the country's petrochemical sector.

46.   With respect to the WTO, Trinidad and Tobago's efforts to bring its legislation into accord with its WTO commitments would help ensure that the environment for trade and investment continued to be positive. Trinidad and Tobago had started applying the WTO Agreement on Customs Valuation, although, as a developing country, it had until end 1999 to bring its valuation system into conformity with the Agreement.

47.   However, further actions could be taken to improve the trade and investment environment. He noted that a number of loss-making state-owned enterprises remained; he also noted the continued existence of licensing procedures as well as import surcharges on a number of products, particularly in the agricultural area. These appeared to be vestiges of earlier policies which could be further liberalized. Government revenues had weakened because of the drop in world oil prices. Divestment of loss-making state enterprises and improved, simplified tax administration could help to offset this trend.

48.   The United States believed Trinidad and Tobago had made tremendous progress in liberalizing its trade regime and urged it to continue down this track.

49.   The representative of the European Union stated that the relations between the European Union and Trinidad and Tobago were governed by the revised Lomé IV Convention, which had been signed in Mauritius on 4 November 1995 and which expired in February of the year 2000. Trinidad and Tobago benefitted from the trade and services provisions of the Convention as well as from special arrangements for sugar, rum and other commodities. The Convention granted preferential

access to the EU market on a non-reciprocal basis to goods from Trinidad and Tobago. The trade provisions of the Lomé Convention were the most valuable part of the agreement for many ACP countries. The new EU-ACP Convention, to enter into force in March 2000, should take into account the limitations of the current Lomé provisions based on preferential market access and the developments resulting from the conclusion of the Uruguay Round. The European Union had recently commenced negotiations with its ACP partners for the new Convention, which would take into account the relevant WTO rules and the sustainable development of the ACP economies, by preparing them for an era of services and new technologies and by encouraging them to move away from trade protection to open competitive trade. Trinidad and Tobago needed to take account of such forthcoming changes and to continue to pursue its policy of economic diversification.

50. Trinidad and Tobago was a small country, with a small population and internal market. Despite these constraints, it had been diversifying and opening its economy, in order to respond to the new requirements of global competitiveness and regional integration, with remarkable results.

51. The Government had achieved a good record of political stability and stable macro-economic performance. The energy sector in particular had shown great dynamism, and the financial sector continued to perform well, although interest rates remained high. Tourism activities had expanded, but the agricultural sector had performed unsatisfactorily, in particular the sugar industry. Lower oil prices would have a negative impact on budget revenues in 1998. Another point of concern was the high unemployment rate.

52. The European Union welcomed the Government of Trinidad and Tobago's commitment to a coherent poverty reduction programme; the European Union was fully prepared to reinforce this programme with suitable projects funded under the National Indicative Programme (NIP). These projects could be targeted to develop infrastructure, tourism capacity and export promotion with a view to contributing to economic diversification.

53. The European Union recognized the efforts of the Government of Trinidad and Tobago to comply with WTO rules, to improve competition and the investment climate and to liberalize its economy. Concern was expressed, however, with regard to the range, costs and coherence of the various investment incentives offered by the Government in energy, manufacturing and in some services activities. The European Union would continue providing for economic diversification and employment creation as agreed in 1997 under the NIP.

54. The representative of Japan stated that Trinidad and Tobago's economy relied heavily on production and export of oil and natural gas. After the decline in oil prices in the mid 1980s the Government of Trinidad and Tobago had introduced measures to restructure its economy by reducing customs duties and promoting privatization. Trinidad and Tobago had succeeded in attracting foreign investment, particularly in the energy sector, as a result of stabilization policies and an increased openness of the economy, and since 1994 the economy had recorded positive growth. Trinidad and Tobago's economy was expected to continue to show a positive growth as a result of high foreign direct investment in the energy sector and growth in non-petroleum activities. However, in order to achieve sustainable economic growth and social development, as well as to promote foreign trade, further measures were required such as further diversification of economic activity, the restructuring of the public sector and the development of infrastructure. Japan expected Trinidad and Tobago to implement policies to meet such objectives and to achieve economic development as well as to contribute to strengthening multilateral trading system through further liberalizing its trade regime. He appreciated that Trinidad and Tobago had made commitment in various services sectors during the

Uruguay Round and also had participated actively in negotiations on financial services and basic telecommunications services. However, sectors on which Trinidad and Tobago had made commitments were still limited. Japan expected Trinidad and Tobago to further liberalize its services regimes including sectors which had not been committed, and to consider to make commitments in these fields during the coming negotiation. Japan noted that it had posed written questions on tariffs, other duties and taxes, standards and technical regulations, competition policy, banking, telecommunications and maritime transport services.

55.   The representative of Mauritius stated that her country and Trinidad and Tobago had a number of things in common: they were both small island states, small economies and net food importers. She noted that although Trinidad and Tobago was an exporter of agricultural products, it imported some 75% of its domestic food requirements. This was the case for many small island states for whom food security remained of paramount importance. Trinidad and Tobago was a clear example of how food security was not necessarily linked to production capacity but to the ability of a country to generate sufficient foreign currency to import its food requirements.

56.   She stated that while Trinidad and Tobago was endowed with oil and gas, unlike most other small islands, strong reliance on the production and export of these two resources was a matter of concern, particularly bearing in mind that proven reserves were estimated at 12 years' supply for oil and at 55 years for natural gas at the current rate of output. She welcomed the initiative of the Government to diversify the economy away from the energy sector. She noted that the Secretariat report made reference to the development of the services sector, particularly transhipment activities. She felt that it would be interesting to know which other sectors had been identified as alternative and reliable sources of revenue.

57.   Mauritius had noted with interest the introduction by Trinidad and Tobago of a Trade Reform Programme that was closely linked with the objectives of attracting foreign investment and of facilitating the development of the domestic industrial base. She cautioned that the competitiveness of Trinidad and Tobago as an investment center could be hindered by the erosion of preferences and the uncertainty about the future of the Lomé Convention. She, therefore, expressed her understanding of the reasons that had led Trinidad and Tobago to introduce initiatives aimed at attracting foreign investment.

58.   The representative of Costa Rica noted the effort by Trinidad and Tobago to implement its WTO commitment through the amendment of domestic legislation, particularly regarding anti-dumping and intellectual property. Furthermore, it would seem that Trinidad and Tobago was planning to dismantle its system of export incentives in 2000, although, as a developing country it had until 2003 to meet is obligations under the Agreement on Subsidies and Countervailing Measures. He understood that one of the goals of the Government was to diversify foreign investment and to this end a new Foreign Investment Act would be put in place. In this respect, he would be grateful to the delegation of Trinidad and Tobago if it could identify the main changes included in the new legislation as compared to the previous law. Costa Rica would also be interested in receiving more information regarding the expropriation and compensation regime, regulations regarding the transfer of capital and rules related to senior management. It would be interesting to know whether the definition of foreign direct investment included intangible goods, such as TRIPS or other rights. Costa Rica wondered what kind of investment promotion scheme would be adopted by Trinidad and Tobago after the dismantlement of the current system of incentives, and on which key elements it would rely.

59.   The representative of India stated that he believed that the documents provided for the review set out clearly the problems and concerns of small economies in harnessing the dynamics of market

access opportunities as they sought to grow and develop. The authorities of Trinidad and Tobago had made explicit in their trade policy initiatives that growth and expansion of their local productive base could only be realized by the penetration of foreign markets. Trinidad and Tobago's policies were based on the recognition that constraints posed by limited size and financial and economic resources could be offset through the openness of the domestic market.

60. The dual approach taken by the authorities was a pointer to the role of diversification of products and markets in achieving an expanding market share in a sustained and aggressive manner. In this context, India would like to commend the authorities for the reach of their country's external trade policy and the plan of action that had been formulated for facilitating a meaningful integration of the local economy with the globalized trading environment.

61. India noted that the process of liberalization and deregulation initiated by Trinidad and Tobago in the mid 1980s had led to the elimination of a number of restrictions to trade, but that a complex system of investment initiatives and high tariffs in some sectors remained. Previous speakers had noted the beneficial aspect of the restructuring programme which envisaged the diversification of the economy away from its dependence on the petroleum sector, by developing non-oil manufacturing activities as well as services. This programme had envisaged a redefinition of the role of the Government itself. However, he noted that a number of goods and services were subject to price controls and that tax concessions, export allowances in the form of tax credits, and customs duty concessions underpinned the incentives structure for a wide range of manufacturing activities. It would be useful to discuss the manner in which the authorities proposed to address these aspects in their plan of action.

62. The representative of Barbados noted her country's close trade relationship with Trinidad and Tobago, and stated that both countries shared similar experiences and faced the same challenges. Within CARICOM, Trinidad and Tobago was Barbados' largest trading partner; Barbados' exports to Trinidad and Tobago accounted for 19% of total exports to CARICOM countries, and imports from Trinidad and Tobago accounted for 72% of total imports from CARICOM. Barbados welcomed Trinidad and Tobago's effort to liberalize its economy as well as its WTO participation.

63. The representative of Australia congratulated Trinidad and Tobago on its effort to implement economic reform and on amending domestic legislation to comply with WTO commitments. She encouraged Trinidad and Tobago to continue on the path of further integration into the world trading system.

64. The representative of Jamaica congratulated Trinidad and Tobago's on its impressive achievement in economic development, in particular with regard to the role played by trade in its economy. He praised the international competitiveness achieved by the energy-related manufacturing sector in Trinidad and Tobago as well as for light manufacturers. This was a good example indicating that a small island economy had not necessarily been constrained by its size "marginalized" in the global economy. In this regard, he recognized the important role played by the Government of Trinidad and Tobago in attracting foreign investment in the energy and energy-related sectors. Notwithstanding these achievements, he also felt that there was a need for more sensitive treatment in some areas where neither Government nor the private sector by itself could overcome the constraints of a small economy. He also expressed concerns about the impact of anti-dumping or other trade-restricting measures imposed on Trinidad and Tobago's economy imposed by its largest neighbour.

VI. REPLIES BY THE REPRESENTATIVE OF TRINIDAD AND TOBAGO AND ADDITIONAL COMMENTS

65. The replies by the representative of <u>Trinidad and Tobago</u> were divided into three main themes: (i) economic environment; (ii) trade policy measures; and (iii) sectoral policies. Written responses to specific questions were circulated to members (Annex II). Trinidad and Tobago would provide further answers in written form within the time allowed under the TPRM. Following the replies, the Chairperson opened the floor to TPRB members for further comments and questions.

(i) Economic environment

66. The representative of Trinidad and Tobago appreciated delegations' interventions and comments. He stressed that the various policy initiatives undertaken by Trinidad and Tobago were all consistent with its WTO obligations. Referring to the role of the State in the economy, he stated that divestment had been going on for some time, and the main problem now was how to treat successor companies. The Board of Directors of all remaining enterprises comprised representatives from the private sector.

67. Trinidad and Tobago was a net food importer, importing around 75% of food requirements. Recognizing the need for reform in the agricultural sector, the representative of Trinidad and Tobago noted that agricultural policies were under review, particularly regarding import surcharges, sugar, and the role of the state enterprise Caroni, Ltd. The case of this enterprise was special and a Ministerial committee had been appointed to deal with its problems. A possible strategy would be to shift the activities of Caroni away from sugar into industrial activities and services and to divide it into several companies.

68. Virtually all price controls had been eliminated, except on three items: sugar, pharmaceutical products and school text books. Prohibited goods included in the Import Negative List were limited to a few items, such as arms and ammunitions, drugs, left-hand drive vehicles and poultry parts, which were considered to compete unfavourably with local production. The list included also cigarette paper, certain pesticides, ships and boats under 250 TT, and oils and fats due to an agreement within CARICOM. Most prohibitions were for safety or public health reasons.

69. Trinidad and Tobago had made considerable progress in the past 15 years in reducing its dependency on the oil sector, as evidenced by the shift from oil to natural gas production. Natural gas was used both as a final product and as a feedstock for downstream industries. The development of the latter might result in Trinidad and Tobago becoming the largest exporter of methanol in the world in the near future. Another evidence of diversification was the significant increase in tourism experienced in recent years.

70. The large number of projects undertaken in the energy sector in 1997 and 1998 had resulted in a substantial increase in imports of construction material and capital equipment, and this had resulted in a trade deficit, which was expected to be redressed in the near future. The fiscal and monetary policy mix applied by the Government, combined with the application of incentive schemes had resulted in a significant reduction in unemployment, from 19% in November 1995, to 13.5% in November 1998. The Government hoped to reach single-digit unemployment levels by 2000. This would be aided by the implementation of a large-scale tourism programme, the opening of an aluminium smelting plant, and the creation of new down-stream natural gas industries. Regarding investment, existing legislation was being amended and the new Investment Promotion Act would incorporate national treatment as one of its features.

71.   The first discussant commended the representative of Trinidad and Tobago for his complete answers. He thought that the rise in imports due to an increase in investment flows was impressive. He was also impressed by the economic reforms undertaken and the commitment to privatization.

72.   The second discussant noted that Trinidad and Tobago's investment regime had shown positive achievements; she applauded the legal measures applied and the large investment inflows obtained. She noted that the system of tax incentives applied was wide and ran across sectors. With respect to agricultural products, she expressed concern regarding the high ratio of imports to domestic demand for some products.

73.   The representative of Haiti congratulated Trinidad and Tobago for their trade policy performance. Haiti recognized the problems and constraints faced by Trinidad and Tobago as a small island. Haiti was interested in being integrated in the group of Trinidad and Tobago's trading partners. Trinidad and Tobago was a model for Haiti.

74.   The representative of Trinidad and Tobago thanked Haiti for the remarks and advised that Trinidad and Tobago was already Haiti's trading partner. He admitted that agriculture was the weak point of Trinidad and Tobago's economy, but expected things would improve in the sector.

(ii)   Trade policy measures

75.   The representative of Trinidad and Tobago stated that his country would promptly notify its anti-dumping legislation to the WTO. Trinidad and Tobago did not apply any direct export subsidies, since the Export Trade Administration facility had expired a few years before. The system of incentives currently applied was mainly comprised of tax exemptions on income generated outside of Trinidad and Tobago, and although WTO-consistent would be dismantled before 2003. His country was making efforts towards the enforcement of copyrights, including the introduction of the Banderole system. Trinidad and Tobago was one of the few developing countries to have introduced wide-ranging TRIPS legislation. He noted that Trinidad and Tobago had chosen not to delay the application of the WTO Agreement on Customs Valuation as was its prerogative as a developing country.

76.   Trinidad and Tobago had implemented the tariff reductions included in Phase IV of the CARICOM schedule of reductions of the CET; the maximum applied tariff on industrial products was 20%. Reductions on import surcharges on agricultural products had been implemented on a accelerated schedule of five years, in accordance with what had been agreed in the Uruguay Round, with only a few products scheduled for reductions over ten years. Import quotas had virtually been eliminated; the few remaining quotas were applied for national security reasons, safety considerations, or to meet CARICOM obligations. Items subject to quantitative restrictions represented a small share of Trinidad and Tobago's imports, of between 5 and 10%. The representative of Trinidad and Tobago noted that some local standards had been developed, using international standards, basically to protect consumers and for public health reasons. Standards were not meant to be non-tariff barriers to trade. In cases where local standards did not exist, international standards were used.

77.   The second discussant noted Trinidad and Tobago's effort in reducing import surcharges. However, the accelerated implementation of reductions in the agricultural sector resulting from the tariffication of quantitative restrictions in the Uruguay Round referred to tariffs and not to surcharges. The problem in the case of Trinidad and Tobago was that in addition to tariffs there were surcharges and together these were well above bound rates in the WTO.

78. In response, the representative of Trinidad and Tobago stated that surcharges had been used as part of tariffication, and that they were being reduced to achieve compliance with bindings.

79. The representative of the United States noted Trinidad and Tobago's economic progress. The trade deficit registered in 1997 was due mainly to an increase in capital goods imports. He expressed his satisfaction with Trinidad and Tobago's implementation of the Agreement on Customs Valuation. His Government would appreciate a prompt notification of Trinidad and Tobago's anti-dumping law to the WTO. He noted that while Trinidad and Tobago had until 2003 to eliminate the indirect subsidies provided by the incentives system, consideration should be given to an earlier phasing-out, to give breathing space to the domestic industry. There was a lack of transparency regarding the assignation of work permits. Referring to the list of products subject to licensing, as provided by the delegation of Trinidad and Tobago, and the justifications presented, he recalled that obligations under the CARICOM Treaty could not be used as a justification for licensing under the WTO. Similarly, national security could not be used as a justification for the licensing in the case of cigarette paper. With regard to import surcharges, he encouraged Trinidad and Tobago to reduce them to their bound level of 15%.

80. In response, the representative of Trinidad and Tobago stated that his country would be working to address the comments made by the United States.

81. The representative of Japan noted that while most import surcharges had been reduced, Trinidad and Tobago was still bound by its WTO commitment to lower them further to 15%. He asked whether any import surcharges were applied on industrial products. He would also like to know whether all standards were published and submitted to public comment in accordance with Article 2.9 of the Agreement on Technical Barriers to Trade.

82. In response, the representative of Trinidad and Tobago noted that information regarding a standard was made public before the standard was adopted, and that all standards used by his country were WTO consistent. He also noted that Trinidad and Tobago did not apply import surcharges on industrial products, but only on a few agricultural products. Surcharges had been put in place as temporary measures to remove the quantitative restrictions that existed under the Import Negative List, and were now subject, except for sugar, icing sugar and poultry, to an accelerated phasing-out.

83. The representative of Canada sought clarification regarding the quantitative restrictions applied on live poultry. He recalled that, under the Agreement on Agriculture, quantitative restrictions were no longer allowed. He enquired whether the measures applied were in fact quantitative restrictions, or if they were tariff quotas and noted the lack of transparency evidenced by the fact that the size of the quota was not made public.

84. The representative of Trinidad and Tobago responded that the quantitative restrictions were applied to comply with the Agreement on Sanitary and Phyto-Sanitary Measures and were not hidden tariff quotas.

(iii) Sectoral policies

85. The representative of Trinidad and Tobago noted that his country had made substantial progress toward production diversification, and that the economy was undergoing a transformation, moving away from oil to natural gas as well as to down-stream petroleum manufacturing, and services. The energy sector accounted now for 25% of GDP, although export earnings were still mainly dependent on the sector. Trinidad and Tobago had not as yet presented an offer regarding banking services but was working on a position which would be submitted to the WTO before the

deadline agreed, in January 1999. Regarding telecommunications, a committee had been appointed to review the operations of the sector. The review should be completed by December 1998 and implemented before mid-1999. In civil aviation, Trinidad and Tobago was committed to an open-skies policy; operations would be expanded upon completion of the new airport, currently under construction. Trinidad and Tobago had a special interest in developing tourism activities, particularly in the area of integrated resorts, where development had been lagging. A Tourism Development Bill was about to be submitted to Parliament.

86.   The first discussant asked whether any actions had been taken at the CARICOM level to liberalize financial services.

87.   The representative of Trinidad and Tobago replied that two Trinidad ad Tobago banks were already operating in CARICOM and other countries of the region, such as Venezuela. Trinidad and Tobago insurance companies were also operating in the CARICOM area.

ANNEX I

ADVANCE WRITTEN QUESTIONS

QUESTIONS BY CANADA

Telecommunications

In the area of basic telecommunications services supplied through mode 1, we understand that Trinidad and Tobago has committed to not impose any market access limitations, provided that the supplier uses the network of the exclusive operator (qualification valid until 2010). Para. 101 states, "While basic telecommunications services are in the hands of the Trinidad and Tobago Limited (TSTT), there are no restrictions on the provisions of value-added services using the network of the exclusive service provider ...". Please clarify the phrase "in the hands of" TSTT as this seems to imply that provision of basic telecom services is exclusively TSTT's.

According to Trinidad and Tobago's Schedule of Commitments, there will be no market access limitations. However, para. 102 states that "... Those who wish to provide the public terrestrial-based mobile services, internet and internet access and teleconferencing for private use through cross-border and commercial-presence modes must negotiate with TSTT ...". There appears to be an inconsistency between its WTO commitments and this statement. Kindly clarify.

QUESTIONS BY THE EUROPEAN UNION

Secretariat Report (WT/TPR/S/49)

Are the import surcharges on meat and milk going to be eliminated on schedule in 1998/99? What is the rationale retaining the surcharges on sugar, icing sugar and poultry cuts? (paras. 16 and 29)

What steps are being taken to bring the customs valuation system formally into line with WTO rules? (para. 17)

What is the purpose of retaining the licensing system for certain imports, now that QRs are no longer applied? Does the Government have plans for abolishing these residual controls? (para. 21)

Does the Government have any plans to eliminate residual price "controls"? (para. 25)

There is a large gap between the tariff bindings for agricultural products and the actual applied tariffs. Does the Government envisage lowering the bindings? (para. 28)

Given the excessive dependence on the energy sector, what strategy does the Government have for economic diversification and employment creation? Does the Government have a strategy for reducing the persistently high levels of unemployment and pockets of poverty which exist in certain parts of the country?

Government Report (WT/TPR/G/49)

Does the Government have a strategy for diverting itself of its holding in loss-making enterprises such as Caroni? (para. 34)

Does the Government envisage the need to revise the rules applying to the banking sector, for example in terms of reserve asset ratios, in order to reduce the relatively high cost of capital in Trinidad and Tobago, particularly for small enterprises? (paras. 13-15)

How does the Government reconcile its objective of pursuing integration efforts within the wider Caribbean, particularly in the context of the FTAA negotiations, with the parallel initiative which has recently begun in the post-Lomé context, to develop a CARIFORUM FAA with the EU? (paras. 51 and 58)

QUESTIONS BY HONG KONG, CHINA

Tariffs and additional duties

We note that while 44.9% of tariff lines are duty free, 19.2% are still subject to a tariff rate between 15% and 20% after the implementation of Phase IV of the CARICOM CET on 1 July 1998. Moreover, more than 8% of items being exceptions of the CARICOM CET, are subject to a rate above 25%. We would like to know if Trinidad and Tobago has any plan to further reduce and, as far as possible, eliminate the tariffs (WT/TPR/S/49, pp. 34-35, para. 12 and Chart III.1).

We note that Trinidad and Tobago has put in place a scheduled, gradual reduction of import surcharges, for some items, the surcharge will be reduced to 86% by 2004 under the reduction schedule. We are interested to know whether Trinidad and Tobago has any plan to further reduce or eliminate such surcharge as well as other duties and charges (WT/TPR/S/49, p. 43, para. 31).

Standards and technical regulations

We note that under the Standards Act 18 of 1997, the Bureau of Standards may recognize a foreign standard for certification and label verification and may accept certificates from laboratories outside the country. We would like to know how many foreign standards/certificates have been so recognized. Are they done unilaterally or on the basis of MRAs? (WT/TPR/S/49, p. 52, para. 59)

Services overview

In Trinidad and Tobago's schedule, its horizontal commitments provide that the acquisition of more than 30% of equity of publicly traded companies is subject to approval. Will the Government consider relaxing this limitation? (WT/TPR/S/49, p. 92, para. 81)

Financial services

We note that at the end of 1997, there were only five commercial banks and one of which is wholly foreign owned. Would like to know the general criteria for awarding licences. Are local and foreign services suppliers subject tot he same requirements? (WT/TPR/S/49, pp. 92-93, para. 85)

Telecommunications

We note that the exclusive rights on basic telecommunication services are given to Telecommunication Services of Trinidad and Tobago Ltd. (TSTT) which will expire by 2009 (Summary Observations, para. 36). Will the Government consider advancing the liberalization of this sector? (WT/TPR/S/49, p. 98, para. 99)

We note that the Telecommunications Act is currently under revision to include changes necessary to meet GATS obligations. What is the expected timeframe for completion and approval by the Parliament and the President? (WT/TPR/S/49, pp. 98-99, para. 100)

Maritime transport

It is mentioned that there are plans to commercialize cargo handling and marine services and that the shares of the Port Authority will be sold to local and foreign investors. Would like to know more information on the plans including timeframe for implementation and any limitations on foreign investors' participation (WT/TPR/S/49, p. 100, para. 108).

Civil aviation

We note that air cargo handling services and airline facilities and repair services are open to foreigners. What are the general requirements for the provision of these services? Are local and foreign investors subject to the same requirements? (WT/TPR/S/49, p. 101, para. 113)

QUESTIONS BY JAPAN

Tariffs

It is reported that Trinidad and Tobago adopted the CARICOM CET on 1 January 1991 and put in place the tariff reductions called for in Phase IV of the CET implementation process. Have the tariff reductions called for in Phase IV which is to reduce the CARICOM CET to 20% already been achieved? If not, please explain the prospect for the reduction to 20% (paras. 11-12, p. 34 of the Secretariat report).

Other duties and taxes

It is reported that import surcharges of 60% on sugar, 75% on icing sugar, and 100% (or 86% expected in 2004) on some poultry which are considerably exceeding the 15% level bound for "other duties" during the Uruguay Round and included in Trinidad and Tobago's schedule of concessions. Does not this measure lack conformity with Article II of the GATT 1994? (p. 43, para. 31)

Please provide information on whether there remains any other products, including industrial products, on which "other duties" are levied. Please also provide the rate of the "other duties", if any.

Standards and technical regulations

Are all the local standards created by the Trinidad and Tobago Bureau of Standards? If not, please explain on which products or in which field local standards are created by other organizations (p. 51, para. 56).

It is reported that standards, developed by a specifications committee, are published for comment prior to adoption. Is this publication made in addition to the procedures provided in Article 2.9 of the TBT Agreement? If so, please explain if such comment is open for foreign governments or foreign public and private organizations (p. 51, para. 56).

Competition policy

It is reported that a proposal for a Fair Trading Act was presented to Parliament in 1997. Please explain the present situation of the deliberation in the Parliament (para. 99, p. 62).

Banking services

Trinidad and Tobago has made no commitment in banking services. Is there any regulation in the Financial Institutions Act of 1993 which limits Market Access (Article XVI of the GATS) or National Treatment (Article XVII of the GATS)? (p. 93, para. 86)

Does Trinidad and Tobago intend to make any commitment in this field in the coming negotiations?

Telecommunications Services

It is reported that the Telecommunications Act of 1991 is not in effect since it has yet to be assented by the President and that the law currently under revision including changes necessary to meet GATS obligations. The Fourth Protocol entered into force on 5 February 1998 (p. 98, para. 100). Please provide information on when the 1991 Act or the law which meets the GATS obligation is expected to be in effect.

Trinidad and Tobago has committed to eliminate the monopoly of TSTT by 2010 and not to limit on Market Access nor National Treatment as of 2010 in its Schedule of Specific Commitments. Please explain the schedule for the elimination of the monopoly status of the TSTT and the liberalization of the sector to meet this Commitment.

Maritime transport

It is reported that vessels wishing to engage in coastal trade between the islands of Trinidad and Tobago are required to obtain a licence and that this requirement is applied to both local and foreign operators. Please provide criteria to obtain the above-mentioned licence. Do the same criteria apply equally to local and foreign operators? (p. 100, para. 106)

QUESTIONS BY THE UNITED STATES

Export Incentives

According to the report, Trinidad and Tobago applies no export taxes, no direct subsidies and no export performance requirements. An export allowance in the form of a tax credit is granted to companies exporting processed or manufactured products (excluding petrochemical and certain other products) to non-CARICOM markets. The tax credit covers the profits on the proportion of export sales to total sales so that profits on exports are effectively tax exempt. Other forms of export promotion to extra-regional markets include assistance on a 50/50 cost-sharing basis to eligible exporters to assist them with the cost of entering and competing in export markets. Local tax law also allows for a deduction of 150% of expenses incurred in promoting the expansion into non-CARICOM markets. Could Trinidad and Tobago provide a list of all exporters who currently benefit from these programs? Also could more information be provided regarding how the tax credit is determined and what the eligibility requirements are for the 50/50 cost-sharing program? Finally, are there deadlines for the termination of any of the programs? The report indicates that the Foreign Investment Act of 1990 is expected to be replaced by a new investment Promotion Act which seeks to diversify export-related foreign investment. How will the new law differ from the current Act?

Intellectual property rights

What is the status of Trinidad and Tobago's efforts to sign the WIPO Copyright Treaty?

Trinidad and Tobago's 1997 Copyright Act became effective 1 October 1997. While the Act offers protections equivalent to those available in the United States, enforcement remains a concern. The Copyright Organization of Trinidad and Tobago has stepped up its enforcement of unauthorized use of locally produced products, in particular audio cassettes and CDs of local artists such as Calypso artists. However, at the same time, pirated foreign videos, especially U.S. movies and audio cassettes, are rented and sold openly in the street and in stores. What is the status of Trinidad and Tobago's enforcement efforts on video piracy?

Agriculture

According to the report, import surcharges are currently applied on a number of agricultural products. For example, import surcharges of 60% on sugar, 75% on icing sugar, and 86% on some poultry cuts are expected to remain in place beyond 2004, considerably exceeding the 15% level bound during the Uruguay Round and included in Trinidad and Tobago's schedule of concessions. What plans does the GOTT have to bring these charges into line with bound duties?

Licences

Does Trinidad and Tobago plan to liberalize its licensing procedures? Items on the Import Negative List still require import licences and include a broad range of products: livestock, meat, fish, sugar, oils and fats, motor vehicles, cigarette papers, small ships and boats, and pesticides.

Anti-dumping/countervailing duties

The report states that Trinidad and Tobago substantially amended its Anti-Dumping and Countervailing Duties law in 1995, but has not yet notified the WTO of this change. When will the formal notification occur?

Services

Telecommunications remains closed to new foreign investment in key areas. Local and international telephone service is provided by a state-owned TSTT (51%) and Cable and Wireless (49%) monopoly. We understand that Trinidad and Tobago maintains that its agreement with Cable and Wireless does not guarantee a monopoly, but the Government's policy is, nonetheless, not to issue licences to operate in this field to other providers. Since the February 1996 commitment by Trinidad and Tobago to allow open access and national treatment for basic (local and long-distance) services by 2010, there has been some discussion of licensing other basic service providers within the next few years. When does Trinidad and Tobago plan to begin to issue licences for additional basic service telecommunication providers? The Government has recently announced opening the cellular telephone market to competition by the end of the year. This is in advance of Trinidad and Tobago's WTO liberalization commitments. Do you still expect to meet this announced date? What are the Government's plans to liberalize other segments of this sector?

Work permits

Foreign firms have occasionally complained about inconsistencies and a lack of transparency in the issuance of renewal of work permits, particularly for foreign executive level personnel. The U.S./TT BIT, which entered into force in 1996, contains a commitment by the Parties which in spirit addresses this issue. The implication is that nationals of one party should be permitted to enter and remain in its territory for purpose of establishing, developing, administering, or advising on the operation of an investment to which they, or a company of the other Party that employs them, have committed (or are in the process of committing) a substantial amount of capital or other resources. it also permits covered investments to engage top managerial personnel of their choice, regardless of nationality. How is Trinidad and Tobago addressing this continuing issue?

Civil aviation

Trinidad and Tobago has expressed interest in liberalizing its air transportation services and, in the recent past, has indicated an interest in signing an Open Skies agreement with the United States. Can you tell us if such an agreement is still being contemplated?

ANNEX II

RESPONSE TO QUESTIONS

I.   ECONOMIC ENVIRONMENT

Macro-economic Stabilization

<u>European Union</u>

Does the Government envisage the need to revise the rules applying to the banking sector, for example in terms of reserve asset ratios, in order to reduce the relatively high cost of capital in Trinidad and Tobago, particularly for small enterprises? (paras. 13-15 of the Government Report).

The monetary authorities are committed to the reduction in the high reserve ratio in the banking sector to more prudential levels over the medium term.

<u>First Discussant, Andrew Stoler</u>

If the visiting government team from Trinidad and Tobago could shed some light on the nature of the 44% growth in imports in 1997, it would make an important contribution to our understanding of the current macroeconomic context.

Imports of construction materials and machinery and transport equipment for the construction of plants in the petrochemical sector were primarily responsible for the increase in imports in 1997. These new plants include an LNG, ammonia and methanol plants.   Increased investment in infrastructure projects by the Government was also partly responsible for the increase in imports.

<u>Mauritius</u>

Could the visiting team from Trinidad and Tobago comment on whether other sectors have been identified as alternate sources of foreign exchange?

The Government of Trinidad and Tobago has undertaken a trade reform programme which is designed to diversify the economy away from it's dependence on petroleum.   In this regard the government has identified the following sectors for the generation of sustainable export-led growth. These include: (a) Financial services; (b) agro-processing; (c) software development; (d) speciality chemicals e.g. essential oils; (e) engineering goods and services e.g. design, maintenance and repair, fabrication of parts;

<u>India</u>

We note that a number of goods and services are subject to price controls and that tax concessions, export allowances in the form of tax credits and customs duty concessions underpin the incentives structure for a wide range of manufacturing activities. It would be useful to discuss in this Body the manner in which the authorities propose to address these aspects in their plan of action.

In keeping with its objective of liberalizing and deregulating the local economy, Government maintains price controls on only three items. However, an incentive scheme has been implemented in order to foster the development of the private sector, which is another major objective of Trinidad and Tobago's industrialization thrust. In addition, Government has removed import restrictions, exchange rate controls and has divested its shareholdings in a number of state companies. Future economic strategies include continued efforts to attract foreign investors and promotion of the development of the small business, tourism and light manufacturing sectors.

Structural Adjustment

Costa Rica

Can you provide additional information on the following: expropriation and compensation regimes; transfer of capital; rules on senior management? Does FDI (its concept) include non-tangible goods like Intellectual Property or any other rights?

Trinidad and Tobago's Investment Regime is investor-friendly. Bilateral Investment Treaties (BITs) have been signed with the USA, France, the United Kingdom, Canada and the Dominican Republic. These agreements and national practice provide for prompt, adequate and fair compensation in the event of expropriation and free transfer of capital. The Government admits senior personnel necessary for the conclusion of an investment according to its work permit and immigration laws. The definition of investment used is a broad one involving both tangible and intangible property.

What type of investment promotion scheme is Trinidad and Tobago to use to promote growth of other sectors ? (In relation to reducing dependency from the oil sector), and what will be the cornerstone of such a policy for attracting investments to Trinidad and Tobago?

Refer to previous answers on duty concession, tax incentives and the like.

First Discussant, Andrew L. Stoler

The documents provided for this review indicate that the Government of Trinidad and Tobago is considering adopting a competition policy framework as part of a proposed "Fair Trading Act". Would the visiting Government team care to comment on the competitive situation prevailing in the financial services sector and whether this situation might be, in part, a motivation for the introduction of competition policy?

The origin of the competition policy was a logical sequence of the liberalization process instituted by successive Governments following the structural adjustment program in the late 1980s. The reform process included trade reform, financial reform and the de-monopolization of certain sectors. The financial services sector in Trinidad and Tobago is highly competitive. Since the early 1990s the financial system has been restructured and deregulated. These changes have included the elimination of selective credit controls, the elimination of capital controls and the strengthening of the supervisory and regulatory framework.

Would the visiting Government team like to comment on why it feels the necessity to maintain management control in partially privatized entities such as the Iron and Steel Company and the National Flour Mills?

Government no longer has management control in the Iron and Steel Company, which is now wholly-owned by the private sector. With respect to the National Flour Mills and other companies in which Government has some shareholding, the Board of Directors comprises appointees of the Government along with appointees from the private sector which in turn appoints the managers.

Caroni, the only producer of sugar in the country is 100% state-owned. On page 9 of the government submission, the Government of Trinidad and Tobago seems to suggest that it might be willing to divest its interest in Caroni after reorganizing its management and operations. Does the Government plan to eventually sell off its interest in the sugar company?

A Ministerial Committee has been appointed to address the issues of restructuring and possible divestment of Caroni (1975) Ltd.

Japan

It is reported that a proposal for a Fair Trading Act was presented to Parliament in 1997. Please explain the present situation of the deliberation in the Parliament (para. 99, p. 62).

The Fair Trading Bill is presently being reviewed by the Chief Parliamentary Counsel before being presented to Cabinet. It will then be placed before Parliament for its consideration.

European Commission

Does the Government have any plans to eliminate residual price "controls"? (para. 25)

Price controls remain only on certain basic pharmaceuticals, school text books and sugar.

Given the excessive dependence on the energy sector, what strategy does the Government have for economic diversification and employment creation? Does the Government have a strategy for reducing the persistently high levels of unemployment and pockets of poverty which exist in certain parts of the country?

The Government has defined its economic policy objectives in the following documents: (a) The Medium Term Policy Framework 1999-2001; (b) The Industrial Policy 1996-2000; (c) The Trade Policy for Trinidad and Tobago 1997-2001; (d) Creating A Nation of Entrepreneurs 1999-2001: An Action Plan For the Future Direction of Micro, Small and Medium Enterprises Development in Trinidad and Tobago; (e) The Tourism Master Plan. Based on these documents the main thrust of Government's economic and industrial policies is the promotion of sustainable export-led growth and development through the diversification of the economy away from its dependence on petroleum. An additional objective of an overall macro-economic policy is the reduction of unemployment largely through the promotion of private sector growth and development. In essence, the Government is aware of the fact that the expansion of business activity will generate jobs and reduce the overall level of poverty in the economy. As mentioned above, particular emphasis will be placed on the development of the small business sector. The Government holds the view that the establishment of small businesses will provide a large number of unemployed persons with a source of self-generated income and has implemented a number of measures to provide financial and technical assistance. The results of these measures include: an economy that has expanded by 5%; an unemployment rate that is the lowest in 14 years (13.4%); a rate of inflation contained at 5%; an increase in foreign reserves to over US$1 billion; increased emphasis on human resource development and social welfare programmes.

Does the government have a strategy for divesting itself of its holding in loss-making enterprises such as Caroni? (para. 34 of Government report)

Yes. Cabinet has approved a broad philosophical approach for the divestment of the State sector, including Caroni (1975) Ltd. Refer to answer provided to Mr Stoler's question above.

<u>Second Discussant, Claudia Orozco Jaramillo</u>

As regards implementation of the Uruguay Round Agreements, what is the view of the Trinidad and Tobago delegation on the contribution that these Agreements have made to the government's efforts to modernize and diversify the economy?

The modernization and liberalization of the Trinidad and Tobago economy began unilaterally in the early stages of the Uruguay Round. It continued during the negotiations through, for example, the schedule of reduction of the Common External Tariff and the introduction of trade remedy laws. The conclusion of the Round led to the amendment of existing legislation to bring these into line with our multilateral obligations and provided a basis for increasing the pace of liberalization. This placed demands on our institutional capacity. The dependence on export-led growth should have been supported by the market openings of the Uruguay Round. The Round provides a measure of stability and predictability and should allow us to enhance our export performance. On the other hand, preferences have been eroded and a greater demand for full reciprocity has emerged. While Trinidad and Tobago is prepared to take up these challenges future agreements will need to pay more heed to the diversity of the membership.

Could the delegation of Trinidad and Tobago explain the need to have recourse to these Instruments, particularly if one takes into account that the applied tariffs are lower than the bound tariffs, would also be interesting to hear what would be done with these Instruments in the future.

The Government of Trinidad and Tobago has virtually removed its import restrictions. As a consequence of this fact, Anti-Dumping legislation was introduced in order to ensure that the domestic market share of local manufacturers is not undermined by imported goods which are under-priced. The basic principle is that the local market has been liberalized, and although domestic manufacturers will undoubtedly be exposed to competition from foreign goods, such competition should be fair and not due to improper practices. In cognisance of this fact the Government of Trinidad and Tobago amended its Anti-Dumping legislation in 1996 in order to ensure the following: (i) WTO compatibility and consistency; (ii) that implementation of this legislation is conducted in accordance with the WTO Agreements on the implementation of Anti-Dumping Rules. The Government of Trinidad and Tobago also plans to introduce a competition policy legislative framework to regulate the behaviour of monopolies, cartels and similar institutions. The objective of government in this instance is that of ensuring that these organizations do not abuse their position of dominance in the local economy. As mentioned above this policy is consistent with the government's objectives of fostering free and fair competition in the local economy.

It would be interesting to hear comments on the fiscal incentives and the impact on the Government's ability to create a competitive environment which would require investments in physical infrastructure and human development.

The fiscal incentive scheme is operated by the Government of Trinidad and Tobago in a bid to accelerate the pace of industrialization in the local economy. These incentives include a number of tax exemptions for machinery, buildings and equipment which would undoubtedly enhance the human resource base and the physical infrastructure of Trinidad and Tobago as firms seeking to benefit from these incentives establish operations in the country.

Regional Arrangements

<u>European Commission</u>

How does the Government reconcile its objective of pursuing integration efforts within the wider Caribbean, particularly in the context of the FTAA negotiations, with the parallel initiative which has recently begun in the post-Lomé context, to develop a CARIFORUM FAA with the EU? (paras 51 & 58 of the Government report)

The Government does not envisage any conflict in adopting various approaches to expanding market access. We are committed to our CARICOM obligations and to negotiating a Free Trade Area of the Americas. On the other hand, no decision has been taken concerning the eventual negotiation of a CARIFORUM Free Trade Agreement with the EU. Any future arrangements will undoubtedly be WTO-compatible.

II.   TRADE POLICY MEASURES

Tariffs and Surcharges: Applied rates and bindings

<u>Japan</u>

It is reported that Trinidad and Tobago adopted the CARICOM CET on 1 January 1991 and put in place the tariff reductions calls for in Phase IV of CET implementation process. Please explain the detail of the Phase IV, as well as Phase I to Phase III, of the CET implementation process. Are tariff reductions called for in from Phase I to Phase III already put in place ? (Paras. 11 and 12, p. 34 of the Secretariat Report)

The Heads of CARICOM took a decision that the Common External Tariff (CET) will be progressively reduced over a period of five years commencing from 1 January 1993. This will be achieved through four (4) phases culminating in a maximum rate of duty of 20% (with a few exceptions) from 1 January 1998. The plan for the phased reduction of tariffs is outlined in the following table:

PHASE	PERIOD OF APPLICATION	RATE STRUCTURE
I.	1 January 1993 to 31 December,1994	0-5% to 30-35%
II.	1 January,1995 to 31 December,1996	0-5% to 25-30%
III.	1 January 1997 to 31 December 1997	0-5% to 20-25%
IV.	1 January 1998 and onwards	0-5% to 20%

Based on this table it is apparent that Trinidad and Tobago has implemented all four (4) phases on the scheduled dates within the appropriate time-frames. Consequently in effect the maximum tariff applicable to industrial products is 20%.

Hong Kong, China (WT/TPR/S/49, pp. 34-35, para. 12 and Chart III.I)

We note that while 44.9% of tariff lines are duty free, 19.2% are still subject to a tariff rate between 15% and 20% after the implementation of Phase IV of the CARICOM/CET on 1 July 1998. Moreover, more than 8% of items, being exceptions of the CARICOM/CET, are subject to a rate above 25%. We would like to know if Trinidad and Tobago has any plan to further reduce and, as far as possible, eliminate the tariffs.

The Government of Trinidad and Tobago may not alter the rates in the CET without the approval of CARICOM Heads of Government. Based on the fact that Trinidad and Tobago's maximum tariffs have been reduced from 45% to 20% over a five-year period there are no plans to reduce these tariffs any further in the immediate future. (WT/TPR/S/49, p. 43, para. 31)

Other Duties and Taxes

Japan (para. 31, p. 43)

It is reported that import surcharges of 60% on sugar, 75% on icing sugar, and 100% or 86% expected in 2004 on some poultry which are considerably exceeding the 15% level bound for "other duties" during the Uruguay Round and included in Trinidad and Tobago's schedule of concessions. Does not this measure lack conformity with Article II of the GATT 1994?

In the view of the Government of Trinidad and Tobago the implementation of these surcharges is in conformity with Article II of the GATT.

Hong Kong, China

We note that Trinidad and Tobago has put in place a scheduled, gradual reduction of import surcharges, for some items, these surcharges will be reduced to 86% by 2004 under the reduction schedule. We are interested to know whether Trinidad and Tobago has any plan to further reduce or eliminate such surcharges as well as other duties and charges.

Trinidad and Tobago intends to maintain the current schedule of taxes and surcharges as specified in the schedule submitted. Notwithstanding, it should be noted that a study will shortly be commissioned by the CARICOM Secretariat in order to review the Common External Tariff on agricultural commodities, which is currently at 40%.

European Union

Are the import surcharges on meat and milk going to be eliminated on schedule in 1998/99? What is the rationale retaining the surcharges on sugar, icing sugar and poultry cuts? (para. 16) (para. 29)

The Government is committed to eliminating import surcharges on meat and milk as planned in 1998/1999. The Government has imposed surcharges on sugar, icing sugar and poultry cuts in order to offer some measure of protection to the local producers while efforts are underway to enhance their efficiency and international competitiveness.

There is a large gap between the tariff bindings for agricultural products and the actual applied tariffs. Does the Government envisage lowering the bindings? (para. 28)

As mentioned earlier the Government's agricultural policies are being reviewed and consequently present bindings will be re-examined upon the completion of these reviews.

What steps are being taken to bring the customs valuation system formally into line with WTO rules? (para. 17)

Trinidad and Tobago's customs valuation is consistent with WTO rules as stated in WT/TPR/S/49.

Licensing

United States

Does Trinidad and Tobago plan to liberalize its licensing procedures? Items on the Import Negative List still require import licences and include a broad range of products: livestock, meat, fish sugar, oils and fats motor vehicles, cigarette papers, small ships and boats, and pesticides.

Since 1992 the Government of Trinidad and Tobago has been liberalizing its licensing regime. In fact 95% of the products subjected to import licences have since been deleted from the Imports Negative List. The residual items which are still subject to the licensing regime are there for specific reasons as detailed below:

Product	Reason for Licencing Requirement
Live Poultry, Fish, shrimp, Lobster and Crabmeat – live, chilled or frozen	Obligation under CARICOM Treaty
Coconuts (excluding coconut oil)	Obligation under CARICOM Treaty
Oils and fats excluding coconut oil	Obligation under CARICOM Treaty
Left-hand drive vehicles imported for specific purposes as defined in the Customs Act Chapter 78:01	Public Safety
Used right-hand drive vehicles excluding garbage compactors	Public Safety
Cigarette Paper	National Security
Ships and Boats under 250 tons	National Security
Specific pesticides	Public Health

European Union

What is the purpose of retaining the licensing system for certain imports, now that Qrs are no longer applied? Does the Government have plans for abolishing these residual controls? (para. 21)

See answer above on licensing.

Anti-dumping: Notification of Act; Procedures

United States

The report states that Trinidad and Tobago substantially amended its Anti-Dumping and Countervailing Duties Law in 1995, but has not yet notified the WTO of this change. When will the formal notification occur?

Trinidad and Tobago in fact amended its Anti-dumping legislation in order to ensure conformity with the WTO legislation. The Government is preparing the relevant notification documents which will shortly be submitted to the World Trade Organization Secretariat.

Standards and Technical Regulation

Hong Kong, China (WT/TPR/S/49, p. 52, para. 59)

We note that under the Standards Act 18 of 1997, the Bureau of Standards may recognize a foreign standard for certification and label verification and may accept certificates from laboratories outside the country. We would like to know how many foreign standards/certificates have been so recognized. Are they done unilaterally or on the basis of MRAs?

Standards recognized for product certification (Standards Mark) must first be declared as a Standard by the Trinidad and Tobago Bureau of Standards (TTBS), as defined by the Standards Act No. 18 of 1997, Part I and Part IV paras. 19-21. So far no certification (Standards Mark) based on foreign standards has been conducted. However, the TTBS issues batch Certificates of Conformity for products in accordance with any internationally recognized standards. This procedure has already been adopted for products originating in the United Kingdom, United States, and Member States of CARICOM.

Japan

It is reported that standards, developed by a Specification Committee, are published for comment prior to adoption. Is this publication made in addition to the procedures provided in Article 29 of the TBT Agreement? If so, please explain if such comment is open to foreign governments or foreign public and private organizations? (para. 56, p. 51)

Yes, this publication is made as part of TTBS practice in the development of a standard and it is comparable with Article 2.9 of the TBT Agreement. Yes, comments are opened to foreign governments, or foreign public and private organizations.

Are all the local standards created by the Trinidad and Tobago Bureau of Standards? If not, please explain on which products or in which field local standards are created by other organizations.

All the local standards are created by the Bureau of Standards but sometimes other foreign standards are used. Please refer to answer to Hong Kong, China above.

Export Incentives

United States

According to the report, Trinidad and Tobago applies no export taxes, no direct subsidies and no export performance requirements. An export allowance in the form of a tax credit is granted to companies exporting processed or manufactured products (excluding petrochemical and certain other products) to non-CARICOM markets. The tax credit covers the profits on the proportion of export sales to total sales so that profits on exports are effectively tax exempt. Other forms of export promotion to extra-regional markets include assistance on a 50/50 cost-sharing basis to eligible exporters to assist them with the cost of entering and competing in export markets. Local tax law also allows for a deduction of 150% of expenses incurred in promoting the expansion into non-CARICOM markets. Could Trinidad and Tobago provide a list of all exporters who currently benefit from those programs? Also could more information be provided regarding how the tax credit is determined and what the eligibility requirements are for the 50/50 cost-sharing program? Finally, are there deadlines for the termination of any of the programs?

The Export Allowance is utilized by claiming a tax credit based on the proportion of export sales to total sales. This is provided for under the Corporation Tax Act. According to the Budget Speech 1998, this allowance will be eliminated from 2002. The 50/50 cost-sharing program refers to the Export Technical Assistance Facility (ETAF), a matching grant programme, which was administered by the Tourism and Industrial Development Company of Trinidad and Tobago Limited (TIDCO), and funded by the World Bank. The ETAF programme has been discontinued.

The report indicates that the Foreign Investment Act of 1990 is expected to be replaced by a new investment Promotion Act which seeks to diversify export-related foreign investment. How will the new law differ from the current Act?

The Investment Promotion Act will replace the Foreign Investment Act of 1990. Based on the draft, the main differences will be in the promotional nature of the legislation, removing any distinction between local and foreign investors. The Act will include measures to streamline and accelerate the decision-making process.

Costa Rica

What are the most significant changes that the new legislation would introduce? (Referring to Foreign Investment Law)

Refer to earlier answer.

TRIPS legislation

United States

What is the status of Trinidad and Tobago's efforts to sign the WIPO Copyright Treaty?

The Government of Trinidad and Tobago has not taken a decision considering signature of the WIPO Copyright Treaty. Trinidad and Tobago did sign the Final Act at the conclusion of the Diplomatic Conference. It should be noted that Trinidad and Tobago is a member of the Trademark Law Treaty and the Union for the Protection of New Plant Varieties (UPOV).

Trinidad and Tobago's 1997 Copyright Act became effective October 1, 1997. While the Act offers protection equivalent to those available in the United States, enforcement remains a concern. The Copyright Organization of Trinidad and Tobago has stepped up its enforcement of unauthorised use of locally produced products, in particular audio cassettes and CDs of local artists such as Calypso artists. However, at the same time, pirated foreign videos, especially U.S. movies and audio cassettes, are rented and sold openly in the street and in stores. What is the status of Trinidad and Tobago's enforcement efforts on video piracy?

Trinidad and Tobago's enforcement agencies are addressing the problem of video and audio cassette piracy and are committed to enforcing domestic law in this area. The Government is studying the feasibility of introducing the Banderole system.

III.   SECTORAL POLICIES

Agriculture: tariffs and surcharges, sugar

Second Discussant: Claudia Orozco Jaramillo

Could the delegation of Trinidad and Tobago comment on the reasons for the shortfall in domestic production in the face of the prices that result from the high level of protection to which sugar exports are subjected?

Historically Trinidad and Tobago was a net exporter of sugar. Sugar exports from Trinidad and Tobago benefit from preferential agreements with the European Union and the United States. The sugar industry is the major contributor to agricultural GDP and provides the bulk of the foreign exchange earnings of the agricultural sector. It is acknowledged that the industry has experienced some production difficulties but these problems will be addressed by placing greater reliance on farmer-produced canes.

First Discussant: Andrew L. Stoler

Would the visiting Government team like to comment on how it reconciles the apparent inconsistencies between its declared objectives for the agriculture sector and the very many evident problems facing this sector?

Government has implemented a three-year programme designed to restructure the agricultural sector. This programme will address land use policy and administration, the development of agro-based enterprises and enhancing the competitiveness of the sector.

United States

According to the report, import surcharges are currently applied on a number of agricultural products. For example, import surcharges of 60% on sugar, 75% on icing sugar, and 86% on some poultry cuts are expected to remain in place beyond 2004, considerably exceeding the 15% level bound during the Uruguay Round and included in Trinidad and Tobago's schedule of concessions.

What plans does the Government of Trinidad and Tobago have to bring these charges into line with bound duties?

Trinidad and Tobago is committed to reviewing the surcharges on poultry parts, sugar and icing sugar prior to 2004 with a view to ensuring compliance with its WTO commitments.

Second Discussant: Claudia Orozco Jaramillo

There has been a decrease in cocoa and coffee, two of the traditional export crops. Is there any interest in rehabilitating these industries?

During the period of high oil prices, the agricultural sector experienced a labour shortage especially for labour intensive industries such as cocoa and coffee. As a consequence many cocoa and coffee estates were abandoned. However Government intends to revive these industries through the following initiatives: the provision of incentives for the rehabilitation and planting of new estates; the establishment of central fermentaries to improve the quality of beans; the maintenance of germplasm; the divestment of the Nonpareil Estate, a state-owned cocoa estate.

Energy

First Discussant: Andrew L. Stoler

Would the visiting Government team care to share its views as to why, notwithstanding the introduction of diversification strategies, the share of petroleum-related manufacturing increased importantly from 41.5% to 66.4 % of total manufacturing GDP in the 1992-96 period?

The impression is gained as a result of a broad definition of petroleum-related activities to include natural gas-based manufacturing. Activities such as ammonia, methanol and urea production are included. Trinidad and Tobago is a leading world exporter of these products. Over the last five years the contribution to GDP of the petroleum and energy-based industries has averaged 25%.

Services

(a)   Services overview

Hong Kong, China (WT/TPR/S/49, p. 95, para. 81)

In Trinidad and Tobago's schedule, its horizontal commitments provides that the acquisition of more than 30% of the equity of publicly traded companies is subject to approval. Will the government consider relaxing this limitation?

The Government is considering making certain changes to its legislation as it relates to foreign holding of shares in publicly- traded companies.

(b)   Financial services

Hong Kong, China (WT/TPR/S/49, pp. 92-93, para. 85)

We note that at the end of 1997, there were only five commercial banks and one of which is wholly foreign owned. Would like to know the general criteria for awarding licenses. Are local and foreign services suppliers subject to the same requirements?

In Trinidad and Tobago the laws and regulations governing participation in the local financial sector are not restrictive to foreign participation. Moreover, they do not discriminate between national and foreign providers of financial services. In the banking sector, the requirements stipulated for obtaining a licence are basically prudential, relating mainly to capital adequacy and the financial soundness of the business. The other requirements concern the necessary safeguards to ensure that prospective operators are "fit and proper".

Japan (p. 93, para. 86)

Trinidad and Tobago has made no commitment in banking services. Does Trinidad and Tobago intend to make any commitment in this field in the coming negotiations?

Deadlines for making commitments in this area is January 1999 and the Government is still finalizing its position in this area.

Is there any regulation in the Financial Institutions Act of 1993 which limits Market Access (Article XVI of the GATS) or National Treatment (Article XVII of the GATS)?

At present the enabling legislation in the banking sector requires that foreign banks or financial institutions wishing to conduct business in Trinidad and Tobago be incorporated in Trinidad and Tobago.

(c)   Telecommunications services

Hong Kong, China (WT/TPR/S/49, p. 98, para. 99)

We note that the exclusive rights on basic telecommunication services are given to Telecommunication Services of Trinidad and Tobago Ltd. (TSTT) which will expire by 2009 (Summary Observations, para. 36). Will the Government consider advancing the liberalization of this sector?

The Government of Trinidad and Tobago is pursuing the matter of the exclusive rights on basic telecommunications services given to TSTT with a view to advancing the liberalization of this sector. (WT/TPR/S/49, pp. 98-99, para. 100)

Hong Kong, China

We note that the Telecommunications Act is currently under revision to include changes necessary to meet GATS obligations. What is the expected timeframe for completion and approval by the Parliament and the President?

The expected time frame for the completion of the review of the Telecommunications Act is December 1998. Parliament and the President should approve the amendments by the end of June 1999.

Canada

In the area of basic telecommunications services supplied through mode I, we understand that Trinidad and Tobago has committed not to impose any market access limitations, provided that the supplier uses the network of the exclusive operator (qualification valid until 2010). Paragraph 101 states, "While basic telecommunications services are in the hands of the Telecommunication Services of Trinidad and Tobago (TSTT), there are no restrictions on the provisions of value-added services using the network of the exclusive service provider ...". Please clarify the phase "in the hands of TSTT as this seems to imply that provision of basic telecom services is exclusively TSTT's.

A Cabinet-appointed Committee is presently reviewing this Agreement with a view to making appropriate recommendations for the regulation of the telecommunications sector in Trinidad and Tobago.

According to Trinidad and Tobago's Schedule of Commitments, there will be no market access limitations. However, paragraph 102 states that "... Those who wish to provide the public terrestrial-based mobile services, internet and internet access and tele-conferencing for private use through cross-boarder and commercial-presence modes must negotiate with TSTT ...". There appears to be an inconsistency between its WTO commitments and this statement. Kindly clarify.

A written answer will be submitted subsequently.

United States

Telecommunications remains closed to new foreign investment in key areas. Local and international telephone service is provided by a state-owned TSTT (51%) and Cable and Wireless (49%) monopoly. We understand that Trinidad and Tobago maintains that its agreement with Cable and Wireless does not guarantee a monopoly, but the government's policy is, nonetheless, not to issue licenses to operate in this field to other providers. Since the February 1996 commitment by Trinidad and Tobago to allow open access and national treatment for basic (local and long-distance) services by 2010, there has been some discussion of licensing other basic service providers within the next few years.

The roles of both TSTT and Cable and Wireless in the telecommunications sector is currently being reviewed by a Cabinet-appointed Committee which will make appropriate recommendations for regulation of the sector.

When does Trinidad and Tobago plan to begin to issue licenses for additional basic service telecommunication providers?

The Government of Trinidad and Tobago expects to be in a position to pursue the issuance of licenses in 1999.

The government has recently announced opening the cellular telephone market to competition by the end of the year. This is in advance of Trinidad and Tobago's WTO liberalization commitments. Do you still expect to meet this announced date? What are the government's plans to liberalize other segments of this sector?

A written answer will be provided subsequently.

Japan (p. 98, para. 100)

It is reported that the Telecommunications Act of 1991 is not in effect since it has yet to be assented to by the President and that the law currently under revision including changes necessary to meet GATS obligations. The Fourth Protocol entered into force on the 5thFebruary 1998. Please provide information on when the 1991Act or the law which meets the GATS obligation is expected to be in effect.

The Government of Trinidad and Tobago should be in a position to meet its GATS obligations by mid-1999.

Trinidad and Tobago has committed to eliminate the monopoly of TSTT by 2010 and not to limit Market Access nor National Treatment as of 2010 in its Schedule of Specific Commitments. Please explain the schedule for the elimination of the monopoly status of the TSTT and the liberalization of the sector to meet this Commitment.

As mentioned above, a Cabinet-appointed Committee is reviewing TSTT's role in the telecommunications sector.

(d)   Civil Aviation

Hong Kong, China (WT/TPR/S/49, p. 101, para. 113)

We note that air cargo handling services and airline facilities and repair services are open to foreigners. What are the general requirements for the provision of these services? Are local and foreign investors subject to the same requirements?

There are three local companies presently engaged in ground handling activities. However, foreign airlines can also undertake their own cargo handling operations. As far as general requirements are concerned, both local and foreign firms must obtain prior authorization from the Airports Authority to operate a cargo handling service and must demonstrate the capability to perform such services, e.g. having trained personnel, necessary equipment, etc.

United States

Trinidad and Tobago has expressed interest in liberalizing its air transportation services and, in the recent past, has indicated an interest in signing an Open Skies Agreement with the United States. Can you tell us if such an Agreement is still being contemplated?

The Trinidad and Tobago Government has taken a decision to deal with the Open Skies Agreement on a CARICOM level. CARICOM has formed a Negotiating Team to deal with the matter. This Team is to chaired by Dr. Kenneth Rattray of Jamaica with Mr. Reginald Dumas of Trinidad and Tobago as the Vice-Chairman.

(e)   Maritime Transport

Hong Kong, China (WT/TPR/S/49, p. 100, para. 108)

It is mentioned that there are plans to commercialize cargo handling and marine services and that the shares of the Port Authority will be sold to local and foreign investors. We would like to know more information on the plans including timeframe for implementation and any limitations on foreign investors' participation.

The Government is considering a proposal for the restructuring of port operations.

United States (p. 100, para. 106)

It is reported that vessels wishing to engage in coastal trade between the islands of Trinidad and Tobago are required to obtain a license and that this requirement is applied to both local and foreign operators. Please provide criteria to obtain the above mentioned license. Do the same criteria apply equally to local and foreign operators?

Droghers are vessels employed in the conveyance of cargo from some part of Trinidad and Tobago to some other part. To operate as droghers, the vessels must be registered in accordance with the Droghers Act, Chapter 50:07 of the Laws of Trinidad and Tobago and must either: (1) be registered either: (a) in Trinidad and Tobago under the Shipping Act, i.e. vessels of 24 metres in length and over or in a foreign state; or (b) under the Motor Launches Act, Chapter 50:08 of the laws of Trinidad and Tobago (i.e. vessels under twenty-four (24) metres in length); (2) provide evidence of third party liability; and (3) provide evidence of meeting applicable safety standards. All Droghers must be issued a Certificate of Drogher by the maritime Services Division. This certificate is valid until 31 December of the year in which the Certificate is issued. A licence to Navigate Coastwise is issued by the Customs and Excise Division based on the Drogher Certificate. With regard to licensing requirements, the owner of a drogher must submit in triplicate a "Declaration of Ownership" Form together with the following: (a) proof of registration; (b) international tonnage; (c) valid safety certificates (load line, safety construction, equipment and radio or exemption for vessels over 500 tons-gross tonnage); (d) certificate of insurance against damage to third party. Finally, with regard to fees, the Drogher fee is calculated using the rate of $1.60 per tonne or part thereof. In no case shall the fee be less than $10.00.

(f)   Work Permits

United States

Foreign firms have occasionally complained about inconsistencies and a lack of transparency in the issuance of renewal of work permits, particularly for foreign executive level personnel. The U.S./TT BIT, which entered into force in 1996, contains a commitment by the Parties which in spirit addresses this issue. The implication is that nationals of one party should be permitted to enter and remain in its territory for purpose of establishing, developing, administering, or advising on the operation of an investment to which they, or a company of the other Party that employs them have committed (or are in the process of committing) a substantial amount of capital or other resources. It also permits covered investments to engage top managerial personnel of their choice, regardless of nationality. How is Trinidad and Tobago addressing this continuing issue?

The work permit policy enables any investor who requires management with certain skills to be employed in Trinidad and Tobago to benefit from this provision. Several thousand expatriates already reside and work in Trinidad and Tobago. Some have lived in the country for a number of years. Trinidad and Tobago has not enjoyed the same level of reciprocity from developed countries. Where work permits have either been denied or not renewed the criteria have not been observed. The efficiency of the system is reflected in the fact that between 1996 and 1997, 3990 work permits were issued.